ARMOURED OPERATIONS

OPERATIONS

of the Second World War (I)

AF EDITIONS

Originally published in Spanish by AF Editores, 2006. (QUIRÓN EDICIONES)
ARMOURED OPERATIONS OF THE SECOND WORLD WAR (I)

Published by:

AF EDITIONS

C/Cromo P. 18-20 - Polígono Industrial San Cristóbal
47012 VALLADOLID (Spain) - Ap. de Correos nº 2038
Tfno: 983 20 69 28 / 983 39 05 83 / 983 21 31 41
Fax 983 39 53 36 / 983 21 26 76
E-Mail: quiron@alcanizfresnos.com
http://www.libromedia.com/quironediciones

Publisher: Carlos Fresno Crespo.

Art Manager: Luis Fresno Crespo.

By:
Juan Vázquez García

Artwork
Luis Fresno Crespo - Julio López Caeiro

Publishing Team
Desing: Carlos Fresno de Vega
Cartography: Diego Hernández Buzón
Photographic treatment: Santiago Gutiérrez Cortés

Photographic collections
Archivo «Canario» Azaola - Archivo Editorial
Autor collection - Biblioteca Nacional (Madrid) -
Archivo General Militar (Ávila)
Archivo General de la Administración (Alcalá de Henares)
Bundesarchiv (Coblenz)

© 2004 Quirón Ediciones
ISBN: 84-96016-72-2 / 978-84-96016-72-9
Depósito Legal: VA-765/2007

Print:

alcañiz fresno's s.a.
C/ Cromo P. 20
Polígono Industrial San Cristóbal - 47.012 Valaldolid (Spain)

Binding:
San Cristóbal Encuadernaciones, S.A. - C/ Cromo P. 18 y 19
Polígono Industrial San Cristobal - 47012 Valladolid (Spain)

ARMOURED OPERATIONS
of the Second World War (I)

By **Juan Vázquez García**

Artwork

Luis Fresno Crespo *and* **Julio López Caeiro**

AF EDITIONS

ARMOURED OPERATIONS IN THE SECOND WORLD WAR

Although the tank was first used during the Great War, it came to maturity in the Second World War, and this was precisely in the hands of those who had sustained its early impact a quarter of a century before. In 1939, all the countries about to participate in the Second World War had tanks to a larger or a lesser degree, and were conscious of their importance. Some of them, like the Soviets, had a huge number of tanks, others, like the French, had tanks that were excellent for the time. Among the British, there were remarkable theorists in armoured warfare. The Americans had an extraordinary industrial potential for mass production of armoured fighting vehicles. However, only the Germans managed to combine the best of each of these factors and saw all the potential of the tank.

The tank was the most revolutionary weapon to be employed at the beginning of the Second World War, particularly when used in independent mass formations, the epitome of this being the Panzerdivision. It was the weapon that was to make the dream of the Great War strategists a reality, the breakthrough of the enemy's front.

As the war progressed, the tank went through an extraordinary evolution, and during six years of war, the battlefields saw the disappearance of designs of Great War vintage, and their replacement with vehicles that would not look outmoded in the 1950's. Those operations and battles where the tank was the main protagonist were some of the most spectacular, and at times most controversial, pages of military history.

This book concisely describes some of the greatest armoured operations of the Second World War. In its pages can be found details on the entire spectrum of armoured warfare, from the blitzkrieg to the peculiarities of the desert war, and from the titanic clashes on the Eastern Front to other, no less dramatic, events in the West. The chapters will cover operations carried out by both the Allies and the Germans, who perhaps best understood and developed the tank's potential. The aim of this book is not to recount the most famous operations involving the tank (although, of course, this will be inevitable up to a point), but rather to focus on some of the most representative, attempting to show the way in which each of the main participants used their armoured resources during the war, and in doing so to understand the evolution of this revolutionary weapon. As well as describing events, each chapter also includes a short biography of some of the commanders of the most important armoured units, and a few technical notes on some of the most well known tanks of the war.

If, after reading the book, the reader has gained a global view of the nature of armoured warfare during the Second World War, and the extraordinary evolution which the tank went through in just six years, then the author's goal will have been achieved.

THE SOVIET INVASION OF POLAND

The Russo-German Non-Agression Pact of the 23rd August 1939, signed by Ribbentrop and Molotov, left the Soviet Union free to take over the Baltic states, and in a secret clause, partition Poland.

The *Fall Weiss*, the German invasion of Poland, began on 1st September 1939, resulting in a series of declarations of war against Germany. However, despite all the earlier promises and plans, under different pretexts, the Western powers eventually abandoned the Poles to their fate, not only to the Germans, but to the Soviets as well.

The *blitzkrieg* unleashed by the Germans crushed the main Polish defensive line in the first forty-eight hours, in such a way that in the first week, effective resistance had been overcome. Of course, there were still numerous engagements to be fought, many of them savage and costly, but the die was cast.

Stalin decided it was time to intervene in Poland, to the surprise of the Germans and the rest of the world, in order to occupy the territories that had been earmarked to come under Soviet control in the Russo-German Non-Agression Pact. Already, on the

12th, *Pravda* published a strongly worded article denouncing the Polish attitude towards that country's national minorities, as well as writing off the Polish state, as it rightly pointed out that it had been abandoned by the Western powers. On the 17th, the Polish ambassador in Moscow was summoned late in the night to the People's Commissar Office for Foreign Affairs, where he received a harsh communique expressing the Soviet decision to invade Poland, and given the destruction of the Polish state, to protect the Byelorussians and Ukrainians living there, as well, of course, to defend the Poles from the unfortunate war that their irresponsible leaders had started.

That same day, Soviet troops crossed the border. The Polish General Staff, headed by Marshal Rydz-Smigly, stunned and depressed by this sudden blow, went to Romania the following day, after issuing orders to his troops not to fight the Soviets, and to escape to Hungary and Romania in order to establish a new army and fight on French soil.

There was little the Polish army could do to stop the Soviet invasion,

A 37 mm anti-tank Bofors guns. (ECPA)

A Soviet BT-5 tank column in the streets of Bessarabia, 1939.

having already been defeated in the west by the Germans. The Polish armoured forces presented no serious threat to the Russians, as they were organized on the French model, with the tanks distributed in small units amongst the infantry, and with only a few independent units that lacked the necessary firepower to be of any use in confronting the large Soviet tank formations. Only the abundant and excellent 37-mm *Bofors* anti-tank guns, of which the Poles had about 1,200, posed a serious threat to the T-26's and BT's, as they had to the *Panzer I's* and *II's*.

The Soviet high command had started to prepare the invasion of Poland a few days after the signing of the Non-Agression Pact. On the 3rd September, Voroshilov, People's Commissar for Defence, had already issued orders to the Leningrad, Kalinin, Byelorussia, Kiev, Moscow and Kharkov military districts to be ready for any eventuality. General mobilization was decreed on the 6th September, and mass manoeuvres started. On the 13th, all the units were in position for the invasion, grouped into two large "fronts" along the 1,400-kilometre border, the Byelorussian Front in the north and the Ukrainian Front in the south. Each Soviet "front" was made up of infantry, cavalry and tanks The tanks' main mission was to breach enemy lines and penetrate into the country's heartland; the infantry were to follow and consolidate the ground taken.

In the face of this unexpected assault, the Polish defensive system completely disintegrated, already having been defeated by the attacking Germans. Initially, the Polish General Staff issued orders to their border units not to resist the Soviets, except if they were to be disarmed, although those orders did not reach all units. Besides, the invading troops' attitude left few options open. At the beginning, the civil population thought that the Soviets were coming to defend them from the Germans. However, they soon realized their mistake.

The Evolution of Soviet armoured forces

Using foreign models as a basis, Soviet armoured forces were rapidly expanded over a short time.

POLAND (1939)

During the first Five-Year Plan over 5,000 tanks were built, but by the end of the second Five-Year Plan over 15,000 tanks were in service and the Leningrad and Kharkov factories were designing new and revolutionary models.

Samoched pancerny wz 34: with a weight of 2.4 metric tons, this armoured vehicle, of which 80 were built in three different versions, was armed either with a 7.92 mm machine-gun or a mod. 18 Puteaux gun. (Arch. Dc. Mec Warsaw)
Illustration: Julio López Caeiro

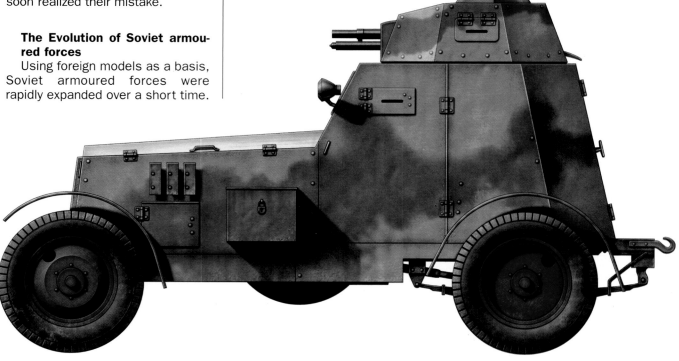

Above: 7 TP jw. The best tank in service with the Polish Army, it was basically a development of the Vickers E. It had a maximum armour thickness of 17 mm, a speed of up to 32 kph and was armed with a 37 mm gun and one or two machine-guns. Some 135 were built.
Centre and right: 7 TP Tank with double turret, each armed with a light machine-gun. It was a derivative of the British Vickers *Six Ton*. (Arch. Dc. Mec Warsaw)

Illustration: Julio López Caeiro

The early models found their inspiration in foreign designs, such as the British six-ton *Vickers-Armstrong* and the American *Christie*, although both these had in fact been rejected by their respective national armies. However, these models were much improved on by

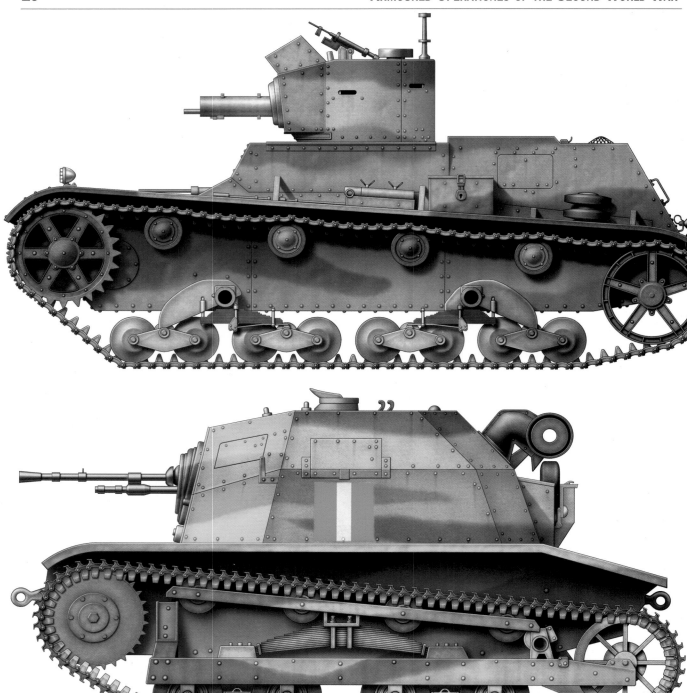

A TK 3: this Polish armoured vehicle was possibly the equivalent of the Panzer I. Badly armoured and with poor firepower, German tanks outclassed them, having their armament mounted in turrets instead of casemates.

A TKS: improved version of the TK-3, armed with a 20 mm gun and with 8 mm of armour, its 42 hp engine giving a top speed of 46 kph. They saw some success in combat against the *2. Panzerdivision*.

Illustration: Julio López Caeiro

the Soviets, particularly regarding armament, the turret and the turret ring, so when the Russians first set eyes on the American M3, it made a very negative impression on them, especially in regard to the tanks armament, the turret turning mechanism and the turret design. The Soviets wanted tanks that were easy to build in large numbers, adapted to the needs of the Red Army, in a short time, using well-proven models to cut development time. The necessary improvements could wait, as their industrial capacity and their engineering experience increased...

In 1939, it is estimated that the Soviet Army had 10,000 light and

Byelorussian Front, 2nd Class *Kommandarm* –Army Commander– Mikhail Kovalov (HQ in Minsk)

3rd Army (*Komkor* –Corps Cder– Vasily Kuznetsov).
4th Infantry Corps (5th and 50th Rifle Divisions)
27th Rifle Division
24th Cavalry Division
Two armour brigades
-22nd Armoured Brigade: 219 T-26s and 3 armoured cars (*Kombrig* –Brig– Lazarev)
-25th Armoured Brigade: 251 T-26s and 27 armoured cars (Polkovnik –Col– Borzikov)

11th Army (*Komkor* Medvedev)
Two infantry corps
Two cavalry corps
15th Armoured Corps (*Komdiv* –Div Cder– Petrov)
- 2nd Armoured Brigade (*Kombrig* Kurkin)
- 27th Armoured Brigade (Polkovnik Zhushchuk)
- 20th Motorized Brigade (Polkovnik Bordnikov)
- Polkovnik Rozanov's Mechanized Group
In total: 461 BT-5 and BT-7 tanks and 122 armoured cars

6th Armoured Brigade (Polkovnik Bolotnikov): 248 BT-7s
21st Armoured Brigade: 29 BT-7s, 105 T-28s and 19 armoured cars

4th Army (*Komdiv* Chuikov)
Two infantry corps
- 16th Rifle Corps: 4th, 13th and 33rd Divisions
- 23rd Rifle Corps: 93rd, 109th and 152nd Divisions
6th Cavalry Corps: 4th, 6th and 11th Divisions
Two armour brigades
- 29th Armoured Brigade (*Kombrig* Krivoshein): 188 T-26
- 32nd Armoured Brigade: 220 T-26s and 5 armoured cars

10th Army (*Komdiv* Zakharin)
24th Infantry Corps (29th, 139th and 145th Divisions)

In total, 1,721 tanks, without taking into account the T-37s and T-38s of the cavalry and infantry divisions and reconnaissance units, which numbered over 800 of those vehicles. As a whole, there were over 2,500 tanks and armoured vehicles in the front.

Ukrainian Front, 1st Class *Kommandarm* Timoshenko (HQs at Proskurov)

5th Army (*Komdiv* Sovietnikov)
8th Rifle Corps: 44th, 46th and 89th Divisions
3rd Cavalry Corps: 7th, 11th and 27th Divisions
36th Armoured Brigade (*Kombrig* Bogomozov): 238 T-26s and 24 armoured cars

6th Army (*Komkor* Golikov)
17th Rifle Corps: 72nd, 96th and 97th Divisions
2nd Cavalry Corps: 3rd, 5th and 14th Divisions
3 armour brigades:
- 24th Armoured Brigade (Polkovnik Folchenkov): 205 BTs and 28 armoured cars
- 38th Armoured Brigade: T-26
- 10th Armoured Brigade: T-28

12th Army (*Kommandarm* Tiulenev)
15th Rifle Corps: 7th, 45th and 60th Divisions
4th Cavalry Corps: 10th, 12ª and 13th Divisions
5th Cavalry Corps: 16th, 25th and 30th Divisions
25th Armoured Corps (Polkovnik Polikarpov)
-1st Motorized Brigade
-4th and 5th Armour Brigades
26th and 23rd Armoured Brigades (T-26 and BT-7)

A total of approximately 500,000 men and over 5,000 tanks and armoured vehicles.

reconnaissance tanks, 1,000 medium tanks and 300 heavy tanks. This was not yet the time of the T-34 and the KV-1, but the basis had been established and soon the huge Russian factories would start production of these two legendary tanks that would rule the battlefields in the second half of 1941.

In 1935, the Soviet Army classified armoured vehicles into four groups. Tanks were either for reconnaissance, combat, breakthrough or penetration and specialist vehicles. Among the tanks, two types were considered, light models, such as the T-26, were for direct infantry support, and the fast ones, like the BT series. Among the breakthrough tanks, there were also differences, those designated medium models, such as the three-turret T-28, and heavy ones such as the five-turret T-35. These two types were organized into special brigades ready to support other units.

The first independent operational unit, a mechanized corps, was established in 1932, and was made up of two mechanized brigades, a machine-gun brigade, and an independent anti-aircraft artillery unit. In total, it grouped together 500 tanks and 200 vehicles of different types. By 1936 there were already four mechanized corps, six independent mechanized brigades, six independent tank regiments, fifteen mechanized regiments of the cavalry divisions and eight tank battalions in the infantry divisions.

THE INVASION

A.- The Byelorussian front
Vilnius was to be the target of three armoured brigades, the 22nd and 25th from the northeast and the 6th from the southeast. On the

A T-38. With a weight of 3.3 metric tons and a crew of two, the T-38 was an amphibious tank used by reconnaissance units. Its 40 hp engine afforded a top speed of 40 kph on the road and up to 6 kph in the water. The armour afforded little protection, as it had a maximum thickness of 9 mm. It was armed with a 7.62 mm DT machine-gun.

17th, the T-26's of the 25-ya Brigada (25th Brigade) crossed the border at five in the morning, and headed for the Plissa-Glebokie sector, which they reached late in the day. The following day, they crossed the Komajka River and at dawn on the 19th, the reconnaissance vehicles

A BA-20 reconnaissance vehicle column on the Polish plain.

Illustration: Julio López Caeiro

A T-28. This 28-ton multi-turret tank, like the heavier T-35, was the result of a fashion which resulted in failure. Its poor mobility, engine and weak armour (30 mm maximum) rendered it vulnerable and useless, despite its powerful (for the time) armament.

The pictures on the left show a parade in Moscow of the giant and useless T-28.

Illustration: Julio López Caeiro

penetrated Vilnius, after driving over 300 kilometres. The 6-ya Brigada fought a fierce engagement with Polish border guards, before finally penetrating the Rakow sector. The next day, after crossing the Berezina, they arrived in the outskirts of the town.

The town had a garrison of eight infantry battalions, a militia battalion and the 20. bateria (20th anti-tank Battery), commanded by Pulkownik (Colonel) Janiszewski. The

T-26 tanks circled from the northeast and the BT-7's from the southeast in the early hours of the morning, and fierce fighting began, with the Polish 37 mm *Bofors* guns knocking out a large number of Soviet tanks (the 37 mm wz.36 *Bofors* was able to pierce 26 mm of armour with a 30º angle at a range of 600 metres, more than enough to face any 1939 Soviet tank). At noon, the 24-ya Kavaleriiskaya Diviziya (24th Cavalry Division) joined the fray. Little by little, the strongest points of resistance, normally made up of groups of officers and students with one or two machineguns barricaded in stone buildings, began to succumb. Finally, at six in the evening, superior Soviet numbers told and the Polish command called for a ceasefire.

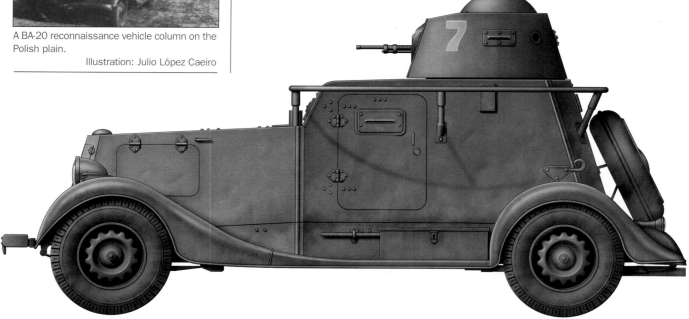

The 22-ya Brigada also saw bloody fighting on the border, but by late in the day it had penetrated over 50 kilometres into Polish territory. During the two days that followed, they advanced in the direction of Vilnius, which had already been captured. Between the 20th and the 22nd, they were busy mopping up resistance on the outskirts, capturing a large number of prisoners and equipment. In the Bezdany forest, they captured a cavalry squadron that was trying to reach Lithuania. The unit covered some 530 kilometres in six days.

The 15-i Korpus (15th Corps) entered Poland after several brief border skirmishes, with the two armoured brigades leading, followed by the 20-ya Mekhanizirovannaya Brigada (20th Motorized Brigade). The first day they covered around 50 kilometres for the loss of one man killed and two wounded. On the 18th, the 27-ya Brigada continued their advance, but the nearby 2-ya Brigada was stopped at the Szcara River, which was crossed once a pontoon bridge had been constructed. On the 19th, the tanks of both brigades were forced to stop for a whole day for lack of fuel. However, once refuelled, the fast BT's drove on again, meeting hardly any opposition, and took Sokófka on the 20th. Some fifty BT-7's of the 27-ya Brigada reached Grodno, their target, which was defended by approximately 3,000 Polish soldiers who had spent the previous days organizing the defences and blocking the bridges over the Niemen.

The reconnaissance group of the 27-ya Brigada, entered the town with twelve BT-7s and a BA-10, followed by two tank battalions (with forty-six BTs). Polish fire was extremely heavy and even though their

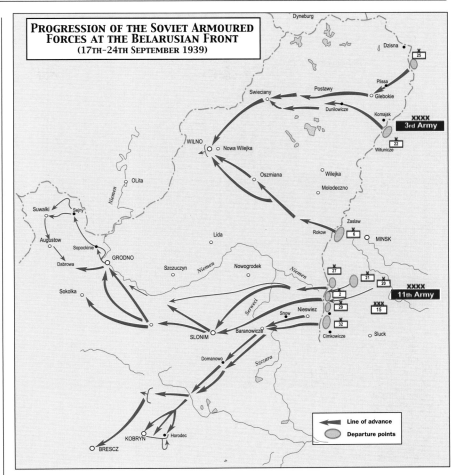

anti-tank guns were not very effective, they began to cause losses among the Soviet tanks. The few infantry accompanying the tanks were pinned down by machine-gun and rifle fire, and Molotov cocktails were also used by the defenders, setting a tank on fire in Liberty Square; a second tank was destroyed by an anti-aircraft gun shortly afterwards, crashing in flames into a shop window. A third tank was captured in Napoleon Street and the populace lynched the crew. A further two tanks were also destroyed by Molotov cocktails nearby. In the face of such furious resistance, the Soviet tank crews resorted to tactics that would be sadly repeated throughout the war. Several children were taken from a local orphanage and tied on the tank turrets, to be used as human shields. One of the teachers, Barbara Majko, was killed when she tried to rescue one of the girls, Tadzia Jasinski. Over 300 Grodno children would die in the first few hours of fighting. Only at the end of the day did the Soviets get the necessary infantry reinforcements to consolidate their positions. These unfortunate incidents would be repeated sixty years later in Grodny, the Chechen town with an eerily similar sounding name.

At 07:00 in the morning of the 21st, the artillery of the 101-i polk and 119-i polk (101st and 119th Regiments) and the 20-ya Brigada started to pound the remaining strongholds of resistance that had been set up in barracks, churches and stately buildings. The 119-i

A T-26 tank advancing in Polish territory. The hatch is open as usual, so that the tank commander, by sticking his head out, could enjoy suitable visibility, although this rendered him vulnerable to infantry fire.

THE T-26 TANK

The T-26 was designed in the 1930's as an infantry support tank, whose main mission, due to its mobility, protection and armament, was to neutralize enemy machine-guns on the battlefield, according to the standards of the time.

In the spring of 1930, the Soviet Union bought several six-ton *Vickers-Armstrong* tanks that the British armed forces had rejected. These models were examined in Leningrad, at the *Dzerzhinsky* Artillery Academy and, after obtaining a licence from the British firm, several prototypes were built for evaluation at the *Bolshevik* factory. In February 1931, without an appropriate evaluation having been completed, the T-26, weighing eight metric tons, was accepted by the Soviet armed forces. The model originally built was armed with two air-cooled DT 7.62 mm machine-guns, placed inside two turrets mounted in parallel. The tank commander sat in the turret on the left. The gunners' seats were fixed and did not turn with the turrets. The driver sat on the left side, beside the gear-box, which had five forward and one reverse gear. The 91 hp engine, based on a *British Armstrong-Siddeley* design, was in the rear compartment. The armour on the early models only offered protection against light weapons and shrapnel. Late in 1931, some 120 of the first models with two turrets had been built. The armament was useless for its intended mission, and other possibilities were studied, the most successful was the installation of a 37 mm gun, as was being tested on tanks in other countries, but the turret would not take the gun so it was totally redesigned in 1933.

The new turret for the 37 mm gun was too unbalanced and, besides, as the loader and the tank commander's seats were fixed to the floor, the gun was too difficult to aim and operate. In the meantime, a new and much more efficient 45 mm gun had been designed and installation work on the tank started. An aerial was also fitted to the command tanks, in the form of a bar around the turret, although this was too visible. Despite this aerial, the range was only about two kilometres, such was the Soviet electronic technology of the time. The 45 mm gun was finally adapted for the tank and this T-26 version was built in large numbers, some 12,000 in 1940.

The T-26 first saw action in Manchuria in 1934 against the Japanese. Over 300 were sent to the Spanish Republic during the civil war (1936-39), and they were first used in combat at Seseña. The T-26 was a shock when it emerged in Spain, as it was very superior to the *Panzer I* and the L3. Two captured tanks were sent to Germany in 1937 to be closely examined. Overall, its firepower, armour and off-road mobility made a serious impression.

The Spanish experience brought several improvements to the T-26, such as the adoption of a conical turret, the use of electric welding instead of rivets and the addition of more machine-guns. The new radio sets were much more powerful and had a lower profile. However, all these improvements could not be tested in the invasion of Poland, as there was hardly any fighting worthy of the name. But, when they were confronted by the Finnish on the *Mannerheim* Line in the winter war, their deficiencies became clear. The Finnish 37 mm *Bofors* guns easily pierced the armour, mechanical reliability left much to be desired, speed was insufficient and balance was not really achieved. Despite that, it was easy to manufacture, maintenance was simple and cheap and the design was the basis for much more successful later types. During the early days of Operation *Barbarossa*, most of the T-26s in service were destroyed by the Germans.

T-26s were built in many versions, as command tanks, engineer tanks, mine clearers, flame-throwers, tank destroyers mounting a 76.2 mm gun, amphibious and anti-aircraft tanks but, except for the OT 130 flame-thrower version, these were rarely successful and had an operational life that was almost insignificant.

Characteristics of the 1937 T-26 Model

Crew:		3
Weight:		10.3 metric tons
Armament:	1 Model 1934 45-mm gun with 165 rounds	
	One, two or three 7.62 mm DT machine-guns with 3,654 rounds	
Engine:	Petrol, 4-cylinder, 91 hp at 2,200 rpm	
Fuel capacity:		292 litres
Top speed:		30 kph
Power/weight ratio:		8.7 hp/ton
Range:		up to 225 kilometres
Specific pressure on the ground:		0.65 kp/sq. cm
Maximum angle of armour:		32º
Dimensions:	Height:	2,410 mm.
	Length:	4,620 mm.
	Width:	2,440 mm.
Armour:	hull: front, side and rear:	15 mm
	Upper:	10 mm
	Floor:	6 mm
	Turret: front, side and rear:	15 mm
	Upper:	10 mm

Strelkovyi polk (119th Fusiliers Regiment) crossed the Niemen in boats, and started to lay a pontoon bridge for the tanks. The fight raged on furiously in the Poniemun neighbourhood all day long. The 20-ya Brigada was blocked by both the river and the heavy fire of the defenders firmly entrenched in a tobacco factory. The railway station was taken in an assault by the 101-i polk, and its 250 defenders were massacred. Finally, on the 22nd, the Soviets gained control of the town. The Poles had lost over 550 killed, many of them smashed by the tanks in the east side, and 1,600 of their men were taken prisoner. The 27th Brigade had lost over fifty men and several BT's. The 20-ya Mekhanizirovannaya Brigada had twenty-three casualties and lost a BA-10. The 2-ya brigada had only thirty-seven BT's left operational. The infantry battalions had suffered over 150 casualties.

After taking the town, the 2-ya Brigada headed for Sopockinie where the remaining Grodno defenders had regrouped, along with an Uhlan regiment. Savage fire-fights were fought around the hamlet of Sylwanowste, where the Polish cavalry destroyed four BT's and caused the Soviets over thirty casualties, before being surrounded by the tanks in the Augustowski forest and forced to surrender. The Polish General Olszyne-Wilczynski, commander of the Grodno defenders, was captured and executed on the spot, being shot in the head.

On the 23rd, the remaining elements of both armoured brigades continued their push, without encountering serious resistance, and reached Suwalki three days later. The 29-ya Brigada crossed the border, occupied Nieswiez and captured two Polish infantry companies. After a forced 40-kilometre march, it arrived at Baranowicze, where 5,000 Polish soldiers, who had been caught by surprise, were taken prisoner. At noon on the 18th they had reached Kosovo, and by the end of the day were forced to stop at Domanovo for lack of fuel.

After restarting on the 22nd, they received orders to occupy Breznad Bugiem (Brest-Litovsk). General Krivochein ordered the 242 tanks of his brigade to speed up in order to occupy the town before the Germans did so. Near Brescz, they

A BT-5 tank column in a Polish street. In the early days of the invasion, the civil population greeted the Soviets, not seeing them as invaders, but rather as allies. They were soon to realize their mistake.

found a group of German officers, sent by Guderian, with orders for them to stop. Krivochein ignored them and entered the town, where he discovered that it had already been taken by the German armoured forces. Guderian himself had already established his headquarters at the town hall, in the town centre. The Soviet general went there, but Guderian made him wait over a quarter of an hour before receiving him. Affectionately, he congratulated him on having got there, while showing him a hall lined with pictures of many Polish heroes from the 16th and 18th centuries. Finally, he proposed a parade in common and thus, in the evening, a T-26 battalion marched with a Panzer II company before Guderian and Krivochein to the music of a Russian military march.

The 32-ya brigada entered Poland encountering hardly any resistance and progressed to Kobryn, 380 kilometres from its start point. But by the time they reached their objective on the 22nd, sixty-nine tanks out of a total of 236 had been left along the way, having broken down. That night there was fighting in the Horodec sector, where over 300 Polish prisoners were taken. During the two days that followed, the brigade was harassed by Polish units, more or less organized and consisting of 100 to 300 men, which caused few casualties, killing around 150 of them. On the 25th, the brigade established a defensive line in the

Kobryn region to block the retreat of the Polish forces, taking several hundred prisoners that same day.

B.- The Ukrainian front

The 36-ya brigada crossed the border with 238 T-26s and twenty-four armoured cars and captured Dubno on the 18th, taking over 6,000 prisoners. After covering a further 50-kilometres in two and a half hours, they arrived at Luck, where the 9,000 defenders surrendered at once, without firing a shot. The unit continued till dusk, reaching Wlodzimierz Wolyaski, where the 13,500-men garrison surrendered the following day and over 150 guns of different types were captured. So far, the brigade had lost one BA-10 and had had five casualties. In the days that followed they reached their final objective, Lublin. On the 25th, they attacked Chelo but by noon the 194 tanks that had started the attack had been halted by the barricades in the town suburbs. After restarting the attack with more determination, the town was taken by six in the evening, with over 8,000 prisoners being captured. On the 28th, the brigade continued its push to Lublin, where they came into contact with elements of the German 4. Infanterie Division and came to a halt. On 5th October they withdrew to the demarcation line

that had been established in the Russo-German Non-Agression Pact. In total, the 36-ya Brigada had driven 710 kilometres, fired almost 2,000 rounds, losing only two tanks in the fighting.

The objectives of the 6th Army's armoured units, a total of three brigades, were Tarnopol and Lwów. The 38-ya brigada arrived in the outskirts of Tarnopol on the 17th and then, in the two days that followed, reached Lwów, 132 kilometres from their first objective.

The 24-ya brigada, with a total of 205 BT's, eight of them being the BT-8 flame-thrower model, and twenty-eight armoured cars, crossed the border at six in the morning, along with a cavalry unit. In the evening they were ordered to cross the Seret River north of Tarnopol, to outflank the town and penetrate from the west. Therefore the over 40 kilometres were covered at night. Due to lack of fuel only ninety tanks took part in this maneouvre. The town was to be attacked simultaneously by both this brigade and the 10-ya brigada, approaching from the southeast. The garrison of about 15,000 men was overcome during the night and a lot of artillery pieces and trucks were also captured. At dawn on the 19th, after a 145-kilometre march, the tanks of the 24th Brigade were in the outskirts of Lwów. As soon as they had arrived they began a night attack, managing to break the weak defences in the sector made up of two barricades and two anti-tank guns, and easily reaching the town centre. But two hours after the attack had

A BT-7. A derivative of the American Christie, this fast tank was the final development in the BT saga, which had received its baptism of fire in Spain. Armed with a 45 mm gun, and two or three machine-guns, with maximum armour of 22 mm, its 450-HP engine afforded a top speed of 53 kph tracked and up to 73 kph on wheels.
Illustration: Julio López Caeiro

started, for no apparent reason, the unit commander gave orders to stop the vehicles and take up defensive positions. At dawn, only the reconnaissance unit was still in the town, the rest of the forces had withdrawn in the direction of Winnik.

At 08:30 German units penetrated the town from the southwest, fighting the Polish defenders, and at the same time coming into contact with the Soviet tanks, which were also under attack from the Poles. Mistaking the the Soviet tanks for Polish vehicles, the German Panzers opened fire on the Russians. Although the latter had initially raised a white flag to warn the Germans of their presence, when the Germans opened fire they withdrew the way they had come. The Germans eventually realized their mistake and ceased firing. At the end of this confrontation, two Soviet armoured cars and a BT-7 were on fire and Russian casualties were three killed (including a commissar) and four wounded.

During the rest of the 19th and the whole of the 20th, discussions were held by the Soviet and German commands in order to reach an agreement whereby the latter would abandon the town, by virtue of the previously agreed Pact, all of this

occurring while at the same time fighting continued with the Polish defenders, as the town was far from having been taken. On the evening of the 20th, the Germans withdrew and the rest of the Soviet brigade concentrated in the outskirts of the town. The final assault on Lwów by the 24-ya brigada and the 2-i Kavaleriiskii Korpus (2nd Cavalry Corps) started on the 21st. After sustaining several casualties at the hands of the anti-tank guns positioned at the barricades, the Soviet tanks entered the town, which surrendered on the 22nd. Early in October, war-booty was taken from the town's streets that included two German tanks and two anti-tank guns (from the sector that had been attacked previously), nine tanks, ten light tanks and some thirty Polish trucks.

On the 17th, the 10-ya brigada detached two T-28 battalions and a reconnaissance company with twenty BT's, which crossed the border over the Zbrucz River. Carrying an infantry battalion on their tanks, they penetrated Tarnopol that evening. On the following day, this unit joined a battle group commanded by Kombrig Wolocha, given the task of capturing Lwów. Due to lack of fuel, only twenty-seven T-26's and six BT-7 tanks took part in the mission. After an extremely fast march, they arrived at Kozlów at five in the evening and the rest of the tanks joined them at dusk. Reinforced with cavalry units, they took up positions west of Jaworów during the following days.

Meanwhile, the 1-ya Mekhanizirovannaya Brigada and the 5-ya bronirovannaya brigada (5th Armoured Brigade) crossed three rivers, the Zwanczyk, the Zbrucz and the Seret, without opposition, and drove 60 kilometres to Zydków, where fighting took place with Polish infantry, who surrendered after sustaining thirty casualties. On the following day, both brigades took the airfield at Buczacz and captured eight aircraft. Shortly afterwards, the reconnaissance group of the 45-ya brigada was attacked by Polish planes, which managed to destroy one BT. However the tanks kept advancing until they arrived at Dobropol, where they became engaged in combat with a Polish battalion, who gave a good account of themselves. After sustaining 300 casualties, the 500 survivors surrendered. The 4-ya brigada meanwhile, penetrated Dobrowoda, where they took several hundred prisoners, as well as capturing an intact TK-3 light tank. By the end of the day, Soviet forces had captured a large part of the Polish 12. Dywizja Piechoty (12th Infantry Division), and taken over 5,000 prisoners.

On the following day, after a 65-kilometre advance, the Dniester was crossed and over 2,500 prisoners captured along with five guns and an anti-aircraft battery. In the days that followed, the tanks kept on advancing and hardly met any opposition until they reached Komarno on the 23rd, where they came to a halt after meeting elements of the 2. Gebirgsjäger Division.

On the 17th, the 26-ya brigada advanced on Buczacz and Zyznomierz, becoming engaged in hard fighting with Polish units fleeing to Romania. Two Polish aircraft that attacked the column were shot down by machine-gun fire. By the end of the day, the brigade had covered over 70 kilometres and captured almost 400 prisoners. On the 19th, on very difficult ground for the tanks, with narrow passes and watercourses, they bumped into elements of four Polish divisions, which surrendered after a short skirmish. In the days that followed, the brigade continued advancing and took a large number of prisoners, including several cavalry units and General Anders, who was to achieve fame later in the war.

A dead Polish soldier. (Arch. Dc. Mec., Warsaw)

The 23-ya brigada advanced along the border with Romania, covering 110 kilometres on the first day. On the 18th, the advance continued with hardly any opposition being encountered, and over 11,000 prisoners and six aircraft were captured. On the evening of the 19th, the Brigade arrived at the Dniester, after covering 120 kilometres in a single day. On the 20th, after a 140-kilometre march, met up with units of the 5. Panzerdivision at Stryj and halted. In the days that followed, they contiued on into the difficult terrain of the Carpathians as far as Boryslaw, where they again encountered German forces, and stopped their advance.

In the final days of the invasion there were several confrontations with German units, despite Hitler's order of the 20 September, after the Soviet intervention, to retreat to the Pisa-Narew-Vistula-San rivers line, established in the Pact signed on 23rd August, and to avoid engaging in combat east of the demarcation line. The German withdrawl began on the 21st, hindered by the need to transport a large number of wounded, broken down vehicles, etc, and, even though the Soviets were supposed to provide cover for the Germans in the case they encountered any pockets of Polish resistance, they did not do so and, in the confusion there were several confrontations between the new allies. Thus, a Soviet cavalry unit sustained over twenty casualties when confronting elements of the 10. Panzerdivision near Ostrolenka.

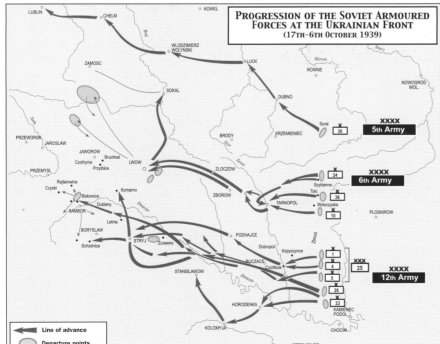

PROGRESSION OF THE SOVIET ARMOURED FORCES AT THE UKRAINIAN FRONT
(17TH–6TH OCTOBER 1939)

Two Soviet officers entering a command post of the German 3rd Army, accompanied by a German officer.

The Polish campaign was officially ended on 6 October.

Russian armoured units, in just over ten days, had occupied all the Polish territory that had been allotted to the Soviet Union in the 23rd August agreement. Favoured by the absence of fortifications or important troop concentrations, it had shown what armoured units could achieve with a deep penetration into enemy territory. Despite the enormously unbalanced forces, the Soviets had sustained considerable losses. Although the official figures mention 737 killed and 1,859 wounded, the real figures are around 10,000 casualties. Forty-two tanks were destroyed and a further 429 broke down and were temporarily out of action. Thirty aircraft were shot down out of the 1,800 which took part in the operation.

As a result of the land operations, deficiencies in the Soviet armoured forces had become evident, the most serious being:

- Lack of fuel stopped several brigades on the second day of the invasion. There were no serious consequences given the circumstances, but if they had faced serious opposition it might have caused the destruction of the brigades. Logis-

Two Soviet tank crew talking nonchalantly. Personal attire and equipment changed little during the war.

tics remained an unsolved issue for the Soviets throughout the war.

- Vulnerability in the face of the anti-tank guns then in service. This shortcoming, which affected all the Soviet tanks of the time, was to be sorted out the following year with the amazing T-34 and, what is more, with the KV series.

- The lack of infantry support in the street fighting caused unnecessary losses among tanks. This circumstance was also to be experienced by the Germans in Warsaw and the French in 1940. Tanks have always been too vulnerable to infantry in towns. Particularly in urban combat, infantry support is needed if they are to survive. The Germans would be the first to develop these

tactics, which they later perfected in the third battle for Kharkov.

These deficiencies did not go unnoticed but nevertheless remained unsolved. In the harsh winter of 1939-40, during the Russo-Finnish War, the battle-hardened Finnish troops took a heavy toll of the Soviet armoured units (as they did with the rest of their forces). Vulnerability of the front tanks in the face of anti-tank guns, determined infantry, fortifications and rough ground became too obvious. Only the commission of new tank types and the change in doctrine, with the use of combined weapons, as well as, of course, the massive advantage in numbers, could change the balance in the fighting.

Despite these negative aspects, the Soviet invasion of Poland in 1939 remains a remarkable example of the massive use of armoured units acting independently to penetrate deep inside the enemy's defensive system, disrupting their defences, leaving the troops of the second wave to consolidate the ground that had been won. The tanks in service at the time were not the most suitable for this mission, which was carried out against all the odds. Only in 1944, during Operation *Bagration*, were the Soviets able to carry out such a manoeuvre, on the central front in this case, and with a crushing numerical superiority, in the face of an enemy of much larger proportions than the Polish Eastern Central Army in 1939.

FROM SEDAN TO ABBEVILLE

According to Manstein's Plan, the *Schwerpunkt* or breakthrough point chosen by the Germans to disrupt the French defensive system in their offensive on the Western Front was at Sedan, once the Ardennes had been crossed. This area was considered impassable for armies, and even more so for armoured units. German strategists were to prove this wrong. The «*Fall Gelb*» intended to lure the Allies into Belgium with their best units, making them think that the Germans would repeat the Schlieffen Plan of the Great War, so as to make the way clear for the main armoured force, which would penetrate through the Ardennes and storm into France and cross the Meuse between Sedan and Dinant. Then, it would rush to the sea, to Abbeville, thus cutting off the best Allied units in Belgium. The German High Command, however, had some reservations regarding the security of such an audacious and revolutionary plan, which was based on the use of armoured units advancing ahead of the slower infantry divisions, which would be tasked with consolidating captured territory. The tanks would dislocate the French defensive system and sow confusion in the rear area. The man in charge of materializing such a plan could be no other than Heinz Guderian, the father of the *Panzerdivision*.

The 1940 *Panzerdivision*

The 1940 *Panzerdivision* was a balanced self-contained unit, ideal for putting the *blitzkrieg* into practice. During the French campaign, there were two types of division. The first type was represented by the 1., 2., 3., 4., 5. and 10. *Panzerdivisionen*, which had two Panzerregiments, each with two battalions. The 6., 7. and 8. Panzerdivisionen, were of the *Leichte Division* type and had just one *Panzerregiment*, with three battalions. The 9. *Panzerdivision* was a particular case and had only one regiment with two battalions.

To give an example, the composition of the *1. Panzerdivision* was as follows;
- A *Panzer brigade*, with two regiments of two battalions each. Each battalion had two light tank companies and one medium tank company
- An infantry brigade
  - An infantry regiment, composed of three battalions, each with two or three infantry companies, a mixed company and a machine-gun or motorcycle company
  - A motorcycle battalion, with four companies
  - A self-propelled artillery company, with six 15-cm sIG 33's.

Deployment of the 7. *Panzerdivision* south of the Somme. (ECPA)

- A *Panzerjäger* battalion, with three anti-tank companies (3.7 cm PaK 35/36) and a machine-gun company
- A reconnaissance battalion, with two armoured vehicle companies, a motorcycle company, a mixed company and an engineers' section *(Pioniere)*
- An artillery regiment, with two battalions, with three batteries each (one with 15 cm guns and the other two with 10 cm guns), and a light battalion, with three 10 cm FH 18 batteries
- An anti-aircraft regiment: with a heavy battery (nine 8.8 cm guns) and two light batteries with twelve 2 cm guns
- An battalion of engineers, with two motorized companies, two pontoon sections and an armoured company
- A signals battalion, of two companies
- Miscellaneous, two medical companies and three ambulance sections, transport, administrative, military police, service units, etc.

The armour forces of each division varied. Thus, the 1. *Panzerdivision* had 161 light (*Panzer* I and II) and 98 medium (*Panzer* III and IV) tanks. The 2. *Panzerdivision* had 175 light and 90 medium tanks and the 10. *Panzerdivision* had 185 light and 90 medium tanks. The 6. *Panzerdivision* had a total of 159 *Panzer* 35(t) medium tanks, whereas the 7. *Panzerdivision* had 110 *Panzer* 38(t)s, both Czech-made.

The *Panzerdivision* was an autonomous independent unit with

Panzerkampfwagen II of the 3. *Panzerdivision*. This tank, with thin armour and armed with a 20 mm gun, was only suitable for reconnaissance missions. Despite this, it contributed remarkably to the success of the *Panzerdivisionen* in Poland and France.

Illustration: Julio López Caeiro.

unprecedented operational flexibility in military history, whose efficiency was based on its very own conception rather than on the individual quality of its tanks. Indeed, only the *Panzer* IV, available in limited numbers, matched or outclassed their French counterparts in combat, if the basic characteristics of a tank are compared. But from the *Panzer* II to the *Panzer* IV, German tanks had a crew that afforded them an unprecedented capability, as well as a complete communications system and tank commanders who had been trained in modern concepts that would materialize in the *blitzkrieg*. Maintenance of the tank was simple, mechanical reliability very high and its use, grouped in independent units, afforded an

The *Panzer* 35(t) was one of the excellent Czech tanks adopted by the German army following annexation, which served in several regiments –with great success– until the early months of *Barbarossa*. The tank in the picture belonged to the 65. *Panzer Abteilung* (6. *Panzerdivision*).

Illustration: Julio López Caeiro.

enormous, unprecedented unparalleled concentration of firepower.

Furthermore, all this was taking place in a very new formation. The first three armoured divisions were established on 15th October 1935, with an organization along very similar lines to the 1927 British experimental unit. Each division was made up of an armoured brigade with motorized infantry and logistics and support units. The armoured brigade

was made up of two regiments, each with two four-company battalions. Each company was made up of thirty-two light tanks (*Panzer* I and II), with a total of 561 tanks per division. The divisional artillery was made up of twenty-four 10.5 cm guns and a 3.7 cm anti-tank gun battalion).

The 4. and 5. *Panzerdivisionen* were established in 1938, and no. 10. in April 1939. These six armoured divisions took part in the Polish campaign, in which valuable lessons were learnt. Tank battalions were reorganized, reduced to a medium company (with *Panzer* III's and IV's) and two light companies (with *Panzer* I's and II's), the total number of tanks was reduced to about 300 per division. With the introduction of medium tanks, and despite these lower numbers, the division's firepower actually increased noticeably. Guderian introduced other modifications, such as, for instance, placing the regimental General Staff closer to the front, and increasing mobility, as well as reducing it to a few armoured vehicles fitted with powerful communications equipment.

The logistics of a *Panzerdivision* was a real challenge for the command, as it could number up to 3,000 vehicles of all type, and some 14,000 men. If the railway network was used for transportation, it required no less than eighty 55-wagon trains each. The capacity of a railway line collapsed for four whole days. Road transportation did not improve the situation, as, on a straight line, the vehicle column could stretch to over 100-

kilometres in length, moving at a desperately slow average speed (5 kph). Breakdowns, passage through towns, damage caused by the passage of heavy tracked vehicles on roads, which made it difficult for the passage of the units that followed, all of this became a logistics nightmare which the Germans managed to master perfectly in 1940. Fuel consumption was extraordinary. A division needed over 3,000 litres for every kilometre covered on the road, and twice as much if it was off-road. Supplies of food and spares parts, the need to rest at reasonable intervals, it was a challenge that a *Panzerdivision* was able to overcome and solve perfectly.

For the Russian campaign the *Panzerdivisionen* were reorganized anew, *leichte* divisions that had proved themselves to be inefficient disappeared, and the number of tanks per division was cut by half, in order to double the number of divisions. Throughout the war, numerous modifications were introduced to adapt to new equipment, new combat requirements, and real numbers of tanks available.

A *Panzerdivision* was much more flexible than any other type of existing division and went hand in hand with the German habit of setting up *Kampfgruppen*, depending on the tactical needs of the time. These "battle groups" were mixed units with a very heterogeneous composition, set up for a particular mission, which were often named after their commander. A typical 1940

Command vehicles such as the *Panzerbefehlswagen* I were an essential instrument in order to give armoured divisions the necessary operational flexibility.
Illustration: Luis Fresno Crespo.

Kampfgruppe could consist of an infantry regiment, a tank battalion, an artillery battalion and several engineer and signals companies. The flexibility achieved by the Germans has never been matched, even though the Americans have claimed the laurels for their task forces, even in current times. This was due to the basic education and doctrine at all levels, according to which any soldier had to be ready to carry out the functions corresponding to one or two ranks above his own. This capability was developed not only vertically but horizontally as well, for which reason, for instance, any tank crewmember was able to take the place of a comrade. During the Second World War, no other army was able to do anything similar and all, without exception, suffered from operational rigidity and a lack of adaptation to the changing circumstances of the battlefield, which was only matched by having resources in overwhelming numbers and by accepting high casualties.

The *Panzerdivision* was the ideal instrument for the *blitzkrieg*. The latter required close cooperation between all arms to be carried out efficiently. One of the key elements was the quality of communications, specifically the wireless, using Morse code. With suitable radio sets, divisional commanders, and even Corps

«FALL GELB»
THE FINAL PLAN

18. Armee Von Küchlev	**Heeresgruppe B** Von Bock 30 divisions
6. Armee Von Reicher	
2. Armee Von Weichs	**Heeresgruppe A** Von Runstedt 44 divisions
12. Armee List	
4. Armee Von Kluge	**16. Armee** Busch
1. Armee Von Witzlet	**Heeresgruppe C** Ritter Von Leeb 17 divisions
7. Armee Dollmann	

red vehicles, one of them with an artillery observer. Motorcycle units explored nearby roads and tracks. The main effort (the *Schwerpunkt*) was to be carried out at weak points, never in the face of fierce resistance. The speed of the advance was vital, and it was preferably to be carried out on the road. The enemy was always be kept in doubt as to where the *panzers* were heading. The narrow front of the advance had to be wide enough to permit the march of two or three columns, which could converge, if necessary, at a single point. Then, the columns should follow different routes to prevent bottlenecks. The real protection of the flanks resided in the air superiority of the *Luftwaffe*, which would stop attacks by enemy aircraft, and smash any threat posed by the enemy's forces.

The Advance of Armee Gruppe A

Three armoured corps formed part of *Armee Gruppe A* (which was made up of a total of 45 divisions), commanded by von Rundstedt, who was in charge of the break through in the Ardennes. In total, seven armoured divisions, deployed in three corps. The XIX *Panzer Korps*, commanded by Guderian, was made up of the 1., 2. and 10. *Panzerdivisionen*. The XV *Panzer Korps*, with the 5. and the 7. *Panzerdivisionen*, was under the command of Hoth, and the XL Panzer Korps, with the 6. and 8. *Panzerdivisionen*, was commanded by Reinhardt. These units were sup-

A *Panzer* II and a *Panzer* I negotiating difficult terrain in the Ardennes, considered by the Allies as impassable for armoured units. (Bundesarchiv 101/382/248/33a)

commanders of the German Army could lead their units on the front, making decisions by the minute, and controlling even the simplest action if they thought it necessary. After the Polish campaign, Guderian urged the commanders of his armoured units to restrict their General Staffs to a few armoured vehicles and stay as close to the front as possible. During the French campaign, after the experience in Poland, Guderian's units, concentrated in an unprecedented way, were to smash the French front and cause its defences to collapse. Carrying out a textbook manoeuvre in their race to the sea.

The theory was well defined. Tank concentrations were only to be used against heavily defended positions. They were to advance in echelon, with a gap of about 50 metres between each tank, making good use of the cover offered by the terrain. The division's commander enjoyed real time information on the progress of his units, and decided whether to use his own forces for an attack or to ask for support from the *Luftwaffe*. Engineers and supporting infantry were to accompany them at the front, keeping pace with the tanks,

as well as anti-tank guns, which were to be in charge of pinning down any enemy tanks that might be met, allowing the *Panzers* to outflank them. After the breakthrough was achieved, the speed of the advance would increase. Reconnaissance aircraft regularly supplied information on enemy forces.

Generally, the spearhead of the advance was made up of three armou-

plemented by five *Panzerjäger Abteilungen* and four *Sturmgeschütz* batteries, respectively equipped with *Panzerjäger* I's and *StuG* III's.

Having crossed Luxemburg with little opposition, they crossed onto French soil. The main problem that they had to solve was the enormous bottlenecks that had begun on the winding roads of the Ardennes for —apart from the naturally difficult task of moving such a mass of vehicles— there was the fact that the routes of several divisions overlapped each other. Despite all these difficulties, the different units were progressing with remarkable speed, much faster than the Allies were ready to admit.

The units advancing in the Ardennes ran into the Belgian *Chasseurs Ardennnais*, who had deployed two divisions. Both retreated in the face of the German advance, without having coordinated at all with the French, leaving the way clear for the Germans. What the *chasseurs* did manage to accomplish was a programme of demolition that had been prepared back in 1935. This included up to 222 demolition tasks along with the defence of several important communication centres by small units that would give cover to one another on the retreat, as the planned demolition was being carried out. The Germans also had a secret, novel plan to accelerate their passage through the Ardennes, called *Niwi*. It consisted in the infiltration of small units behind the Belgian lines in *Fieseler Storch* aircraft in order to disrupt their communications and spread chaos in the rearguard until the arrival of their own forces. Shortly after six in the morning, the tanks of the 1. *Panzerdivision* crossed the Luxemburg border at Wallendorf and crossed into Belgium. An unevenly matched fight took place at Bodange, where the *chasseurs* managed to stop the 1. *Panzerdivision* for almost six hours, at high cost. Finally, the firepower of the armoured division was overwhelming and the resolute Belgian defenders surrendered. For their part, the 2. *Panzerdivision* had to neutralize a point of resistance at Strainchamps. There, the German tanks clashed with a Belgian 47 mm self-propelled gun, which managed to knock out a *Panzer* III. The combination of infantry, artillery and tanks soon caused the Belgian resistance to crumble. The Ardennes was an obstacle no more.

The French air force, particularly the reconnaissance squadrons, carried out several missions in that direction, but ran into the *Luftwaffe* umbrella and were not able to find the bulk of the German forces advancing in the woodlands. An additional difficulty was the demolition work and barriers set up by the Belgians, which caused difficulties not only for the Germans, but for the French units as well. The French High Command had no idea of the German intentions, and took the strange movements detected in the sector for an attempt to outflank the Maginot Line, as a secondary manoeuvre in the framework of the main offensive taking place in Belgium.

On the 11th, the 2. *Panzerdivision* had taken Libramont and taken the first French prisoners, whereas the 1. *Panzerdivision*, having gone beyond Neufchâteau, advanced on Bertrix. Practically the only difficulties encountered were the demolition and obstacles set up by the Belgians, which forced the engineers to work hard to clear the way. The 10. *Panzerdivision* originally had to cover the southern flank, but was alternatively diverted by Guderian and Kleist, depending on their attitudes, which were more aggressive or more cautious respectively. This tension between both commanders finally exploded on the 17th. Reconnaissance aircraft kept on supplying updated information on the enemy, and the advance was only hindered by the level of destruction in their way. At 15:15, elements of the 1. *Panzerdivision* entered Bertrix, meeting hardly any opposition.

On the 12th, Guderian's forces crushed the cavalry units of the French 2e *Armée* and, before dusk, took the historical town of Bouillon, hometown of Godfrey de Bouillon, one of the leaders of the First Crusade. Bouillon was defended by a motley heterogeneous group of units that were soon beaten by the combi-

The *Panzer* IV *Ausf* D was the most powerful tank the Germans had in 1940. However, its L/24 75 mm gun was not really efficient against contemporary enemy tanks.

Illustration: Julio López Caeiro

ned fire of tanks and artillery and an accurate attack by a *Stuka* squadron. In the afternoon, the German position in the town was now well established, and a bombardment by the French heavy artillery in the evening only caused several civilian casualties.

All the bridges over the nearby Semois River had been demolished, but the reconnaissance units discovered several fords that the engineers soon made passable for the tanks. At dusk, they had reached the banks of the Meuse, the last great barrier before reaching ideal tank country. Huntzinger, the commander of the French 2ᵉ *Armée*, thought that German intentions were to attack the Maginot Line from the rear, and placed his best units to protect it. On the other hand, he used 2nd class divisions to defend what was to be the critical sector, at the Meuse.

The land was really suitable for defence. The Meuse itself was an amazing obstacle and, besides this, there were a good number of fortifications along its banks to conceal support weapons of different types and artillery of different calibres. But most of the divisions in charge

A *Panzerjäger* I of the 521. *Panzerjäger-Abteilung*. This tank destroyer was the first German attempt to take the chassis of an obsolete tank and fit it with armament that was far superior to that mounted on the original tank. In this case, a Czech 47 mm anti-tank gun on a *Panzer* I Ausf B chassis.
Illustration: Julio López Caeiro

of the defence were of low quality, poorly trained and equipped 2nd rate units. To make things worse, the 55ᵉ and 71ᵉ divisions defending the sector that was to be the target of the main attack exchanged positions, which added noticeable confusion to the mess prevailing among these second class units.

Disaster at Sedan

The French command was so sure that there was no danger in the Sedan sector, that the 2ᵉ *Armée* had no forces to organize a second defensive line. And the situation had not changed even on the 12th, when the crossing was imminent. Such was the degree of deception achieved by the Germans and the poor results of the few reconnaissance flights made by the overburdened French air force over the Ardennes.

Reinhardt's LXI *Panzer Korps* succeeded partly because of Guderian's breakthrough at Sedan. Upon reaching the northern bank of the Meuse on the night of the 12th, Guderian's troops were getting ready to cross the river the following morning. The French did not expect an attack within 96 hours, according to traditional doctrine. The attack, however, could not start until the afternoon, because the French artillery, well entrenched on the Marfée hills, where advanced observers were deployed, harassed the German units throughout the morning, preventing any concentration for the assault. No matter how effective,

the French artillery could not exploit its advantageous position because their ammunition stocks were limited, as the High Command did not think that the main German effort would be unleashed in that sector.

Given the situation, Guderian asked for support from the *Luftwaffe*, which proved devastating. Row after row of *Stukas*, He 111's and Do 17's, and even fighters, bombed French batteries and positions for four hours, neutralizing most of the positions, the guns either being destroyed or their crews demoralized. All this devastation occurred along a corridor of a depth of about 20 kilometres by over 700 aircraft. At three in the afternoon on the 13th, with direct air support, and under cover of the 8.8 cm guns and field artillery which was by then in place, the first units of 1. *Panzerdivision* started crossing the river. The sector was defended by a 2nd rate French infantry division, the 55ᵉ, which, with its defences smashed by direct fire from the 88's, could do little (most of its soldiers were over 35 years old and its establishment of officers were well below the required number and also of poor quality). The infantry regiment of the 1. *Panzerdivision*, along with the *Grossdeutschland* Regiment, crossed the river, and consolidated the area at Ignes. The earliest crossings were carried out at four different points, by 6/8-men sections in rubber dinghies.

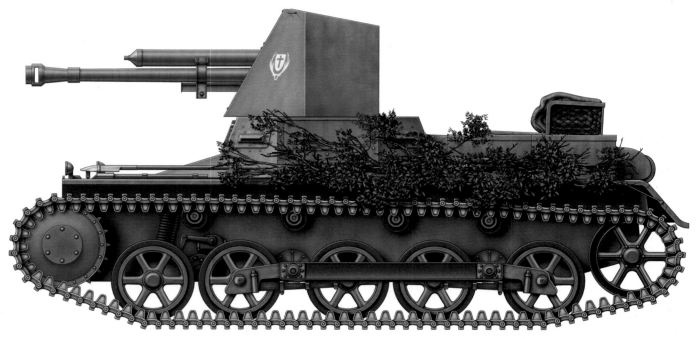

In the meantime, the 10. Panzer-division ran into more serious difficulties trying to cross the river at Wadelincourt, a sector defended by the 75 mm guns of the 71ᵉ division. The French, in the face of the push by the infantry of the 1. *Panzerdivision*, soon abandoned their positions, letting the Germans advance on the Marfee hills. At dusk, reconnaissance units of the 2. *Panzerdivision* had crossed the Meuse at Doncherry. An eight-kilometre deep bridgehead was established.

The French 55ᵉ division, in full retreat despite the efforts of its CO, Général Lafontaine, hindered the arrival of two reinforcing infantry regiments. At that moment, a chain reaction began that caused panic and a stampede among the French troops, which then spread to the nearby 71ᵉ division. Although there are many hypotheses to explain this, such as the presence of fifth columnists, communist elements, French tanks confused with *panzers*, etc., the truth is that the cause of the panic was the devastating air raid and the rapidity of the infiltration by the German assault troops, which disorganized the whole defensive system, and completely disoriented the French command.

Despite this debacle, the German bridgehead was not yet consolidated, and was only being secured by infantry units. If the French were able to organize a counterattack with all their available units, there was still a chance to stop the gap. But the German *Pioniere* gave them no chance. In 38 minutes they had organized the first ferry, and the first pontoon bridge was ready, after three and a half hours work, at eleven that night. The first vehicle crossed it ten minutes later. Shortly after six in the morning on the 14th, the tanks of the 1. *Panzerdivision* started to cross the Meuse.

At about the same time, 06:20, the French began their first counterattack in two directions, using an infantry regiment and one FCM 36 tank battalion (with 45 tanks apiece). The conditions were adverse, as the French were not aware of the enemy's situation, lacked reconnaissance and had many difficulties in advancing against the stream of refugees and stampeding

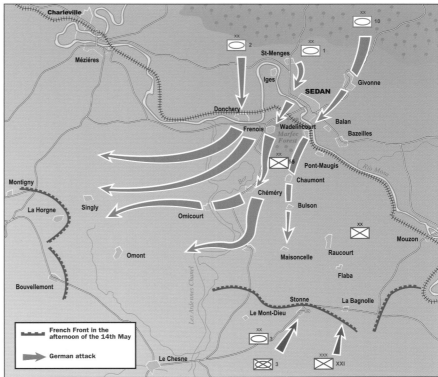

French Front in the afternoon of the 14th May

German attack

troops. The 213ᵉ Infanterie and the 7ᵉ BCC attacked at the Chéhéry-Bulson sector, taking over five hours to advance five kilometres. Initially, they destroyed two German 3.7 cm anti-tank guns, but the infantry stopped in the face of German fire and the tanks carried on alone. Although the first German infantry units they met broke contact quickly, they soon ran into German tanks. The deficiencies of the 3.7 cm SA 18 gun, and the one-man turret of the French tanks were soon to be left in evidence. The first *Panzer III* sustained twelve point-blank hits, without suffering serious damage. In the first company, only three FMC 36's returned, credited with knocking out just one *Panzer* III. Another company lost nine out of their thirteen tanks, but at least managed to immobilize two *panzers*. The second company began an engagement that lasted over two hours, scoring numerous hits on German tanks but without knocking any out, and retreated with only three surviving tanks (out of their initial thirteen). In total, the 7ᵉ BCC had lost 70% of their tanks and 50% of their men, without having reached their objectives. The infantry that should have supported them were stuck on the ground and did not take an active part in the fighting.

After considerable losses, both counterattacks were aborted, and the French troops started a retreat that soon became a total disorder. At noon, the Germans had captured four bridges, and the stream of troops across the Meuse was ceaseless. *Luftwaffe* support was constant and deadly, although on some occasions it hit the wrong target. On one of those occasions they bombed a column of the 1. *Panzerdivision* by mistake, destroying several vehicles and killing several members of the General Staff of the 2. *Panzerregiment* 2.

Despite the French attempts at assaulting Guderian with their three heavy armoured divisions during the 14th, they were not able to organize them in time. The attack on Hoth by the 1ᵉ DCR on the 15th ended in disaster. The 2ᵉ and 3ᵉ DCRs aborted their attacks and were used as a stop-gap, whereas the Germans penetrated some 10 kilometres and secured the hills at Stonne. On the evening of the 14th, the XIX. *Armee Korps* (motorizet) had accomplished their mission, and the contact between the II. and IX. *Armee* was broken. A breakthrough had been achieved.

The disorganized French counterattacks did nothing but waste good units that, if they had been employed otherwise, could have played a

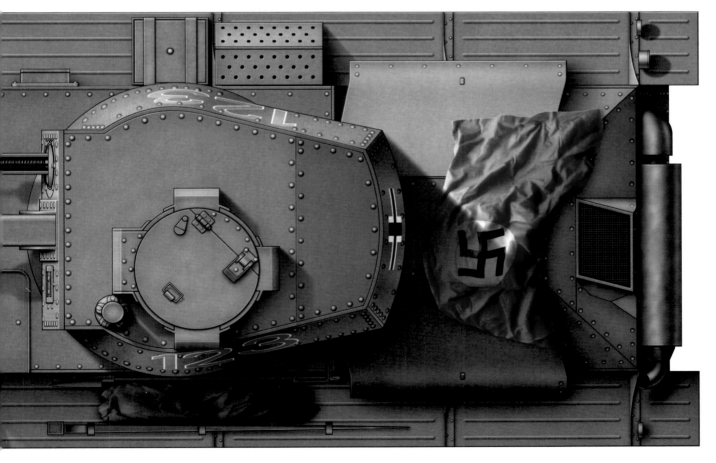

Panzerkampfwagen 38(t)

In the years before the war, Czech industry had achieved a remarkable degree of quality, which placed its products among the most advanced in the world. One of its armament factories, CKD (Ceskomoravská Kolben Danek), had designed a tank that was chosen by the army for series production, but this could not be started before the German annexation of Bohemia and Moravia on the 15th March 1939. This tank, called the TNHP-S, whose prototype had done over 5,500 kilometres in three months without noticeable problems, and had shown remarkable capability over broken ground, apart from minimum maintenance needs, was called *LT vz 38* by the Czechs. The Germans were soon aware of its virtues and adopted it at once in May 1939.

Apart from the 150 initially ordered by the Czech army, the Germans ordered an additional 325, and called it the *Panzerkampfwagen* 38(t). They also adopted another Czech tank in service, the *LT vz 35*, built by Skoda, to which they added a fourth crewman in the turret: the loader.

One hundred and fifty *Panzer 38(t) Ausf As* were built from May to November 1939. The Germans added a fourth crewman, the loader, as they had done in the Skoda. In order to place him, apart from lacking a seat and sights, three containers, each holding six shells, were discarded.

From January to November 1940, a further 325 of the B, C and D models were built, each with small modifications, such as the addition of smoke grenade launchers, suppression of the huge aerials and the installation of German lighting systems. From November 1940 to October 1941, an additional 525 tanks of the E and F models were built, following experience gained in Poland and France, these were fitted with additional armour plates of 15 to 25 mm in thickness. Ninety S type units, initially ordered by Sweden, were built and 500 of the G model, although only 321 of the latter, fitted with much thicker armour, were completed as tanks.

The *PzKpfw 38(t) Ausf A* had a weight of 9.4 metric tons, and a four-man crew, consisting of the tank commander/gunner, radio operator/gunner, driver and loader. The armament was made up of a 3.7 cm *Skoda A-7* gun and two 7.92 mm machine-guns, one coaxial and the other in the hull in a ball mount. Armour was 25 mm at the front, 15 mm on the sides and 10 mm at the rear. It was propelled by a water-cooled six-cylinder Praga EPA petrol engine, with a maximum output of 125 hp at 2,200 rpm that afforded a top road-speed of 40 kph and a range of about 250 km. It could take ninety 3.7 cm and 2,400 7.92 mm rounds.

The turret had a manual turning mechanism that could be disengaged so that it could be moved by the tank commander with a shoulder support. The gun was aimed by a coaxial gun sight, and elevation, also attained by means of the shoulder support, ranged from -10º to +25º. The turret lacked a stowage bin and the crew were standing on the hull floor, as there was only a seat for the commander. The fixed cupola had four periscopes.

The radio was of the *FuG 37(t)* model, and was installed at the front on the left hand side, greatly restricting the space for the operator. Depending on the aerials used, range was one to five kilometres. Although it lacked an intercom, the commander could send some orders to the driver by means of a system of coloured lights.

The first unit to put it into service was the *Panzerabteilung* 67 of the 3. Leichte Division in Poland, which used 59 of these tanks, seven of which were damaged, although all were later repaired. A small number took part in the Norwegian campaign, and in the French campaign 229 were used by the 7. and 8. *Panzerdivisionen*. Again, total losses were really very rare and this tank became famous for its extraordinary mechanical reliability. In Russia things changed, and it is estimated that almost 800 were lost during the first six months of the campaign. It had reached its operational limits.

But if its career as a light tank was finished, a new one had started, that of the variants or of the vehicles developed on its chassis, such as the *Marder* and the amazing *Hetzer*.

Indeed, after it became obsolete as a tank and was seen as too slow for a reconnaissance vehicle, the chassis was reused in 1942 and fitted with a gun that had been captured in large numbers during *Barbarossa*, the magnificent Soviet 76.2 mm gun, ZIS 3. The *Panzerjäger 38(t) für 7,62 cm Pak 36(r)*, or Sdkfz 139, also known as the *Marder III*, was created, 366 of which were built. The Pak 40 was fitted to 417 tanks, late in 1942 and in 1943, giving rise to the *Sdkfz 138 Ausf H*. 975 of the M were built, in 1943 and 1944, and was an excellent tank-hunter, 350 of which were still in service in February 1945.

It was also fitted with the 15 cm sIG 33 infantry gun, in several versions, and was known as the *Grille*. Almost 400 vehicles were thus transformed. It was also used as an anti-aircraft tank, with a 2 cm *KwK38* gun (140 built), as a reconnaissance tank, with the 2 cm *Hängelafette* 38 turret, as a munitions vehicle, etc. However, the most numerous and most successful development was the amazing *Hetzer*, 2,584 being built up to the end of the war. Armed with the 7,5 cm Pak 39 L/48, protected by sloping armour up to 60 mm thick, and with a top speed of 42 kph, the small *Hetzer* became one of the most efficient tank destroyers of the Second World War. After the war, it was used by both the Czechs and the Swiss.

decisive role. For instance, the 1e Brigade de *Cavalerie* and the 3ᵉ *Brigade de Spahis* took over one third casualties at La Horgne in a useless attempt at stopping the advance of the 1. *Panzerdivision*. The regimental CO's were killed in combat, and the CO of the *Spahi* brigade was seriously wounded.

The fight for Stonne is representative of the useless nature of French efforts. The town was taken by the infantry of the *Gross Deutschland* and the French counterattacked with their tanks without infantry support. Unable to consolidate the ground, and subject to aggressive infantry fire, the French tanks retreated and the Germans regained their positions. When at last a French infantry regiment was able to capture the town, the French tanks had to leave the position to re-supply and the German infantry and artillery forced the French to retreat. At night, a raid by British Fairey *Battles* was fruitless, as they were not able to identify their targets properly.

On the 15th, the VIᵉ *Armée*, commanded by Général Touchon, was hastily deployed to fill the gap between the IIe and the IXᵉ *Armées*. The units that were to form the reserves to launch a counterattack were being used in a piecemeal way to shore-up the front. The stream of troops in retreat, the speed of the German advance and the lack of suitable information, hindered the French ability to manoeuvre. With hardly any opposition, Reinhardt rushed to Montcornet. The French were still without a clear picture of German intentions, and tried to bar the way to Paris and defend the exposed left flank of the *Maginot* Line.

The 16th saw another French counterattack, again in the Stonne sector. Two B1bis tank companies of the 41ᵉ BCC formed the spearhead, followed by an H-39 company of the 45ᵉ BCC and two infantry companies of the 51e RI. Advancing fearlessly under German fire, the B1 bis entered the town, where they encountered several tanks of the 10. Panzerdivision. The tank commander of the first company, *"Eure"*, sustained over one hundred 2 cm and 3.7 cm hits, without serious damage. In the narrow back streets of the town, firing was at point blank range, often at less than 50 metres, and the Germans could not manoeuvre. Several of their tanks, including some *Panzer IV's*, were knocked out, as well as several of the useless 3.7 cm guns. With the arrival of the French infantry, the Germans withdrew, losing about 100 men, killed or taken prisoner. On the following day, however, the arrival of elements of

The Sdkfz 251 was the ideal vehicle for the grenadier units of a Panzerdivision, but their numbers were always too few to equip all units.

Illustration: Julio López Caeiro.

the 2. *Infanterie Division (motorized)* turned the tables and the French were definitively chased out of the town. A last-ditch French counterattack the following day ran into firmly entrenched German infantry and artillery, and was repelled with heavy losses by the B1 bis.

The French found it impossible to regroup their dispersed units for a cohesive and decisive action, due to the speed and power of the German advance. Three factors had been decisive for the breakthrough. Firstly, Guderian's decision to attack at

Engineer units were essential for the successful advance of a Panzerdivision. The picture shows a pontoon bridge being crossed by an improvised ambulance and French prisoners. (Bundesarchiv).

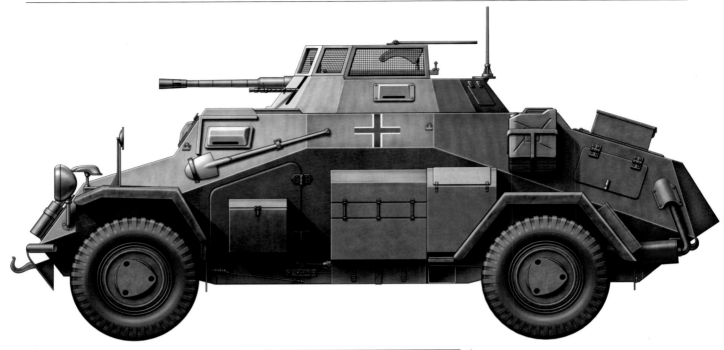

The Sdkfz 222 was an excellent reconnaissance vehicle by 1940 standards and remained in service throughout the war. Rapid and manoeuvrable, it was armed with a 2 cm gun and a 7.92 mm coaxial machine-gun.

Illustration: Julio López Caeiro

once on a narrow front, without giving the enemy time to react. Secondly, the panic created among the French troops by the speed of the German advance (some units did not stop before reaching Reims, almost 100 kilometres away), and the presence of the tanks, which had a really demoralizing effect, no matter if their efficiency in combat (even the *Panzer* I's managed to cause panic) was real or not. And finally, there was Guderian's decision on the afternoon of the 14th to advance westwards without waiting for the infantry, contrary Kleist's opinion.

The race to the sea

On the 16th, Guderian's units and, further to the north, Rommel's, had reached ideal tank country, large plains and isolated farms, where the French artillery could not establish blocking positions, and armoured units could move freely. However, an unexpected setback endangered the breakthrough achieved by Guderian.

A line of *Panzer III* tanks, followed by an ammunition vehicle (in the foreground), penetrating a French region. The number of fuel drums can be seen at the rear part of the tanks. (Bundesarchiv 101/382/248/11th)

On the night of the 15th, Kleist ordered the XIX *Panzer Korps* to stop, fearing that his exposed flanks might be the targets of an Allied counterattack, and in order to wait for the slower infantry divisions. Guderian managed to convince him to advance for the next 24 hours, but on the morning of the 17th, he was again ordered to stop. The German General Staff, including Hitler himself, were afraid of their own success, and were not confident with the evolution of events. There followed a serious

The Sdkfz 263 was the command and communication version of the excellent Sdkfz 234. Although not built in large numbers some remained in service to the end. The one depicted here was General Erwin Rommel's vehicle during the battle of France.

Illustration: Julio López Caeiro

argument in which Guderian even resigned from his post, but after von Rundstedt's personal intervention, Guderian was allowed to carry out what he called a "reconnaissance en force". Such a reconnaissance manoeuvre, in an interpretation that was both loose and lucky, was carried out by no other than the armoured units and infantry of the 1. and 2. *Panzerdivisionen.*

The morning of the 17th also witnessed the first serious French attempt at a counter-attack, in a disorganized advance by the recently established 4ᵉ DCR, commanded by de Gaulle, on Montcornet. The powerful French tank units entered directly into combat as they arrived, without coordination, and were beaten without much effort by the few

It is a widely held belief that in 1940, the German army was totally motorized. This is far from true, as most of the infantry divisions had numerous horse-drawn wagons for transport. Only the *Panzerdivisionen* and *Leichtedivisionen* were reasonably equipped with motor vehicles in a wide variety of roles like this Grosser *Nachrichtenwagen* Kfz 62 on a Krupp L3H163 chassis.

Illustration: Julio López Caeiro

8.8 cm anti-aircraft guns deployed there, as well as by the determined defence made by several infantry units, well entrenched within the towns. The counterattack was a failure that hardly worried the Germans. This action, however, will be the subject of more detailed attention in a later chapter.

At nine in the morning on the 18th, the 2. *Panzerdivision* entered St-Quentin. The crossing of the

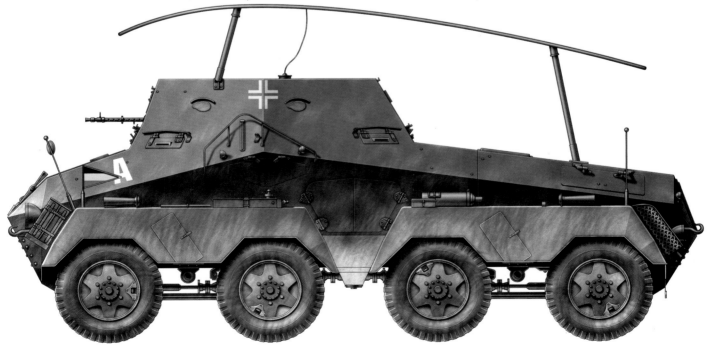

Oise represented the breakthrough of the last French line of defence, after which Guderian's tanks would not come across any further obstacles before reaching the sea. The 1. *Panzerdivision* arrived at the Somme at Peronne and crossed it without trouble, capturing a large group of French officers of the General Staff who had nonchalantly approached the dynamic front line, unaware of the close presence of German troops.

Further to the north, after fierce fighting, the 6. *Panzerdivision* annihilated the remains of the French 2e DCR, a B-1 bis battalion. Rommel ran out of fuel and, after defeating several French units in the vicinity of Le Cateau, he established an improvised *Kampfgruppe*, with some tanks, several anti-aircraft guns and a mechanized infantry battalion. With this unit, he advanced on a wide front to Cambrai, creating such a dust cloud that the French defenders took them for a whole armoured division. By dusk, he had taken the town.

In the meantime, the French High Command kept on deploying their units as fast as they could to defend Paris, establishing a defensive line behind the Aisne. Standing between the Germans and the

sea were two British territorial divisions, the 12th and the 23rd, short on artillery and made up of inexperienced troops. The movements of the French and British units were now hindered by the stream of refugees that crowded the roads. The capture of Giraud with his whole General Staff on the following day made things even worse for the Allies given the already chaotic situation they were in.

On the 19th, de Gaulle tried to carry out one more counterattack on Guderian's left flank from Laon, in the Crécy sector, using the 150 tanks that the mauled 4e DCR still had. Again, lack of coordination, the combined action of the German tanks and anti-tank guns and the sudden appearance of the *Luftwaffe* spoiled the attempted attack, causing the French serious losses.

Late in the afternoon of the 19th, Guderian was given permission to advance the next day towards Amiens, as all the available information from the reconnaissance units suggested that the French had no reserves to pose a threat on the left flank of the XIX *Panzer Korps*. This was symbolic ground for the Germans, for it was near Amiens that Ludendorff's offensive had finally been brought

to a halt in 1918. History would not repeat itself.

At 04:00 on the 20th, Guderian's troops started their advance and Balck's tanks reached Amiens at noon, a distance of over 50 kilometres. The *Royal Sussex Regiment* was annihilated in a brief but fierce fight for the control of this town. In total, both British territorial divisions, which held an improvised defensive line along the *Canal du Nord*, were smashed by the 2. Panzerdivision and ceased to exist as combat units.

The units of the 1. *Panzerdivision* advanced to establish a bridgehead south of the Somme, which was consolidated at noon, to a depth of six-kilometres. The 10. *Panzerdivision*, after crossing the Somme, established a defensive line east of Corbie.

The 2. *Panzerdivision*, for their part, advanced on the right towards Abbeville. Initially, this division showed signs of fatigue, requesting

The 15 cm. sIG 33 (Sf) auf Pz.kpfw. I Ausf B was a failed attempt at equipping the infantry with a genuine self-propelled gun. Although it enjoyed notable firepower, the chassis was too light for such a large calibre gun.

Illustration: Julio López Caeiro

more fuel before starting their advance, but the energetic Guderian, after checking their supplies, soon made the armoured units set off. One of his comments became famous: *"when commanders are tired, fuel lacks."* After these incidents, the 2. *Panzerdivision*, reached Abbeville at the end of the Somme estuary at seven in the afternoon. Their entry into the town, which lacked an efficient defence, was preceded by a heavy air raid that spread chaos and panic with the advance of the German tanks, apart from causing numerous fires in the town. At dusk, their reconnaissance units, commanded by *Oberstleutnant* Spitta, rolled up at Noyelles-sur-Mer. The German tanks had reached the sea. They had covered over 400 kilometres in ten days, crossing rivers, destroying powerful French units, beating off several counterattacks, capturing main towns and disrupting the whole French defensive system. Never before had such a comparable been achieved. The German General Staff was surprised and scared of its own success and, throughout the 20th, *Gruppe Kleist* neither received or issued any orders regarding the development of operations.

The race to the sea had finished. The best French, British and Belgian units had been cut off, and victory was just a question of days. On the 21st a race along the coast started, when Guderian's units advanced on Boulogne and Calais, whose garrisons were hurriedly reinforced by British units.

On the 22nd, the French launched their last counter-attack on the German pincers in the Cambrai sector which was also repulsed after a moderate initial advance. This was the last demonstration that while the French may have had the equipment and men for a war of movement, they lacked suitable commanders at the highest levels.

The 2. *Panzerdivision* met serious French resistance at Samer on the afternoon of the 22nd, but this was overcome by the combination of the whole potential of the armoured division. Two battalions of the French 21[e] DI managed to slow down the 1. *Panzerdivision* at Desvíes until noon on the 23rd before they were routed. Then, several Allied naval units joined the fight, and the

advancing German units that were sticking to the coast were bombarded by several destroyers. The *Luftwaffe* came to their aid and soon the French destroyer *l'Orage* was sunk and two British destroyers, *HMS Keith* and the *HMS Vimy*, were seriously damaged.

On the 23rd, the Germans entered Boulogne, although the fight in the town continued for two days. Five thousand British and some French soldiers were evacuated by sea. The British troops belonged to the Guard's Brigade, and the last ones were evacuated on the morning of the 24th. The French command was not informed of this manoeuvre, which caused the whole French defensive system in the town to crumble. Some British units were also not evacuated, either by error or through lack of coordination, and were left behind. On the 25th, the 2,000 surviving defenders entrenched in the citadel surrendered.

On the 24th, Calais was surrounded by the 10. *Panzerdivision*, whereas the 1. *Panzerdivision* reached the Aa canal. On the same day, when Dunkirk was the only usable port left to the Allies, and which was about to be stormed by Guderian's units, Hitler, to the former's despair, ordered the tanks to stop outside the town.

The fight for Calais gives an idea of the confused situation for the Allies in those dramatic days in May. The stream of British reinforcements arriving in the port was ceaseless. The 3rd RTR, with twenty-one Mark VI's and twenty-seven cruiser tanks, arrived on the 22nd. After a confused series of orders and countermands, they advanced towards St-

Omer, where they ran into the German tanks. After a brief fight, in which twelve tanks were lost, the 3rd RTR returned to Calais. On the 23rd, a reconnaissance squadron, en route to Dunkirk was almost annihilated by the tanks of the 1. *Panzerdivision*. It was clear that there was no way out of the defensive perimeter established around the town and the nearby Gravelines. Three Panzerdivisionen besieged the town. Despite Hitler's order to stop, the commander of the *Leibstandarte* decided to take Mount Watten, crossing the Aa canal on the 25th. This small 72-metre-high hill was vital in order to dominate the surrounding area and, by taking it, the German forces were ready to storm the town. After another encounter with the German tanks, the 3rd RTR was reduced to twenty-one tanks. After almost two days of air raids, the Germans attacked the town, which eventually fell on the 26th. Now there was only Dunkirk left as an escape for the isolated Franco-British units.

Epilogue

The *Panzerdivisionen* had proved all of their potential and had developed the *blitzkrieg* concept perfectly at the hands of its creator, Guderian, and all this in spite of the fear and continuous interference from the high command, distrustful of the new and wonderful weapon in their hands. Something which had not been achieved in four years of war in 1914-18, the new *Panzerdivisonen* had accomplished in just over ten days. A new and revolutionary chapter in the art of war had been opened.

German Infantry (posing for the camera) taking up positions in a ditch by a marsh, among several destroyed French vehicles.

HEINZ GUDERIAN

Born on 17th June 1888 at Kulm, he was the son of a Prussian soldier. He attended school at Colmar and St.-Avold and later the cadet school in Karlsruhe and at the *Gross-Lichterfelde*, near Berlin. His first posting was at the (Hannover) 10. Jäger Battalion, at Bitche. In 1912 he attended a one-year communications course in Koblenz, a subject that caught his attention. He had two sons, Heinz Günther and Kurt.

His service record during the First World War was not particularly outstanding. He was posted to the General Staff during the battle of Verdun as an intelligence officer and later as a liaison officer to von Brauchitsch to carry out coordination tasks between land and air forces.

After the armistice, he joined the Freikorps forces fighting left-wingers, later working at the *Reichswehr* Ministry where he spent thirteen years studying the influence of the use of motorized units on military tactics and strategy. Unlike other theoreticians on the subject, he managed to perfectly define the concept of the tactical use of armour. In 1931, after promotion to *Oberstleutnant*, he became inspector of motorized troops. In Hitler, two years later, he found an enthusiastic supporter of his theories on the use of tanks. Thus, in 1935, he was made the commander of the recently established 2. *Panzerdivision* which he organized according to his ideas.

In 1936 he published the book «Achtung! Panzer!», where he described and defended the simultaneous use of tanks, artillery and aircraft. He saw the armoured division as being independent of the infantry units, an autonomous unit with extraordinary mobility to penetrate the enemy defensive system, disrupting their forces and spreading chaos in the rearguard, leaving the slower infantry units to consolidate ground.

In 1938 he was the commander of the *Armee Korps* (motorized) that occupied Austria. Problems detected in the use of tanks, particularly in regard to logistics and maintenance, were quickly solved. Shortly afterwards, he took part in the occupation of the Sudetenland. In November he was appointed General Inspector of Armoured Troops. In September 1939 he took part in the Polish campaign as commander of the XIX *Armee Korps* (motorized), which honoured his theory by penetrating deeply into the Polish defensive system, according to the principles of *blitzkrieg*. He made contact with the Soviet troops at Brescz (Brest Litowsk), a town that he had taken after fierce fighting with the Polish defenders.

A great advocate of the *Fall Gelb*, during the French campaign he assumed command of the XIX *Armee Korps* (motorized), regrouping the 1., 2. and 10. Panzerdivisionen, and reinforced by the *Grossdeutschland* Regiment, the elite of the German infantry. He made the *blitzkrieg* a reality, by disobeying the orders of his superiors and made his units advance, putting to the test the resistance of both men and machines. This resulted in the collapse of the front and he obtained a real breakthrough, the dream of the General Staffs of the Great War, and spread chaos in the French rearguard, cutting communications, capturing General Staffs that did not expect such a deep and rapid penetration and making any attempts at closing the breaches useless.

Before the start of «Barbarossa», he was promoted to *Generaloberst* and appointed chief of the 2. *Panzergruppe*. Shortly after the start of the operation, he was awarded the Oak Leaves but, due to his constant disagreements

with his superior, von Kleist, who became alarmed at the rapid and risky advances of his tanks, he was dismissed.

In February 1943, following the disaster at Stalingrad, he was appointed General Inspector of the Armoured Forces, and given the task of reorganizing the Panzerwaffe and adapting production to the realities of service at the front. He was on good terms with Speer, and the pace of tank production speeded up. He personally introduced many improvements in designs and, with his characteristic vehemence, he maintained continuation in the production of the *Panzer IV*, against Hitler's idea to concentrate exclusively on the production of the *Panther* and *Tiger*, which, given the situation of German industry at that time, would have caused the collapse of tank production and disaster in a few months.

Although he was appointed Chief of the General Staff in 1944 following the failed attempt on Hitler's life, after a violent discussion with the *Führer*, he was again dismissed in March 1945. He was captured by the Americans in May but was not tried at Nuremberg. Set free in 1948, he published several books on the war and the Panzerwaffe, until his death on 14 May 1954.

His subordinates nicknamed him Heinz "the Swift", and he was universilly appreciated. However, this was not the case with his superiors, who had to put up with his energetic and violent character. In fact, he was one of the few who discussed openly and vehemently with Hitler, and did not hesitate to give up command if he did not get the support he judged necessary. Despite such friction, time and again he was called on by the *Führer* to try and restore the situation when the latter became desperate. He had a profound knowledge of the possibilities of each armoured vehicle, both in theory and in practice, and knew their limits, which he transmitted to his men. His extraordinary virtues as a tank commander –probably the best ever– were never appreciated by the most conservative elements of the German General Staff.

MONTCORNET, 17TH MAY 1940

In comparison with their German or British counterparts, French tank units did not play a brilliant role on the Western Front in 1940. However, it was neither because of the poor quality of the materiel nor the fact that armour was a novelty for the French army, but rather it was down to strategic and doctrinal error. As a matter of fact, in the First World War, the French had had tanks before the Germans and the first armoured division in the world was created in 1930 by order of the French Chief of General Staff, Général Weygand. The *1ère Division Légère Mécanique* (light mechanized division or DLM) was ready in 1933. In the 1920's, Général Jean-Baptiste Eugène Estienne (1860-1936) had preached in vain the possibilities of armoured warfare, like the British Liddell-Hart, but it was not until a decade later when his ideas were taken seriously, by both General Staffs and governments.

The DLM was a balanced force, and the French General Staff started the conversion of cavalry divisions into DLMs but, unlike the Germans, these large units remained under the control of the infantry. Each French armoured division had half the tanks a German *Panzerdivision*. At the beginning of the war, the French had more tanks than the Germans, but fewer armoured divisions, as they distributed tanks in independent battalions for infantry support.

Individually, French tanks were better than their German counterparts, particularly the SOMUA S 35 and the B-1. As a matter of fact, the SOMUA S 35 combined the three fundamental elements of a tank, speed, firepower and armour, with much more efficiency than any German tank in 1940. Not all was advantages, of course. The one-man turret of the French tanks was a very serious handicap, which overburdened the tank commander with the task of loading and aiming the gun, apart from leading the tank and localizing targets. Besides, if he was a section or a squadron leader, his task was virtually superhuman. Range was very limited and commu-

nications very poor, as most French tanks lacked radio communications equipment. Besides, in general, they lacked the capability to evolve and develop in the same way that German tanks enjoyed (for instance, in its later versions, the *Panzer IV*, already in service in 1939, was still a very effective tank even in 1945 and a rival to many more modern Allied designs, which was a real tribute to the German engineers who designed it in the 1930's).

All in all, the worst scourge of French armoured forces was doctrine. In a memorandum dated 3rd September 1939, Colonel Charles de Gaulle, commander of the armoured units of the *Ve Armée*, stationed in Alsace, supported by politicians like Paul Reynaud, advocated the creation of an independent armoured shock force, but his proposal was turned down by the government and the General Staff. In the spring of 1940, along with three DLMs, they had three *divisions cuirassées de réserve* (DCR, or reserve armoured divisions), but with a fundamen-

A German reconnaissance motorized column. These units were fundamental in making the advance of the tanks effective. The French lacked similar units and consequently paid a high price. (Bundesarchiv 101/054/1525/09).

tally defensive role. These DCRs were not intended to operate independently, but in conjunction with the DLMs, which did have divisional reconnaissance and support units.

The first two DCRs were created on the 16th January 1940 and the third one on the 20th March. Although they were to be initially equipped with B-1 or B-1 bis tanks, insufficient production resulted in only half of the tanks being of that model (a *demi-brigade*), the other half were Hotchkiss H 39 light tanks, armed with the 37 mm SA 18 gun, instead of with the new SA 38, much more effective against armoured vehicles. Likewise, the

mechanized infantry had only one battalion, in Lorraine 38L vehicles, or *Laffly's*, instead of the two planned. Even worse, the 160 tanks belonging to each division were virtually blind, as they lacked the divisional reconnaissance units.

The 4e DCR, hastily established on 15th May, was commanded by Colonel de Gaulle, who was 50 years old at the time, and it was noticeably reinforced, on paper at least, when compared to the other three DCRs.

The Bullfighter's Rapier

On Friday, 10th May 1940, after nine months of the so called *drôle*

de guerre, the *Phoney War* or *Sitzkrieg* for the Germans, a phase of virtual inactivity on the Western Front, the Germans unlashed their *Fall Gelb* (Yellow Plan), the expected offensive in the West.

In the north, Armee Gruppe B, commanded by von Bock, with 29 divisions (three of them armoured), attacked the Low Countries, to advance later on Belgium and pin down the elite of the Allied forces. Indeed, according to the Dyle-Breda Plan, the best units of the Franco-British army, as the German attack started, would march into Belgium to face the enemy on Belgian soil and defeat the German army, which presumably would try to repeat the *Schlieffen* Plan of the last war. There was no other option, as the *Maginot* Line was shielding the Franco-German border, and the Ardennes were seen as impassable for armoured units. The Germans did not see it the same way. Armee Gruppe C, commanded by von Leeb, with 18 divisions, formed a

The FMC 36 light tank had the shortest life among French tanks. The one hundred built in 1938/39 disappeared during the 1940 battles.

Illustration: Julio López Caeiro.

screen along the *Maginot* Line to prevent a possible French attack on that front. The main attack, the *Schwerpunkt* or breakthrough point, was to be carried out by Armee Gruppe A, commanded by von Rundstedt, with 45 divisions (seven of them armoured). The target, according to the Manstein Plan, was to penetrate the French defensive system, between Sedan and Dinant, to continue on to the sea as far as Abbeville and then encircle the bulk of the Allied Army that had entered Belgium. In Liddell-Hart's words, von Bock's attack was the bullfighter's cape that the Allied army would charge on, and the coup de grace was to be administered by the bullfighter's rapier, the attack through the Ardennes that would trap the enemy.

Von Rundstedt's spearhead was the *XIX Armee Korps* (motorized.), with three armoured divisions (1., 2. and 10.), and the *Grossdeutschland* Regiment, commanded by General Heinz Guderian, father of the *Panzerwaffe*, who would cross the Meuse at Sedan, thus disrupting the

French defensive system. On the evening of the 12th May, Guderian's forces reached the Meuse, in a sector defended by the French infantry of the 55e division, a second rate division of middle-aged reservists. At noon on the 13th, after an intense and prolonged bombardment by the Stukas and heavy artillery, the men of the 1. *Schützen-Regiment*

The excellent French roads were ideal for the rapid movement of German armoured units (Bundesarchiv 101/12770396/13a).

commanded by *Oberstleutnant* Balck from the west, and the *Grossdeutschland* from the east, started the assault between Glaire and Torcy, crossing the river and over-running the French defences.

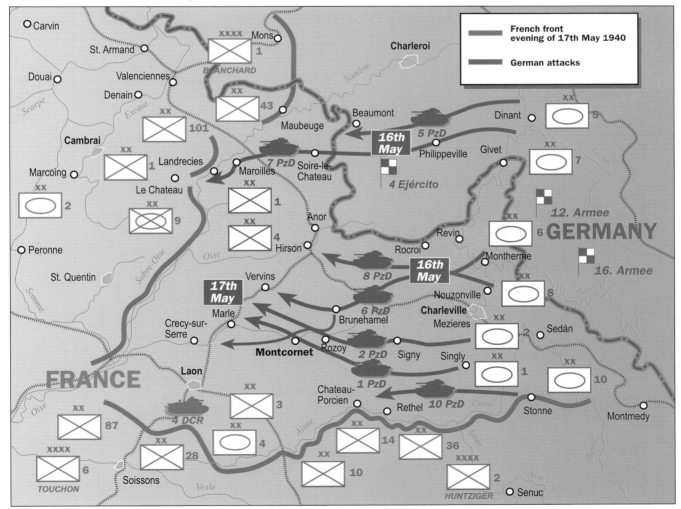

Panic spread among the French troops and by the end of the day the tanks of the 1. *Panzerdivision* were south of the river.

On the following day, the French counter-attacked with the thirty-nine *FCM36* tanks of the 7ᵉ BCC, twenty-nine of which were destroyed on the spot, unable to stop the *panzers*. The French line was broken and the French command, totally disoriented regarding German intentions, thought that the armoured divisions were trying to encircle the *Maginot* Line, for which reason they called back the units available to defend the fortified line in the rearguard. This left the way free for the German tanks, which did not waste the opportunity that the enemy had given them.

Advancing in the midst of changing opposition, while one of the *panzer* divisions successively centred on the target obtained by the others, the Germans went beyond Montcornet on the 16th, leaving behind a breach of over 100 kilometres in the French defensive system, between the IIe *Armée*, in the south, and the IXe *Armée*, in the north. Général Touchon, commander of the newly established VIe *Armée*, was ordered to close this huge gap. The French units were being used piecemeal to try and close the breaches that were emerging, without trying to concentrate them for a large scale counter-attack. The French "masse de manoeuvre", which the Allied defensive strategy was based on, was no more. The speed of the German push and the breakthrough point chosen had ruined the Dyle-Breda Plan.

One of Touchon's first orders was for the recently established 4e DCM, commanded since the 11th by the energetic Colonel de Gaulle. On paper, this unit was a powerful force, able to penetrate the exposed flank of the *Panzerdivisionen*. In actual fact, it was going through a hasty and chaotic process of concentration and training east of Laon and the units that made up this force –in theory– were significantly different from each other. Thus, the artillery was of very good quality, equipped with off-road vehicles and very well trained gunners. The B-1 bis tanks were new but the crews had had hardly any training. The D2

ORDER OF BATTLE OF THE 4E DCR

- *6ᵉ Demi-brigade*
  - 46ᵉ BCC (35 Renault B1 bis)
  - 47ᵉ BCC (35 Renault B1 bis)
  - 19ᵉ BCC (45 Renault D 2s)

- *8ᵉ Demi-brigade*
  - 2ᵉ BCC (45 Renault R 35s)
  - 24ᵉ BCC (45 Renault R 35s)
  - 44ᵉ BCC (45 Renault R 35s)
  - 74ᵉ Compagnie de transporteurs de chars

- Cavalry
  - 3ᵉ *Cuirassiers* (40 SOMUA S 35s and 40 Hotchkiss H 39s)
  - 10ᵉ *Cuirassiers* (40 AMD Panhard P 178s)

- Artillery
  - 322ᵉ RATT (Cannon 75 modèle 97/33)
  - 5ᵉ BDAC (Cannon de 47 antichar SA modèle 1937)
  - 1020/404 Batterie DCA

- Other units, two Compagnies de Sapeurs (engineers), three medical transport units and an air observation group.

---

tanks badly needed overhauls, although the crews were generally good. The best crews, however, manned R 35s, which had already served under de Gaulle, but these were the poorest combat tanks in the division. The state of the 3e *Cuirassiers* was pitiful, lieutenants, just out of St-Cyr, had no experience with armour, 80% of the tank commanders came from *Spahi* units, men had little knowledge of each other and most tanks drivers had hardly any training. The situation at the 7e RDP was no better: there were hardly any machine-guns or 81 mm mortar ammunition, AMRs would take days to arrive, most of the 25 mm guns were obsolete and about 100 men of the second battalion even lacked helmets.

On the 15th, at a General Staff meeting at Montry, Général Doumenc ordered de Gaulle's unit to attack the Germans, in order to give time to Touchon's recently established VIe *Armée* to deploy its infantry along the Aisne. Later, the armoured division should reinforce the defensive system, thus giving up any use it may have had as an independent unit, in the style of the *Panzerdivision*. De Gaulle returned to Bruyères, south of Laon, where he established the division's General Staff and prepared the attack with his Chief of Staff, Lieutenant Colonel Rimebruneau.

Contrary to myth and propaganda, most of the German units were horse-drawn and, at best, had bicycles. Despite this, the speed of the infantry's advance was remarkable, although far from that of the *Panzerdivisionen*. (Bundesarchiv 101/127/0396/13a).

On the same day there was a dramatic battle between the B-1 bis of the 28ᵉ BCC and the *Pz 38(t)'s* of the 7. *Panzerdivision*, which, impotent in the face of the well armoured French tanks and 75 mm guns, refused combat after losing some thirty tanks and continued their push westwards. Shortly afterwards, the 5. *Panzerdivision*, in conjunction with the 7. *Panzerdivision*, in a classic converging manoeuvre, attacked the 1ᵉ DCR, most of whose tanks were refuelling at the time and therefore stationary, and so the latter was wrecked as a fighting unit (over 65 tanks were destroyed). Rommel's forces continued westwards. Further to the south, Guderian's group was going to confront de Gaulle.

The attack on Montcornet

De Gaulle's first step was to set up an anti-tank barrier to blockade the enemy's likely axis of advance from Montcornet, the place where the German tanks had been reported for the last time. It should be remembered that the 4ᵉ DCR had no reconnaissance units, communications were poor and so information on the movements of the rapid German units was inaccurate, doubtful and even worse, it came too late. In order to blockade the German advance, three positions were established, one blockading the road to Laon, northeast of the forest of

---

THE 4ᴱ DCR (*GROUPEMENT DE GAULLE*) ON 17ᵀᴴ MAY 1940

- *6ᵉ Demi-brigade*
    46ᵉ BCC (34 Renault B1 bis) *Commandant* Bescond
    345ᵉ CACC (14 Renault D 2s) *Capitaine* Idée
- *8ᵉ Demi-brigade*
    2ᵉ BCC (45 Renault R 35s) *Commandant* François
    24ᵉ BCC (45 Renault R 35s) *Commandant* Delatour
- Cavalry
    3ᵉ *Cuirassier*s (19 SOMUA S 35s) Col. François
- Artillery
    322ᵉ RATT (Cannon 75 modèle 97/33) Col. Anselme

Samoussy, a second one on the road from Sissonne to St-Erme and the third one at Neufchâtel. Each position was made up of a section of three R-35 tanks, a battery of 75 mm guns and an infantry platoon. In order to make up for the lack of suitable reconnaissance, several officers on motorcycles headed for the northeast and came back with inaccurate information on German motorized units advancing towards St-Quentin. The French units were coming in dribs and drabs and, on the basis of the information and means available, de Gaulle, aware of the limitations of his unit, planned a very simple manoeuvre. Basically, he would advance to the northeast, towards Montcornet, on a front of about twenty kilometres. By taking Montcornet and Lislet, he would protect Laon, and would give the infantry the time they so badly needed to deploy into their new defensive positions.

In the evening of the 16th, elements of the French division reached Chivres, where they ran into German reconnaissance units, which retreated after losing several motorcycles and an armoured vehicle. During the night of the 16th/17th, the different units regrouped east of the Samoussy forest.

At 04:15 on the 17th May, the attack on Montcornet finally began. The French units advanced along two axis. The main force, made up of the *6e demi-brigade* (with thirty-four B-1 bis and fourteen D2 tanks), commanded by Lieutenant Colonel Sudres, advanced along the Laon-Montcornet road, while the *8ᵉ demi-brigade*, with 90 R-35 tanks, (the infantry of the 4ᵉ BCP had not arri-

With a weight of 10.6 metric tons, a top speed of 20 kph, armed with a 37 mm gun and machine-gun and with 40 mm of armour, the Renault R 35 was the French army's most numerous tank in 1940.

Illustration: Julio López Caeiro

ved in time for the start of the advance), commanded by Lieutenant Colonel Simonin, protected its flank, advancing along the La Maison Bleue-Sissone-Lislet line. It would enjoy artillery support from the II/303e RALT and, acting as makeshift infantry, some 400 artillerymen of the 4e GAA.

The left wing advanced in two columns, the *B-1 bis* on both sides of the road, and the *D2s* along the railway line. Shortly after the start of the advance, six *B-1 bis* became bogged down in a marshy area just ouside Liesse, although five of them were recovered during the afternoon. The *D2's* had their baptism of fire when they were attacked by several *Pak 37's*, lying in ambush along the railway line, but, to the Germans' dismay, their solid armour withstood the hits of the 37 mm armour-piercing shells with no problem and continued with their advance, neutralizing several of the anti-tank guns without great difficulty.

Shortly afterwards, a German artillery convoy belonging to the *615. Artillerie Abteilung* with 21-cm ammunition and towing two 77-mm guns which had taken the wrong turn (it was heading for Marle instead of Laon) came under fire from the French tanks, losing twenty vehicles and suffering over 60 casualties, killed, wounded and taken prisoner. Several trucks were left burning spectacularly on the road, a sight that raised French morale.

The German units in the area to be attacked by the French tanks were made up of the 56. *FlaK* Battalion, of the *666. Pioniere Abteilung* at Montcornet itself, the 90. *Panzer Aufklärungs-Abteilung* and of *Aufklärungs-Abteilung* of the 10. Panzerdivision.

Around noon, the first tanks arrived at Clermont-les-Fermes, a few kilometres from Montcornet, but the bulk of the unit had lagged behind at Bucy, refuelling. Indeed, the B-1 bis and D2s had a much higher fuel consumption than was officially estimated, which was already very high, a handicap that was worsened by the fact that they progressed slowly, in short hops, as the lack of reconnaissance units called for extreme caution.

The 8ᵉ *demi-brigade*, equipped with the *R-35* tanks lights, advanced faster. The objective of the 24ᵉ BCC was Montcornet, and they advanced with two companies leading the march and the third in the rearguard, while the 2ᵉ BCC covered their flank. By noon they had reached the plateau towering above Montcornet from the south. The 13ᵉ BLM took defensive positions at the farm at St-Acuaire. The tank commanders had a short meeting and attacked, shortly after noon, the second company against Lislet, and

The 1939 *modèle Lorraine* chassis was the basis for a complete family of vehicles, from tank destroyer to munitions transporter or artillery observation, to be developed by the Germans.

Illustration: Julio López Caeiro

the other two against Montcornet. At Lislet there was a PaK 37 section and six tanks (probably *Panzer III's*) that were being repaired and about to leave to return to their unit, as well as part of the General Staff of the *1. Panzerdivision*, with its commander, General Kirchner, who had been wounded two days earlier in a road accident. One of his officers, Wenck, left at once to report to Guderian.

Eight R-35 tanks of the second company entered the town, without any infantry support, but were met by point-blank fire from the German 37 mm anti-tank guns. Two of the R-35s were knocked out in a few minutes. At such short distance, even 37 mm shells could be devastating. Besides, forced to stay inside the turret, the tank commanders had many difficulties in identifying targets, and even more in

The high consumption and slow refuelling system of the French tanks was a handicap which was to have devastating consequences.

firing at them, both with the machine-gun and the short, inefficient 37 mm gun. So, short on fuel, without infantry support and little resources to face the aggressive pak and the determined German infantry, the rest of the French tanks withdrew in the direction of St-Aquaire.

Montcornet was defended by the 3. Kompanie of the *666. Pionier Abteilung*, which had mined the approaches from the southeast. Anti-tank defence was in the hands of elements of the 59. Flak Battalion, which had a single battery of four 8.8 cm guns. The first French tanks to reach the outskirts of the town were the R-35s of the 1e compagnie of the 24e BCC. The B-1 bis, which had sufficient armour to stand withstand the enemy fire, were expected to drive in first but these heavy tanks were refuelling and would not be ready for at least an hour. Thus, Capitaine Panet, following de Gaulle's energetic orders, decided to attack with the light tanks. Four of them went past the first houses confidently until fire from the German anti-tank guns destroyed two at once. The other two, again unable to effectively face the infantry or anti-tank guns, hurriedly retreated back to Boncourt.

In the meantime, the 2e compagnie of the 2e BCC had taken Dizy-le-Gros and was advancing towards Ville-aux-Dames, when it was fired on by three PaK 37s of

the *10. Panzerdivision*. Fire from the R-35s was totally ineffective, whereas the Germans, who had started to receive reinforcements, knocked out two tanks. The light tank company, totally disorganized, withdrew to St-Acquaire. At the same time, the recently arrived infantry of the 4e BCP, after getting off the buses that had brought them, started to overpower the few pockets of resistance around Chivres. These were the only reinforcements the French tanks recieved all the day.

The D2 tanks, refuelled at long last, continued with their advance around three in the afternoon but

came under fire from three 8.8 cm guns, west of Montcornet, and three of the tanks were knocked out in succession. The deadly '88', which had been first used in Spain, once again proved its reputation as an effective anti-tank gun. The advance was stopped dead and the tanks sought cover. Late that afternoon, the rest of the D2s would withdraw to Bucy.

At four in the afternoon, once the refuelling had at last been completed (it took about four hours!, hardly acceptable for a war of movement), the B-1 bis continued on their way to Montcornet, in combat formation, with two companies leading and another one at the rear. They had orders to reach the town and bombard it for ten minutes, then withdraw. The French tanks drove through Clermont-les-Fermes, destroying a German reconnaissance vehicle. Lacking maps, they mistook the town that could be seen at the other end of a plain as their objective, headed towards it and bombarded it for fifteen minutes. But the town they had attacked was actually Ville-aux-Dames, although no one realized at that time. As they started their retreat, after accomplishing their orders, company leader's tank, the *"Berry-au-bac"*, broke down and was immobilized within sight of the enemy. The crew boarded another tank, the *"Sampiero corso"*, which was destroyed shortly afterwards, at 18:15, by two 8.8 cm shells

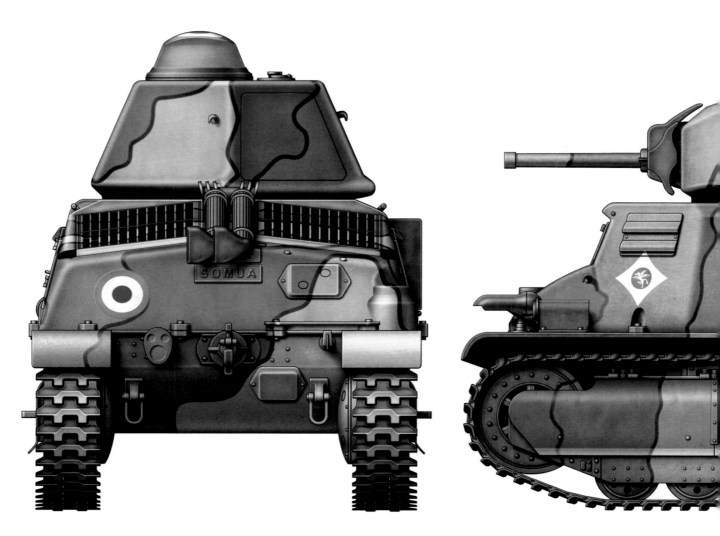

SOMUA S.35

Probablemente el mejor carro del frente occidental en 1940, el SOMUA S.35 tenía un peso de 19,5 toneladas. Su motor de 190 caballos le daba una velocidad máxima de casi 45 km/h, con una relación potencia/peso de algo más de 9 caballos por tonelada. Su autonomía era de más de 250 kilómetros. Su dotación era de tres hombres, uno de ellos, el jefe de carro, situado en la torreta. Estaba armado con un eficaz cañón de 47 mm y un ametralladora de 7,5 cm. Su blindaje era más que suficiente para derrotar a los cañones contracarro alemanes de 37 mm, con un espesor máximo de 50 mm en la torreta y 40 mm en el casco.

El primer prototipo de S.35 vio la luz en abril de 1935, sólo siete meses después del comienzo de los estudios, y fue el resultado de las estrechas relaciones industriales entre Schneider, casa matriz de SOMUA, y la checoslovaca Skoda, que estaba fabricando carros tan destacados como el futuro Pz 38(t) y el Pz 35 (t). De hecho, el tren de rodaje del S35 era similar al de los carros Skoda-Id y LT 35. En este sentido, conviene destacar que, en mayo de 1940, sólo tres carros de combate en el mundo eran capaces de efectuar una etapa de más de 250 kilómetros sin mantenimiento: el Pz 35 (t), el Pz 38 (t), y el S 35. Ni el *Panzer III* era capaz de superar los 150 km/día.

El motor derivaba de un modelo fabricado por Hispano-Suiza, ya en fase de desarrollo. El gran volumen del motor obligó a que el casco tuviese una altura superior a la deseada, lo que, al elevar el centro de gravedad, reducía la velocidad en todo terreno y la capacidad de superar obstáculos, pero su elevada velocidad y autonomía compensaban con creces estos defectos. Mejor aún, su capacidad de marchar durante ocho horas a una velocidad media de 35 km/h lo hacía ideal para la guerra de movimiento.

Su blindaje de 40 mm en el casco y hasta 50 mm en el frente de la torreta le hacía invulnerable frente a los cañones anticarro alemanes, exceptuando el 88 mm. Su armamento principal, de 47 mm, era más que suficiente para batir a los carros alemanes con los que se tenía que enfrentar, a las distancias normales de combate en 1940, desde una relativa invulnerabilidad.

Como defectos, hay que destacar sus pobres cualidades en terreno quebrado, la mala ergonomía, que contribuía a provocar un cansancio excesivo a las dotaciones, la carencia de radio, que limitaba notablemente su operatividad, y como no, la ubicua torreta de un solo hombre, que mermaba gran parte de la eficacia del carro en combate. Estos eran defectos comunes a casi todos los carros franceses de la época. A pesar de ello, el S.35 era el mejor de que disponían los franceses, y estaba al nivel de los carros alemanes para la guerra de movimiento, mientras que estaba en condiciones de batirlos en combate singular. La pésima doctrina táctica de las unidades acorazadas galas impidieron que este magnífico carro demostrase lo que era capaz de hacer en el campo de batalla.

fired from 2,500 metres. It was the fourth gun of the anti-aircraft battery, positioned one kilometre south of Montcornet. The eight crewmembers died, including the company leader, Commandant Bescond. One more B-1 bis, the «Duguesclin», was also destroyed by the same German gun. This was a foretaste of what the powerful '88' would accomplish during the Second World War. Shortly afterwards, again very low on fuel and subject to the relentless pursuit of the *Luftwaffe*, the rest of the tanks retreated towards Bucy.

The objectives of the attack of the 4e DCR were far from having been met. One of them was to establish infantry positions on the Serre-Montcornet line, and Rutaud to Lislet. Not even the tanks had managed to maintain those positions. They had not managed to slow down the advance of the German tanks at all, as the hold-up that day was due to the disputes among the German General Staff. Although de Gaulle dreamt of the

possibilities of a powerful armoured force to trap the German units, penetrating independently in depth, in 1940 only the *Wehrmacht* was in a condition to do this. The technique and operational possibilities of the French armoured units (and the rest of the countries), were well below the necessary level.

In any case, De Gaulle had reasons for some satisfaction, as he had attacked and raised the troops' morale in really adverse conditions, these were units that he had just taken command of, hurriedly regrouped, were incomplete, lacking artillery and air support, or reconnaissance units, unable to coordinate due to the lack of radio communications, heavy tanks that had the huge burden of their poor range and an incompetent refuelling system, etc. All the potential of the French armoured units in this first phase of the French campaign were wasted due to the erroneous doctrine and was only timidly put to good use in the three actions carried out by de Gaulle.

The 88 mm guns placed west of Montcornet neutralized the attack of the D2 and B1 tanks, up to then invulnerable. One of the B1 bis was destroyed from a distance of 2,500 metres! (Bundesarchiv 101-769-0231-11).

Illustration: Luis Fresno Crespo.

For the Germans, the French attack was an unpleasant surprise but caused no panic at all. The 17th was critical, however, as the high command was pondering the vulnerability of the southern flank in the face of a likely counter-attack coming from the region of

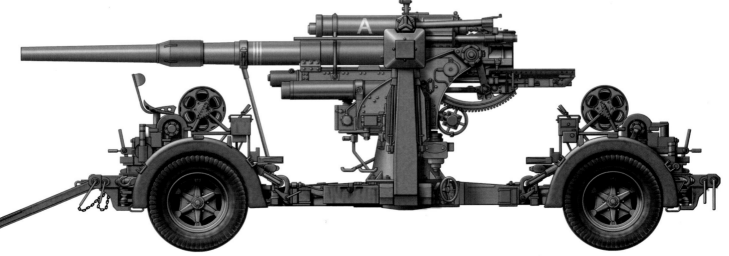

Laon, when de Gaulle's attack took place. Perhaps surprised by the unexpected speed of the advance following the breakthrough at Sedan, the German General Staff was not fully convinced of the security and convenience of such a rapid progression of the armoured units, leaving the slower infantry units behind, without totally securing the supply lines or the flanks, as advocated in traditional doctrine. Guderian wanted to continue his race to the sea at any cost, aware that the success of the plan was based on speed, so as to disrupt the French defensive system, which, as a matter of fact, is what was actually occurring. With that situation, in the midst of a dilemma on which course of action to be taken, the timid attack by the French tanks seemed to support those who took a more traditional view. On the 17th, before having news of the French counter-attack, Guderian was summoned by von Kleist at 07:00 and ordered to stop the advance of the armoured units. The origin of this decision still remains controversial. It is not clear whether it was von Rundstedt or Hitler himself who was responsible. The latter was for a rapid advance to the northeast, whereas the General Staff preferred a more conventional push, further to the south. Whatever the case, this temporary hold-up of the advance, along with

a similar occurrence a week later off Dunkirk, would give the Allies precious time to withdraw, which Guderian would not have given them. Besides, the pre-existing tension between Guderian and his superior, von Kleist, who was of the old school and a much more cautious follower of academic tactical concepts than his subordinate, came to a head in the meeting.

The encounter between Guderian and von Kleist was very stormy, with mutual reproaches, and Guderian asking to be relieved of his command, which initially von Kleist agreed to, passing it on to the next general in the order of seniority, Veiel. The chief of the XII. Armee, List, came in person to the

The Hotchkiss H 39, with a weight of 12 metric tons and similar armament and armour, was noticeably faster than the R35, reaching 36 kph.

Illustration: Julio López Caeiro

command post to try to solve the situation and, on von Rundstedt's behalf, cancelled the dismissal and ordered the momentary continuation of the advance of the Panzers. It was the afternoon of the 17th but Guderian was not too worried about the French attack at any time. All of his energy on that

The German 3.7 cm anti-tank guns were totally useless against the French heavy tank, and had serious difficulties when facing even the light ones, which had 40 mm of armour. (Bundesarchiv 101/127/0391/21).

With a weight of 31 metric tons, armed with a 75 mm gun in a casemate and a 47 mm gun in the turret, protected by a maximum of 60 mm of armour, the B1 bis was invulnerable to the German 3.7 cm anti-tank guns. But the 8.8 cm AA gun or the 105 mm field guns proved devastating when used in the direct fire role. It was very vulnerable in towns too, without infantry support. (Bundesarchiv 101/057/1669/15).

day was devoted to his quarrel with von Kleist and to restore the impetus of the advance of his tanks.

By 11:10 on the 17th, the *Luftwaffe* had already identified French armoured units near the forest of Samoussy. The tank regiment and the *Aufklärungs-Abt.* were ordered to advance at once towards the south of Montcornet, to protect the flank. At 12:00, Guderian thought that the French objective was the General Staff of the Army Corps, but considered that the threat was not serious enough and paid little attention to it, given the internal problems he had to deal with. It was not until after seven in the evening that the *10. Panzerdivision* was ordered to deploy a battalion, reinforced by anti-tank guns, to the west of Montcornet, because of the persistence of the French armoured forces in that area.

The *1. Panzerdivision* operational diary pointed out the following facts on the 17th,

- the most important losses corresponded to the ammunition convoy that had gone the wrong direction, without giving precise figures.

- the 3.7 cm anti-tank guns proved ineffective when facing the French heavy tanks and it was necessary to resort to the 8.8 cmm anti-aircraft guns to stop them.

- the auxiliary units of the division were insufficiently armed.

The Germans had suffereed about one hundred casualties, most of them in the ammunition convoy which the French had caught by surprise. The French had fourteen killed, six wounded and nine missing. The Germans, on the other hand lost no tanks, whereas the French had lost twenty-three by the end of the day, out of a total of eighty-five tanks that had actually participated in the action.

From the psychological point of view, the Germans gave hardly any importance to the attack, whereas for the French troops taking part as well as other nearby units it was a morale booster, and this also affected the civil population, who stopped fleeing for some time. And all that despite the low spirits of the 46e BCC crews, who had seen their beloved commander killed in action.

What de Gaulle actually gained was a remarkable personal political victory, as he was able to exploit the situation very well and, with the government support he enjoyed at the time, he managed to report the facts in his favour. However, two days later, on the 19th, he made a similar attack on the enemy's southern flank in the Crécy area, with similar results, and failed again on the 28th in his attempt at overwhelming the German bridgehead in the Abbeville sector, south of the Somme.

The attack on Crécy
Following tyhe Montcornet operation, Général Georges ordered

a new attack on German communication lines two days later. The objectives would be Crécy and Montceau, an operation that was to be carried out by the 4e DCR, with forces that, on paper, were closer to their theoretical establishment. In reality, there were only about thirty B1 bis and just over forty D2s and S35s, the only ones really effective against the German tanks. The rest were R-35s, whose short 37 mm gun rendered them useless at over 400 metres. The probabilities of hitting the target were minimal at such a distance and, should they manage to do so, they had hardly any chances of piercing 8 mm of armour. For this operation, the French would benefit from the presence of the AMD Panhard reconnaissance vehicles of the 10e *cuirassiers*.

At 04:15 on the 9th May, the 4e DCR attacked again. On the left, the 8e *demi-brigade*, on the right, the 10e *cuirassiers* and the S 35s of the 3e *cuirassiers* and, in the middle, the *6e demi-brigade* with the B1 bis.

Once again the B1 bis proved to be apt for anything but the war of movement. After covering about ten kilometres in just over one hour, they were forced to a halt to refuel. Finally, at 08:00, they started off again. Once more, lacking radio communications, the light tanks led the march without support and were the first to contact the enemy at Crécy and Chalandry. A savage exchange with the German anti-tank guns followed, and the latter, after destroying French several tanks, withdrew to the north. The D2s joined the fight and entered Crécy, where the first two were immediately lost to mines. It was clear that, without the necessary support from the infantry, they would never be able to take a town.

Different paint schemes on the Char B1 bis during the May-June 1940 period. The first one, one of the most famous B1 bis, is the «Sampiero corso» for quite dramatic reasons, as its eight-man crew were killed when it was hit by two 8.8 cm rounds, fired from a distance of over two kilometres.

Illustration: Julio López Caeiro

But the infantry never arrived. They still depended on the buses for transport and German pressure on the right flank of the division was increasing. They did not manage to reach Crécy, and the D2s waited in vain, fearless in the face of enemy fire, outside the town until six in the evening... At 10:45 de Gaulle had already ordered the retreat, conscious of the useless and dangerous nature of the attack. There was fierce fighting on the right flank of the division, especially in the Chambry sector, where about twenty AMD *Panhards*, and three infantry companies held back the Germans until five in the evening, giving time for the tanks to retreat to their start positions, under the ceaseless harrying of the *Luftwaffe*. In total, the division lost over 70 tanks and armoured vehicles that day. The 4e BCP alone had sustained over 170 casualties. The delay caused to the German advance at the end of the day was probably no more than one hour.

On the evening of the 28th, at Abbeville, de Gaulle launched his third attack, with the 150 tanks he had left, and again the same story was repeated. After penetrating about fours kilometre into the German bridgehead on the Somme, their armour invulnerable to 2 cm and 3.7 cm guns, the combined action of German tanks, artillery and aviation, on the German side, stopped the French advance dead in its tracks, forcing them to return to their starting point, unable to overpower the German positions. At the end of the day, there were less than a hundred French tanks left operational.

Conclusions

- These operations represented the only attacks by the French tanks that posed any danger to the German advance, as well as the one at Abbeville a few days later. All in all, they remained timid attempts that caused hardly any worries for the German armoured units.
- The Germans did not worry much about these raids. The French units proved tactically inferior, having objectives that were not very ambitious and with unsuitable means to achieve them.
- The individual superiority of the French tanks over the German ones was proven in that phase of the war, if the three main characteristics of an armoured vehicle are to be taken into account, i.e. armament, armour and mobility. The paradigm was the S 35, probably the best tank in service on the Western Front. But such an advantage was only theoretical, as the poor operational capability of the French vehicles cancelled out their advantages. The tactics used were childish, without grasping the whole potential of tanks. The French heavy tanks proved useless for the war of movement. Their excessive fuel consumption, excessive refuelling time and lack of radios made them vulnerable and of little operational value.

Their armour rendered them invulnerable to the 2 cm and 3.7 cm German guns and only the 7.5 cm anti-tank shell and, of course, the 88 were able to pierce their armour. The French SA18 37 mm gun proved too inefficient but not so the 47 mm, probably the best anti-tank gun in service in 1940. The 75 mm gun of the B1 bis was also able to knock out a German tank, at normal combat ranges. Beyond 400 metres, the French were hardly able to hit any targets. The morale of the French tank crews was very inferior to their German counterparts' as a whole.

German doctrine and training was very superior. The speed and tactical flexibility of the German tanks, thanks to their communications equipment and five-man crews (three of them in the turret) made advances possible in order to disrupt the French defensive system.

Montcornet was mainly a propaganda victory for de Gaulle. He presented the battle as a victory that had allowed the French precious time to reorganize the defence, and had stopped the rapid German advance. He exaggerated German losses disproportionately and claimed the initiative of the attack for himself, against his superiors' orders; whereas he had actually just followed the orders he received. It is no less true that little could be done with the means available, but he proved extremely careful and cautious in the management of his armour, unlike his German counterpart. Although his defenders have wanted to present him as Guderian's French equivalent, actually any comparison in that sense is almost ridiculous.

Another B1 bis knocked out in a town. The tank has suffered an internal explosion that has destroyed it. (Bundesarchiv 101/382/0201/09)

CHARLES DE GAULLE

Born in Lille in 1890, he graduated at St-Cyr in 1912, 13th in his class, later joining the 33e Régiment d'Infantérie, commanded by Colonel Pétain. He was wounded while a captain and taken prisoner by the Germans in 1916 at Verdun. He made five unsuccessful escape attempts. After the Great War, he was sent to Russia as an attaché with the Polish Army. In 1921 he was a military history teacher at St-Cyr and later was part of the General Staff of the Rhineland Army, as well as the Beirut General Staff.

De Gaulle expressed his ideas on armoured warfare in his book «**The Army of the Future**», published in 1934, in which he criticized the theorists favouring a static war of defence, whose paradigm was the Maginot Line, and advocated the creation of a motorized and armoured army. The book was unpopular with the government and the General Staff and, in 1936, de Gaulle was "punished", seeing his promotion barred.

In 1938 he published «**France and her Army**», which was criticized by Petain, as the latter thought it was a plagiarism of a previous work by the General Staff for courses at the War College.

At the outbreak of the Second World War he was appointed commander of the armoured units of the *Ve Armée* in Alsace. He was soon frustrated with the ideas of the General Staff, oblivious to the importance of masses of tanks acting independently and supported by aircraft.

A wrecked B1bis heavy tank, probably destroyed by a direct hit from a 10.5 or 15 cm gun.
An internal explosion has displaced the turret. (Bundesarchiv 101/125/0277/09)

He wrote a memorandum at the beginning of the offensive, together with fifty fellow officers, defending the use of the armoured units as an independent force, following the German example, which caused bitterness in the General Staff and the Government. After commanding the 4e DCR for a few weeks, on 6th June, president Reynaud appointed him as undersecretary of state for defence and war. From that position, de Gaulle proposed that, in case of need, the government should leave the home territory to continue the fight. After the armistice, on the 16th June, he left for London, where he broadcast the famous appeal of the 18th June, when he announced that the French would continue the war with the British. In October he organized the empire defence committee, and tried to gather the soldiers and the colonies that had not accepted defeat. He failed in Dakar, but succeeded in Chad, French Equatorial Africa and Cameroon. Finally, after the liberation of Paris, he arrived in the capital on 25th August 1944 and re-established the authority of the central government and started important structural reforms. It was the beginning of a political career that took him to the presidency of the Republic on several occasions, until his final resignation in 1969. He died a year later from natural causes, aged 80.

He was an arriviste in character, egocentric and ambitious, energetic and intransigent, with good friends in the government, an opportunist and with a view to his political future. A good politician, as a soldier he was maybe above average compared to the 1940 French command, but very far from being on par with the German commanders.

Although he was a pioneer in the publication of works on the use of the armoured units, in actual fact his thesis on mechanized warfare had been known for some time in French military circles. De Gaulle, with no basis, claimed authorship of such ideas for himself. Similarly, his book «**The Army of the Future**» is too theoretical and vague, without concrete, practical proposals on the use of tanks, practically a philosophical exercise. Besides, although he later wanted to claim the ideas of direct support of tanks by aircraft to be his own, he actually only regarded the air arm as a specialized reconnaissance unit, nothing to do with what would be the *blitzkrieg*. It can be considered as a mere declaration of intentions, not comparable at all to Guderian's mythical «***Achtung! Panzer!***»

A German soldier posing by one of the numerous knocked-out R 35 tanks. Although classified as a light tank, it was very slow.

THE COUNTERATTACK AT ARRAS

After the breakthrough at Sedan, German armoured units began an extraordinary advance to reach the coast at Abbeville, as part of the Manstein Plan, to isolate the elite of the Franco-British units in Belgium. The *British Expeditionary* Force (BEF) had crossed into Belgium on the 10th May, at the commencement of the *Fall Gelb*, in accordance with the Dyle Plan in order to start decisive operations against the German forces in Belgium, thus repeating the opening phase of the First World War. Three BEF army corps entered Belgium to take up positions along the Louvaine-Wavre line, between the Belgian (on their left) and the French armies (on their right).

The First Army Corps was made up of the 1st, 2nd and 48th Divisions and was on the right wing; the Second Army Corps, on the left wing, was made up of the 3rd and 4th Divisions and, finally, the Third Corps regrouped the 42nd and 44th Divisions and, along with the 5th and 50th Divisions, made up the reserves. The British units moved into Belgium without difficulty, with the reconnaissance units leading, equipped with *Vickers* Mk VIb light tanks and *Bren Carriers*. A curious story occurred with the 3rd Division, commanded by Major-General Montgomery,

when it was stopped by Belgian border guards demanding written permission to cross the border. As for the rest, the Belgian population cheered at the arrival of the Allied troops.

The BEF had a few days of relative tranquillity, from the 10th to the 15th May, while the French front crumbled at Sedan and Guderian's *Panzerdivisionen* started the race to the sea. During the afternoon of the 15th, watching the turn of the events, the Allies decided to withdraw towards the Schelde. This retreat was carried out perfectly, keeping the cohesion of the units, although it should be stressed that it was done under no pressure. At the time the BEF was intact and had seen hardly any combat, therefore it was to be called on to play a very active role in the fighting to come along the Somme. On the 19th, Weygand replaced Gamelin and overnight the subtle condescension that the French had shown towards the British so far for their small forces vanished and was replaced by hurry and the need to urge the British to carry out a decisive manoeuvre against the apparently unstoppable German advance.

Lord Gort, the British commander-in-chief, was surprised at this change of attitude and very upset. He was

Matilda I tanks undergoing maintenance in a French *château*. Totally obsolete by 1940, their only virtue was the thickness of their armour, up to 60 mm, which rendered them invulnerable to German 3.7 cm guns. However, their tracks and wheels were very vulnerable.

not only reluctant to maneouvre his army for the benefit of the French, but was fully aware of his situation. His lines of communication stemmed from Cherbourg and Brest and, if the German forces cut them, the BEF would be as overwhelmed as the French *1e Armée* had been. As a matter of fact, he had already received orders from London to plan a withdrawal to the Channel in order to try to ensure if necessary a possible re-embarkation. A meeting to set up a strategy between Billote, nominal C-in-C of the BEF, and Lord Gort took place on the 19th. Although the idea was to carry out a concentric attack from the south and the north on the German line of advance, the battle of Montcornet two days earlier had proved, among other things, that any attack from the south was unviable at that time. Leaving Belgium hurriedly was not a politically feasible option, so there was only one possibility, evacuation by sea. This option would lead to the abandonment of practically the entire equipment of the best Allied units and their neutralization as

combat units but, luck permitting, would ensure the salvation of the soldiers. Gort asked London for instructions and the answer on the following day was not very clear: *"The BEF must carry out a movement to the south in the direction of Amiens, attacking all the enemy forces it may meet, and take up positions on the left of the French army"*. After several discussions, the British and French commands decided to use a combined force, each army supplying two divisions, to carry out a southwards attack, in the sector of Arras and

A Vickers Mk VI, with a camouflage scheme that would see hardly any changes during the second half of the 20th century.
Illustration: Julio López Caeiro.

Cambrai, with the objective of cutting the German line of advance and isolating their most advanced forces. The British *War Office* considered the Germans to be exhausted after their hurried advance and thought that maybe this was the time to launch an offensive on their exposed flank.

Despite these early intentions, Lord Gort was very conscious of his limitations, and was more concerned with saving his army than helping the French. Events started to gather pace and the speed of the German advance made all plans obsolete in hours. On the morning of the 20th, the British right flank had already been overpowered and Gort wanted

to prevent a repetition with the left if their links with the Belgians were broken. For that reason, as time went by, he decided to carry out a much more modest and limited operation. Rather than attempting a breakthrough to the south, this would be a mopping-up operation in the Arras sector to evacuate the besieged garrison of the town and threaten the German lines of communication. Instead of a resolute attack to the south, Gort was thinking of a hurried escape to Dunkirk, to re-embark for the United Kingdom. If the French were not able to close the enormous gap in the Allied defensive system, neither was the BEF.

The forces available were also very weak. Command was entrusted to General Franklyn and he would have two infantry divisions, nos. 5th and 50th, but with two brigades each instead of three. Two would defend the eastern approach to Arras, from Cambrai, which the Germans had already taken. One brigade would be kept in reserve, leaving only one (with three battalions) for the attack itself. In support would be two battalions of the 1st Armoured Brigade, equipped with 76 tanks, but only six-

An A 13. cruiser tank armed with an efficient but limited two-pounder gun, its speed did not make up for its poor protection.
Ilustración: Julio López Caeiro.

teen of these were armed with a 2-pounder gun, the rest were *Matilda* Mk.I's, which were well armoured but very slow, rather unreliable and armed with just a *Vickers* machine-gun. To make things worse, the French could only muster the 3^e DLM (equipped with about 70 *Hotchkiss* tanks) for the attack, and the tanks of the GBC 515. Although it was not possible to imagine a decisive breakthrough to the south with these forces, it was, nevertheless, the first great counter-attack to be carried out against the Germans since their breakthrough along the Somme front.

The 7.*Panzerdivision*, under Rommel, attacked in the Arras sector in the early hours of the 20th, with the commander leading in person, and reached Beaurains at six in the morning. But the fusilier regiments had not managed to keep pace with the tanks, so Rommel turned back in a half-track to try and speed up his advance. On the way, he got caught up in the midst of French armoured units that were heading south. After a close shave, he managed to join an infantry regiment advancing on a forced march, reinforced by a field artillery battery. In this situation, the French withdrew to the north. By the 21st, the 7.*Panzerdivision* had encircled Arras and pivoted to the northwest, with the SS Totenkopf giving cover on the left flank, and the 5. *Panzerdivision* were advancing to the east of Arras.

In an order to General Franklyn on the 20th, Gort stated that his initial intention was to *"support the garrison of Arras and blockade the roads south of Arras, cutting the German lines of communication from the east."* After sending this order, Gort received instructions to collaborate and coordinate his movements with the French, who were to make the main effort. Billotte, after a meeting with the British command, decided to use two divisions for the counterattack of the 21st and agreed to coordinate his actions with Franklyn. But the latter did not receive new orders from his superiors and, when the French asked him for cooperation,

Franklyn agreed only to those actions for which he had clear instructions. This was just one more dramatic example of the remarkable, chronic lack of coordination between the Allies during the French campaign. The need for personal meetings to make combined decisions and conduct operations in parallel, as well as acting independently and without coordination, contrasted sharply with the speedy German decision making on the spot to exploit opportunities as they arose. However, the French promised to give cover to the Bri-

Motorcyclists of the *50th Infantry Division* socializing with Belgian women. (*Royal Tank Museum*).

tish flank, even at the expense of their own security, and would keep their promise.

The counter-attack

For the attack, the British forces would split up into two columns that would start from a position west of Arras to advance later to the south, following more or less parallel paths and, after having gone beyond Arras, head east. In command of the forces involved was *Major-General* Martel. To support the main attack, the 150th Brigade, that was northeast of Arras, would march to the south, later to turn to the west and thus encircle the town, linking up with the two mixed columns.

The British plan got off to a bad start, as the starting point was in the middle of land now occupied by the Germans. This was due to lack of suitable reconnaissance by the Allies and the speed of the German advance. As a matter of fact, the British were not aware that they were going to confront the 7.*Panzerdivision* and SS *Totenkopf*, or that the 5. *Panzerdivision* was approaching fast east of Arras.

The lack of suitable reconnaissance was chronic among the Franco-British forces too, as were the errors of interpretation of the enemy's intentions and the correct evaluation of German forces. Actually, there were reports on the presence of enemy tanks and strong concentrations of motorized infantry in the area that the British had to cross and, even worse, north of the start point. Despite this, the plan went ahead accor-

ding to schedule. Although in theory two infantry divisions and a tank brigade were to be used, as we have seen, the forces actually involved were much smaller. Instead of two divisions, a little over two battalions were actually used, and the tank brigade had only 58 *Matilda I*'s and 16 *Matilda II*'s, many of them without suitable maintenance after having covered many kilometres. There were also the light Mk VIb reconnaissance and command tanks, the only ones fitted with radios in this engagement. It was obviously an insufficient force for the task that it was being asked to perform.

Martel conceived the attack as a push by two parallel columns, each made up of a tank battalion, an

infantry battalion, a field artillery battery, an anti-tank battery and a motorcycle company for reconnaissance. They should cross the Arras-Doullens road at two in the afternoon. The infantry were to march about twelve kilometres, in the midst of a stream of refugees and a major traffic jam, to reach their start positions. There was very little time to study the orders and none for suitable reconnaissance.

The right column

The right column set off at 13:15, after the tanks had waited for the infantry for over one hour. An important feature was that the *Matilda* tanks had no radios and only the light Mk VIb's were able to send orders. Their rapid destruction by the German *Pak's* was to result in an enormous lack of control. These light tanks were used by the reconnaissance units, both of the infantry and the armoured divisions. They were also used by battalion commanders, which rendered them extraordinarily vulnerable. After a one-hour march, at around 14:30, the light reconnaissance tanks encountered German infantry at Duisans, eight kilometres from the planned start position. They came under fire from several anti-

Right Column	Left Column
7ᵗʰ RTR (23 *Matilda Is* and 9 *Matilda IIs*)	4ᵗʰ RTR (37 *Matilda Is* and 7 *Matilda IIs*)
8ᵗʰ Battalion (*Durham Light Infantry*)	6ᵗʰ Battalion (*Durham Light Infantry*)
365ᵗʰ Battery, *92nd Reg. RFA* (12 x 25-pounders)	368ᵗʰ Battery, *92nd Reg. RFA* (12 x 25-pounders)
260ᵗʰ Battery, *65th AT Reg* (12 x 2-pounders)	206ᵗʰ Battery, *52nd AT Reg* (12 x 2-pounders)
One AT platoon (3 x 25-mm)	One AT platoon (3 x 25-mm)
One platoon 4ᵗʰ *Northumberland Fusiliers*	Major-General Martel's General Staff

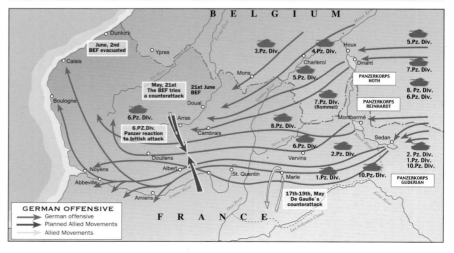

The rapid and efficient action of the German engineers combined with pontoons allowed natural barriers to be crossed without great difficulties, much to the defenders' surprise. (Bundesarchiv: 101 I-146-2005-48).

tank rifles at once, which caused no casualties. In the meantime, French tank units moving on their right further ahead, reported the presence of German tanks advancing westwards (it was the 25. *Panzerregiment*, of the 7. *Panzerdivision*). These French tanks were also seen by the British light tanks which took them for Germans; although contact was broken off minutes later. The *Matildas* arrived at Duisans and the few German forces present abandoned the town.

The tank column, headed by the light Mk VI's, advanced without opposition as far as Wagnonlieu and Dainville. Although the tanks passed without difficulties, the infantry marching behind them soon found themselves having to fight in order to keep up with the tanks and gain control of the towns. After about four hours of combat, the first elements of the *Durham Light Infantry* finally arrived at the intended start line. Two infantry companies and two anti-tank sections stayed at the town of Duisans. A German air attack by several Ju 87's twenty minutes later caused few losses but managed to prevent any push by the British infantry in that sector. In the meantime, the tanks had continued alone,

A *Panzer IV Ausf D* of *Pz.-Rgt.7*, the most powerful German tank in service in 1940.

reaching Wailly and spreading chaos in the enemy ranks. The first German units that the *Matildas* found after crossing the start line belonged to the SS *Totenkopf*, who panicked at Wailly in the presence of the British tanks. Several motorized units were intercepted and many trucks were set on fire. However, casualties were not as high as they would have been had the British infantry been there. Although many prisoners were "captured", as the tanks continued with their push and the accompanying infantry lagged very far behind, it is highly improbable that any of the "prisoners" headed for the British lines on their own.

After going beyond Dainville, German resistance became stronger

and the British tanks started to attract more and more intense fire. Most of the light reconnaissance and command tanks, the only ones fitted with radios, were knocked out, either by 3.7 cm anti-tank shells that pierced their thin armour or by artillery of various calibres that immobilized them by damaging the vulnerable tracks and wheels. Some of them were even knocked out by anti-tank rifles and hand grenades thrown point blank by the infantry.

But the *Matilda* tanks, with their thick armour, were an unpleasant surprise, as the German 3.7 cm anti-tank guns, and especially the anti-tank rifles, proved useless when faced with the British tanks. The commander of the 7. *Panzerdivision*, who was regrouping the fusilier bri-

A destroyed Vickers VIC. This type, like the one below –belonging to the *10th Hussars, 2nd Armoured brigade, 1st Armoured Division*– was armed with a 15-mm machine-gun.

Illustration: Julio López Caeiro.

to advance further and there was no artillery or air support. The British attack in this sector was over.

The left column

The 4th RTR progressed faster than its neighbouring regiment, although once again without infantry support, which lagged one hour behind the tanks. The burden of the attack was on the *Matilda* I's, armed with a *Vickers* machine-gun and a speed of no more than 10 kph. The seven *Matilda* II's, borrowed from the 7 RTR, were the reserve company and drove a little further behind. Despite all this, the tanks progressed slowly, crushing a surprised German infantry column, belonging to the 6. *Infanterie Regiment* of the 7. *Panzerdivision*, on their way west of Dainville. Ten kilometres to the east, six *Matildas* crushed a 3.7 cm gun battery. Shortly afterwards, north of Achicourt, the *Matildas* bumped into an 8.8 cm gun battery, hurriedly placed in position, which caused the first losses among the British tanks. In view of this unexpected obstacle, the reserve company, with the *Matilda* IIs, was placed on the first line and reoriented their push towards a small valley northwest of Mercatel. There they

gades to support the *Panzerregiment*, was unpleasantly surprised by the British advance and asked for the use of the 8.8 cm anti-aircraft guns to stop the British tanks, which they did with great efficiency. Indeed, Rommel, once again showing the legendary capability for improvisation of the *Wehrmacht*, managed to set up a veritable wall of fire to stop the British tanks. He placed the guns of the 78. *Artillerie Regiment*, the 86. Flak Leichtes Batterie, the 3. *Abteilung* of the 59. *FlaK Regiment,* the 2. Abteilung of the 23. *FlaK Regiment* and elements of the 42. *PaK Battalion* among Tillois, Beaurains, Vailly and Warlus. The 8.8 cm armour-piercing shells and HE 10.5-cm cm

shells soon showed their worth and several of the British tanks began to burn. The German forces at Wailly, where Rommel himself was leading the defence, were able to repell the British attack.

In this situation, once the initial surprise caused by the enemy was over, the *Matildas* withdrew towards Warlus, where they finally made contact with the infantry of the *8th Durham Light Infantry* that had already consolidated the town. A timid attempt at an advance from there was stopped by German mortar and machine-gun fire that caused many casualties. The infantry were too few and the tanks were not in condition

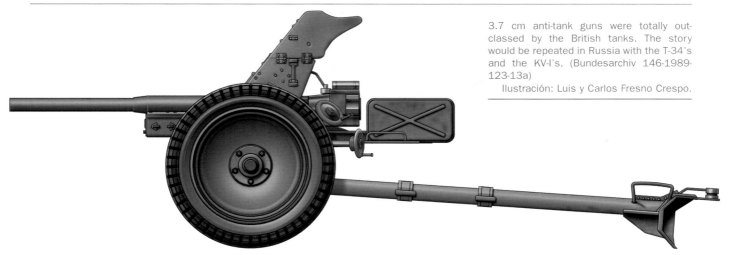

3.7 cm anti-tank guns were totally outclassed by the British tanks. The story would be repeated in Russia with the T-34's and the KV-I's. (Bundesarchiv 146-1989-123-13a)
Ilustración: Luis y Carlos Fresno Crespo.

met more German infantry and logistics units of the 1. *Battalion* of the 6. *Regiment*, who were totally caught by surprise by the British tanks. Despite the intense fire from the 3.7 cm anti-tank guns and the anti-tank rifles, the *Matildas* advanced fearlessly, spreading chaos and destruction in the German formation. Without single loss, they left a trail of trucks and motorcycles in flames, smashing guns and corpses. Unfortunately, they did not enjoy infantry support to exploit their success. Only the motorized company of the *4th Northumberland Fusiliers*, reinforced by several armoured vehicles, continued eastwards, to their final objective, Wancourt and the Cojeul River. However, after reaching their objective, they became isolated a few hours later and almost all of their crews were taken prisoner.

The infantry that followed the tanks occupied themselves with consolidating Achicourt, Agny and Beaurains but stopped in the last town. The *Matildas* had caused heavy

casualties among the fusiliers of the 1. *Battalion* of the 6. *Regiment* and the soldiers of the *Totenkopf*, destroying a large amount of materiel, but the artillery line set up by Rommel between Agny and Beaurains using the 8.8 cm anti-aircraft guns and the divisional artillery, equipped with 10 cm and 15 cm guns, stop-

ped them dead with this remarkable concentration of direct fire, which was more than the slow British tanks could take and were destroyed one after another. Indeed, the 8.8 cm guns had no problem in piercing the 78 mm armour of the *Matilda II*'s from over 2,000 metres and, on this occasion, combat distances were no more than 1,000 metres. The HE shells of the 10 cm and 15 cm guns also proved remarkably efficient. Although they did not pierce the armour, the effects on the crews and mechanical components were devastating. What is more, the tracks and wheels of the extremely slow *Matilda I*'s were particularly vulnerable to HE fire. An 8.8 cm battery destroyed nine *Matildas*. The field artillery claimed the destruction of a total of twenty-eight British tanks. The left column had been halted.

As the attack by the two British columns was taking place west of

Field artillery joined the barrage with direct fire to try and stop the British tanks. (Bundesarchiv: 101-054-1527-14).

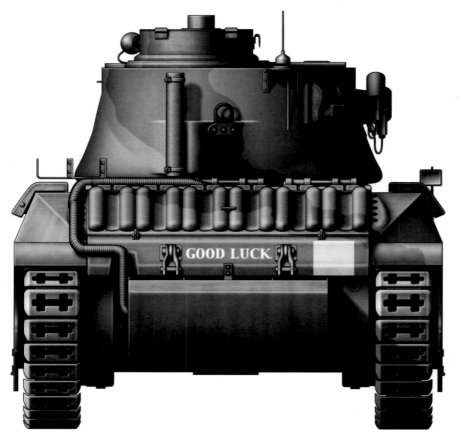

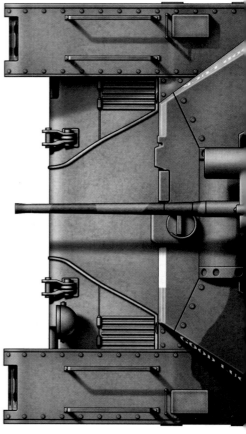

THE MATILDA Mk II TANK

In 1934, following the experience of the Great War, a study was begun on the design of a tank that would be simple, well armoured and armed with a machine-gun to overcome enemy defences. The *Master-General of the Ordnance*, Sir Hugo Elles, very influenced by the First World War, favoured a small infantry tank, due to the limited budget.

October 1935 saw the start of the design of the tank called the A11 or *Matilda,* a small vehicle with a two-man crew armed with a machine-gun. Its armour would have a maximum thickness of 60 mm at the front and would be powered by a 70 HP *Ford* engine. With a weight of 11 metric tons, top speed was 12 kph, which was thought to be suitable to accompany the infantry. The first contract was signed in 1938 with *Vickers Armstrong* to build 120, enough to equip two battalions, but in January 1939, with the perspective of an imminent war, it was obvious a tank would be required to equip six battalions. The new tank would be called the *Matilda Senior.*

The tank's origins date back to September 1936, with the start of the study for an infantry tank with thick armour, a three-man crew to be armed with a two-pounder gun. Although a gun capable of firing HE rounds was preferred, as the main mission of the tank was to protect the infantry from enemy tanks, it was thought that the two-pounder anti-tank gun, which by that time was very effective as such, was best suited. As there was not a suitable engine, it was decided to use two currently in use on buses, in parallel. This was the 87 hp water-cooled six-cylinder AEC diesel. A "Japanese type" so-called suspension, developed by *Vickers* in 1928 for the C medium tank, sold to Japan. The armour was the most remarkable feature, as it had a thickness of 78 mm at the front, and a minimum of 20 mm. Thus, the tank would be able to withstand any anti-tank shell then known and even most artillery shells in service. The general structure of the tank was extraordinarily solid, conceived to withstand a high off-road speed.

The drivers compartment was remarkable, as was the thick armour, with its cast hull, and which required a large number of man-hours to construct, posing a problem for the series production of the tank. There was no machine-gun in the hull. The suspension, unlike the A11, was totally protected by a complex system of plates and panels, but this rendered maintenance work complex and costly in terms of work time.

The turret was cast with a riveted top and a cupola for the commander on the left and a hatch for the loader on the right. The loader doubled as radio operator. The gunner was positioned in front of the commander, and was in charge of the two-pounder gun and of the co-axial *Vickers.* 303 machine-gun. On each side of the turret there were two pairs of four-inch smoke canisters. Because of the heavy weight of the turret, a hydraulic turning system was installed. But, as British doctrine of the time established (quite optimistically), when firing on the move, the gun would be raised and depressed by means of a device resting on the gunner's shoulder. For that reason, a great section of the chamber was placed well behind the trunnion hole, thus occupying a lot of space inside an inherently constricted turret.

A total of 2,890 *Matilda* Mk IIs, as the new tank was known, were built in several versions. The last ones were built in 1943, when it was clearly obsolete. They made their operational debut in France, in May 1940, where they proved an unpleasant surprise for Rommel, due to their heavy armour. A few months later, in North Africa, they were decisive in Operation *Compass,* when the Italians were smashed. Only with the arrival of the *Afrika Korps* would the balance be re-established. During 1941 the *Matilda* took part in a lot of fighting in the African theatre, where the Germans soon developed specific tactics to confront it. Initially, only the '88' was able to pierce its armour without problem. With the standardization of the long-barrel 5 cm gun, either the PaK 38 or the L/60 on the *Panzer* III, the days of the *Matilda* were numbered. Its poor mechanical reliability in the harsh conditions of the desert and its slow speed, together with the difficulty of introducing appreciable improvements or modernizations, relegated it to the second line.

As usual, there were several versions as successive modifications were introduced. The first consisted of the replacement of the water-cooled *Besa.* 303 machine-gun with the air-cooled British version of the ZB. This was called the *Mark* IIA. The *Mark* III was powered by *Leyland* engines. The CS (*close support*) version was armed with a three-inch howitzer that used HE or smoke shells only, exclusively intended for infantry support. Special versions were developed to fill in ditches, minefield clearance, flame-throwers, rocket-launchers, etc... Perhaps the most curious version was the CDL, fitted with a searchlight.

One thousand *Matildas* were sent to the Soviet Union, 750 of which arrived, but were of little use in the difficult Russian landscape. New Zealand got thirty-three *Mark* IV CSs but handed them over to Australia in 1944. This country had a few more than 400 of these tanks, which proved extremely useful in the jungle. Its armour proved very efficient against Japanese weapons and its armament, particularly the three-pounder howitzer, was very suited for destroying Japanese bunkers. Several remained in service until 1955.

Arras, the 150th Brigade, northeast of the town, started a timid advance, crossing the Scarpe River and progressing to Tillois, as part of the second arm of the counter-attack. But the scarcity of forces and their unsuitability for the intended objectives soon became evident; the attack halted in the face of the tanks of the 25. *Panzerregiment* and the British withdrew. Just in time, as the first elements of the 5. *Panzerdivision* were approaching Arras from that direction and they were nearly cut off.

The counterattack by 25 *Panzerregiment*

Once they had got over their initial shock, with their usual adaptability to the changing circumstances on the battlefield, the Germans did not take

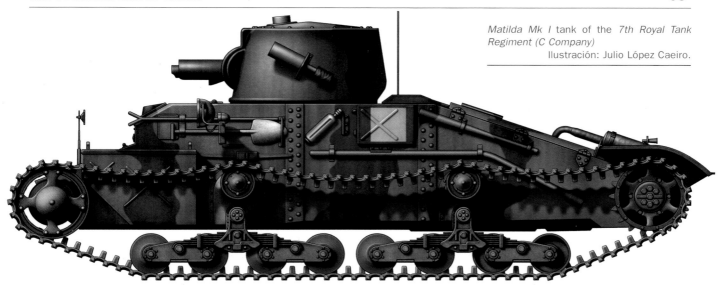

Matilda Mk I tank of the *7th Royal Tank Regiment (C Company)*
Ilustración: Julio López Caeiro.

long to react effectively. It should be stressed that, for the first hours of the battle, the British tanks were only confronted with infantry and artillery units, not tanks. As a matter of fact, the 25. *Panzerregiment*, commanded by Oberst Rotheburg, had already overtaken the British units. Rommel took control of the situation in a short time and, after organizing the defensive line with the artillery available, he then prepared the counterattack. Everything was very confused at the start. Rommel headed for Wailly, where he attracted machine-gun fire from the British tanks. In the village the situation was chaotic, with a large number of troops and vehicles seeking cover. On the way, west of Wailly, he had found some destroyed *Panzer 38(t)'s* and several 3.7 cm and 2 cm *FlaK* guns with their crews in hiding. After reestablishing some order in this chaos, Rommel managed to concentrate several guns against the enemy tanks, which finally halted near Wailly.

The German tanks turned back and went onto the attack against the Allied forces. First they met elements of the French 3^e DLM and, later, the *8th Durham Light Infantry*, which was entrenched at Duisans and Warlus. Instead of attacking both towns, the German tanks surrounded them, cutting off all exits. A section of tanks made a feint at one of the towns, but attracted the fire of several 2-pounder anti-tank guns. In the subsequent duel, the Germans lost five tanks, whereas all of the British anti-tank guns were destroyed.

The crews of the anti-tank guns had hardly any possibilities in the open against infantry tanks.

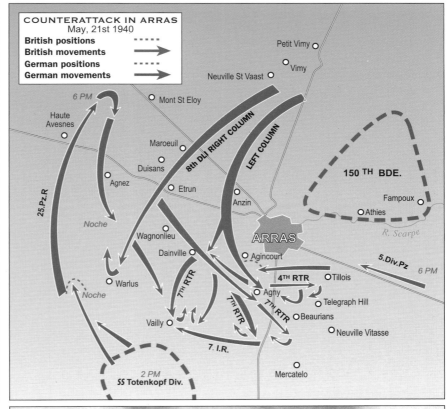

COUNTERATTACK IN ARRAS
May, 21st 1940
British positions
British movements
German positions
German movements

Petit Vimy
Vimy
Neuville St Vaast
6 PM
Mont St Eloy
Haute Avesnes
Maroeuil
8th DLI RIGHT COLUMN
LEFT COLUMN
150 TH BDE.
Duisans
Agnez
Etrun
Anzin
Fampoux
Athies
Noche
R. Scarpe
Wagnonlieu
ARRAS
Dainville
Agincourt
5.Div.Pz
6 PM
Warlus
4TH RTR
Tillois
7TH RTR
Noche
Aghy
Telegraph Hill
7TH RTR
7TH RTR
Beaurians
Vailly
Neuville Vitasse
7. I.R.
2 PM
Mercatelo
SS Totenkopf Div.

BRITISH EXPEDITIONARY FORCE (BEF)

The BEF consisted initially of two Army Corps, each with two infantry divisions. The I Corps comprised the 1st Division (Alexander) and the 2nd Division (Lloyd), and was commanded by General Barker. The II Corps comprised the 3rd Division (Montgomery) and the 4th Division (Johnson), and was commanded by General Brooke. In December 1939, it was reinforced with the 5th Division. Later, in January, three territorial divisions were sent, the 48th *(South Midlands)*, the 50th *(Northumbrian)* and the 51st *(Highland)*. The latter was sent to the Sarre, under French command, to reinforce the Maginot Line. The rest of the BEF deploying along the Belgian border, as part of the French IIIe *Groupe d'Armées*, under Billotte's nominal rather than effective command.

The position of the BEF and its commander Lord Gort in the chain of command proved very complicated and ambiguous. Although on paper it was part, along with the 1st, 2nd, 7th and 9th Armies, of the Iere *Groupe d'Armées* commanded by Général Billotte, directly subordinated to the Commander-in-Chief of the Northeast Theatre, Général Georges, who in his turn, was directly responsible to Gamelin. Despite this nominal subordination to French command, which was also divided by internal dissent, Gort had the faculty to act independently of the orders received and follow his own criteria, providing that he had previously conferred with his own government.

The Divisions numbered 42nd *(East Lancashire)*, 44th *(Home Counties)*, 46th *(North Midland & West Riding)*, 12th *(Eastern)* and part of the 23rd *(Northumbrian)* joined in April. Finally, in May, the 1st Armoured Division, commanded by Major-General Evans, arrived. The BEF by then totalling some 394,000 men.

Even though the campaign was already doomed, more forces were sent in, such as the Canadian 1st Division and the 52nd Division *(Lowland)*, in the second week of June. In final days of the campaign, the 20th Guards Brigade was sent to Boulogne and the 30th Brigade to Calais, to support the overburdened defenders.

On 12th June the encircled 51st Division surrendered at St Valéry. The last British soldiers abandoned French soil on 18th June. The BEF had sustained over 68,000 casualties, and had lost all its equipment.

The BEF was essentially an infantry force, fundamentally established on the Great War model. Each infantry battalion had a nominal force of 780 men, fifty machine-guns, fifteen mortars and twenty anti-tank rifles. There were specialized machine-gun and motorcycle battalions (with 150 motorcycles, *side cars* and armoured cars). Armoured battalions had about twenty-eight light tanks and forty-four Bren carriers per divisional cavalry regiments, and fifty-two *Matilda I's* or *II's*, or cruiser tanks in the case of the Armoured Regiments. It should be made clear that what the British called a *Regiment* corresponded to battalion-sized units in the rest of the armies. Artillery regiments were of different types, depending on the calibre (field, medium, heavy and super heavy), and had six to twenty-four guns. Anti-tank regiments had forty-eight 25-mm (of French origin) or two-pounder guns. Anti-aircraft artillery was abundant and of good quality; each regiment had either thirty-six or forty-eight 40 mm Bofors or twenty-four or thirty-two 3.7-inch guns.

Compared to other armies, British infantry were well motorized and enjoyed extraordinary mobility. Thus, each infantry division had about 3,000 vehicles of all types. But in practice things were different. In May 1940, Lord Gort complained that of the 624 tanks of all types available in theory, a little over one hundred were actually operational.

The only armoured division was considered by the French command as a "caricature" of a division. Its tank complements were not complete. Its infantry force was so small that it rendered it useless for many of the missions a *Panzerdivision* was in condition to carry out without difficulty. In theory, it only had two motorized infantry battalions. The mixed anti-aircraft/anti-tank regiment itself had only six anti-tank guns, instead of the nominal total of forty-eight. It was made up of the 1st Reconnaissance Armoured Brigade (Brigadier Norman), with the *1st Fife & Forfar Yeomanry* and the *1st East Riding Yeomanry*, the 2nd Reconnaissance Armour Brigade (Brigadier Clifton), with the *5th Royal Inniskilling Dragoon Hussars* and the *15th/19th The King's Royal Hussars*, and the 1st Tank Brigade (Brigadier Pratt). This brigade had two armoured regiments, the 4th RTR and the 7th RTR, that were equipped with a total of 100 tanks, but only twenty-three were *Matilda II's* (in the 7th RTR), the rest were *Matilda I's*. The *4th/7th Royal Dragoon Guards*, *12th Royal Lancers*, *13th/18th Royal Hussars* and the *1st Lothians & Border Yeomanry* were assigned as independent tank units, but they were in the wrong place with the wrong material.

In this first phase of the war, the United Kingdom had still not grasped the idea that the war would be one of movement, although it had been a pioneer in the use of the tank and would gain a resounding victory in North Africa in the face of an enemy superior in numbers by using its greater mobility. Its strategic conceptions were not that different from those of the Great War, and the doctrine for the use of armoured forces was a reflection of this. These were infantry support units that, as a whole, would not operate as independent units. As a matter of fact, due to its composition, the British armoured division was able to do very little. The battle of Arras was an event of a purely tactical nature, without any repercussion or strategic objective. Neither the command nor the equipment was ready for anything else but a tactically limited action. The Matildas were not suitable for the war of movement and the cruiser tanks were not suitable for tank-to-tank combat. Only the light tanks were suitable (and with many limitations at that) for reconnaissance. Coordination among the different arms was virtually non-existent and the traditional British tendency to stick to the regimental system made it very difficult to integrate the different units for a combined operation. As a whole, the BEF was an amalgam of small units, each of good quality individually but with very little polyvalence, and the armoured forces were a living example of this. Although they might represent an unpleasant surprise for the enemy at certain times, it was very unlikely that they would be able to do more than that. Events in France would soon show this to be true.

At dusk, the German infantry started to harass the British with mortar fire and took positions for the assault on both towns, but the latter tried to escape to the north. In this attempt, they were joined by the few surviving elements of the 3ᵉ DLM, although by pure chance, not as a result of a coordinated action. Indeed, during the night, several tanks of the French 3e Battaillon, along with the General Staff, arrived at Warlus, where the leading vehicles came under the fire of several German anti-tank guns that caused several casualties among the officers. The British fired as well, initially on the French units, but luckily with poor accuracy. However, despite these setbacks, the tanks and the French infantry managed to get inside the village, whereas the few German lead units present withdrew. There they linked up with the British, whose commander thanked them warmly for their help, to the astonishment of the French officers. The *Matildas* had long departed the battlefield. In the midst of the German fire, six Hotchkiss tanks and two armoured infantry transports tried to give cover to the retreating British forces in the early hours of the morning. Although several groups managed to escape, many were taken prisoner.

The forces entrenched at Duisans also managed to escape during the night, helped on this occasion by the anti-tank guns that had remained as reserves and the *Bren Carriers* of the 9th *Durham Light Infantry*.

The tanks of the 25.*Panzerregiment* continued their march eastwards and

a furious battle with British tanks, mostly *Matilda* II's (7th RTR), took place in the outskirts of Agny. In the course of the fight, the Germans lost three *Panzer IV's*, six *Panzer 38(t)'s* and several light tanks, *Panzer I's* and *II's*, before they managed to push back the British to the north.

At dusk there were scenes of great confusion, as enemy units mixed up. In one instance, the General Staff of the *4th RTR* was surrounded by tanks that he initially mistook as British. These were actually *Panzer 38(t)* tanks, apparently hard to mistake for *Matildas*. Their commander, *Major* Fernie, was killed in the subsequent action.

South of Arras, in the outskirts of Beaurains, the German attack started at about nine in the evening. Companies C and D of the *6th Durham Light Infantry* were dispersed and started a messy retreat to the north. About two hundred men reached the British lines during the next morning. A small group, completely lost, but showing a rare ability for survival, managed to arrive

in Dunkirk, where they re-embarked for the United Kingdom. Another group of British soldiers succeeded in reaching Boulogne.

A French unit, the 3ᵉ DLM, reinforced by the 515 GBC (battalion), made up of 47 Renault and Hotchkiss tanks, played an important role in the battle. Initially, their task was to give cover to the British right flank. They set off at three in the afternoon but, shortly after starting their advance, several units became the target of 10.5 cm guns and tanks from Bernaville. Some *Hotchkiss* managed to reach Warlus, but stopped there, as we have seen, only to withdraw in the early hours of morning, aiding the British in the process.

Balance
The battle of Arras had finished. Despite all the propaganda, especially after the war, it had no great influence on the course of events, neither could it have been otherwise. No doubt, it was a coup on German morale, but in no way could it have changed the final result.

Actually, it has to be put in context on a purely tactical level. It was the first occasion when British tanks, *Matildas* to be exact, equipped with heavy armour, unprecedentedly scored ephemeral partial victories on the Ger-

In theory, British infantry divisions were generously equipped with Bren Carriers, like most of the cavalry regiments which had 44 of them.

Illustration: Julio López Caeiro

GERMAN LOSSES:

7. Panzerdivision: 89 killed, 116 wounded and 173 missing (mostly POW's)

SS Totenkopf: 100 wounded and killed and 200 POW's.
9 tanks (total loss)

ALLIED LOSSES:

46 out of the 74 British tanks (only two *Matilda II's* returned)

4th Northumberland: 16 out of its 21 armoured reconnaissance cars were lost 50% of the infantry units

13ᵉ BCC: 10 Hotchkiss tanks

and, to their credit, it must be concluded that they individually managed to make good use of the limited armour equipment they had available. And these good results must be attributed both to the virtues of the tanks and the professionalism of the crews and intermediate commanders, who were very often ahead of their superiors, the latter still not having grasped the possibilities of tanks.

For the Germans, it was a blow to their morale that Rommel himself recognized. The flanks of an armoured unit are always at risk and difficult to protect. Von Rundstedt admitted that it had been a critical moment, as did von Kluge and von Kleist, who both became alarmed at the evidence that they could have confronted a very dangerous crisis that could have slowed down the advance of their armoured units.

mans in France. As it would later be proved in the African desert, the *Matilda's* greatest virtue was its solidity but it was only fit to fight light tanks, and useless for the war of movement. The Germans soon learnt to fight it with suitable arms and tactics.

As for the rest, cooperation among the different arms was virtually non-existent for the British. Whereas the Germans had perfected the rapid coordination between the different types of artillery, tank units and a variety of infantry units, not to mention the notable role of the *Luftwaffe*, the British acted as independent forces, with the tanks totally distanced from the infantry, with practically non-existent artillery and an RAF that did not show up. The disastrous reconnaissance, or rather the lack of it, is another noticeable factor in the battle. Both contenders were operating with doctrines that belonged in another war. The British, as if it was still the Great War and the Germans, with a doctrine that, with the obvious technological adaptations, is fully in force in the 21st century.

Despite all this, the counterattack at Arras was the only significant action involving British armoured forces during the French campaign in 1940

A knocked out A 9 tank. They proved totally unsuitable when facing German tanks.

THE BRITISH COMMANDERS

The United Kingdom was not exactly the ideal place for the creation and development of great tank commanders during the Second World War. As is usually the case with the victors, their stratagists remained anchored in the Great War and saw the tank as an infantry support element, although this could appear paradoxical given the use of cruiser tanks and the extraordinary mechanization achieved by the BEF, as well as having one of the greatest theoreticians on the potential of tank warfare, Sir Basil Liddell Hart, whose books were indeed put to good use by such notable commanders as Guderian.

The BEF was basically an infantry unit. Lord Gort was no tank expert, despite his brilliant military career. Born into an aristocratic family, he was educated at Harrow and joined the army in 1905. He later studied at Sandhurst and joined the *Grenadier Guards*, with whom he fought in the Great War with the rank of captain. During the war he showed remarkable courage, being mentioned in despatches a total of nine times, he was awarded the *Military Cross*, the DSO and, above all, the *Victory Cross*. His idea of the tank corresponded to that of the First World War and so, in general, he did not use them to any real advantage in France. However, it was not at all his fault alone. The quantity and quality of

the equipment he had could not have given better results. On the 31st May, in the midst of the evacuation of Dunkirk, he ceded command to Major-General Alexander.

Harold Rupert Leofric George Alexander was, with Montgomery, the best-known British general of the Second World War. Born in 1891, the third son of the fourth Lord Caledon, his early youth was devoted to sport, painting and enjoyment. He entered Sandhurst in 1910, for family tradition rather than choice. As an officer in the *Irish Guards* he proved himself to be of excellent quality during the

Harold Alexander.

First World War, winning the *Military Cross*, the DSO and ending the war as a *major*, one of the most decorated and respected officers in his regiment. At 31 he was a lieutenant colonel and a *brigadier* by the age of 43. After a time in India commanding the *1st Infantry Division*, he was sent to France with the BEF. Enjoying Churchill's favour, in August 1942, he was appointed chief of the Middle East Theatre of Operations, replacing Auchinleck. Although critical of Montgomery's methods, he gave him freedom of action. He led the British forces in the Tunisian campaign, with a cool head, efficiency and professionalism (very unlike his American allies), and avoiding unnecessary losses. Later, he conducted operations in Italy, until he was appointed Field Marshal and Chief of the Allied forces in the Mediterranean Theatre, in November 1944. Cold and calculating, methodical, he was not noted for originality or aggressiveness, despite the ever increasing means available to him.

Claude John Eyre Auchinleck was born into a military family at Aldershot, in 1884. After Sandhurst, he was sent to India. During the Great War he took part in the fighting against the Turks, particularly in Mesopotamia, where he was conscious of the useless and costly price of the futile frontal attacks, so cherished by the British command and politicians. In 1919 he was promoted to lieutenant colonel, fought in Kurdistan and was sent to India. At the start of the Second World War, as a lieutenant general, he led the Expeditionary Corps in Norway, in part due to his mountain experience, and was later to organize the home defence. In 1941 he succeeded Wavell to command the troops in North Africa. Upon his arrival in Africa he found a critical situation following the defeat of Battleaxe, with morale at a very low ebb. He insisted on the training of the troops and the need for more equipment before the start of further offensive action. In November he launched Operation Crusader to liberate Tobruk and repelled the Italo-Germans up to El Agheila, but Rommel's counterattack forced him

to withdraw again, with heavy losses, up to Gazala. In July, he managed to stop Rommel at El Alamein. Then he withstood pressure from Churchill to attack until he had the necessary equipment. However, for political reasons, Churchill decided to replace him with Alexander on 8th August and give Montgomery command of the 8th Army. The latter, very opportunistic and a master of publicity, copied Auchinleck's plans and took advantage of his work to gain the victory at El Alamein. A man of honour and principles who loved his soldiers, an enemy of politicians, had he had Montgomery's power from 1942 to 1945, the course of the war might have been very different.

Archibald Percival Wavell was an atypical soldier. His personal likings were art, history and literature but family tradition led him to take up a military career. He took part in the 2nd Boer war with the *Black Watch* and, later, he was pos-

ted to Russia, a country of which he became a specialist. During the First World War, he was awarded the *Military Cross* and was posted to Palestine when the war ended. In 1935 he commanded the *2nd Infantry Division*, where he had an influence on future officers of note such as Wilson, Dempsey and Horrocks. He stimulated physical and intellectual education, as well as the basic training of soldiers and was a great advocate of mechanization. He was one of the rare British generals who, in the 1930's, grasped the future possibilities of the aircraft and tank working in unison on the battlefield. He saw his greatest success in December 1940 when he annihilated a much superior Italian army during Operation *Compass*. He could not exploit this victory as Churchill deprived him of part of his force and necessary supplies to give priority to the foolhardy adventure in Greece, which ended in a new disaster for the United Kingdom. After the failure of operations *Brevity* and *Battleaxe* against Rommel, his post was taken over by Auchinleck.

With regard to armoured warfare, perhaps the only British general in his own right was Richard Nugent O'Connor, although his was a rather short career. Born in India in 1889, he was very aggressive and loved difficult tasks. He arrived in Egypt in June 1940, as a lieutenant general, and took charge of the *Western Desert Force*, which comprised two divisions (the

4th Indian Infantry and the 7th Armoured). His handling of armoured units during Operation Compass, which wiped the Italians out of North Africa, was brilliant given the limited equipment available. Captured by the Germans in April 1941, he escaped in 1943 in Italy but played no more truly remarkable roles, in spite of taking part in the fighting in Western Europe.

Bernard Law Montgomery leaves no one indifferent and cannot be left aside. Born in 1887, he was appointed chief of ground forces in Normandy under Eisenhower, which to him was an offence. A master of logistics, extremely methodical, he knew how to galvanize his men in times of crisis and handle propaganda admirably to climb up the social ladder, and to show his comrades up. His best moments were when he enjoyed full superiority, lots of equipment and time to organize an operation. When short on time or needing to go off the well-worn paths, it ended in disaster, like the most unfortunate operation *Market Garden*. His handling of the battle of El Alamein, the campaign of attrition around Caen, his intervention in the battle of the Ardennes and later the crossing of the Rhine are good examples of his savoir faire when he was in an advantageous position. Certainly, this was a general who never lost a battle, except for Market Garden, but he only fought those where he had all chances of winning. Obviously, despite his association with tanks, he was not precisely a paradigm of an tank commander.

O´Connor and Wavell in a snap taken at Bardia on 4th January 1941.

Monty and Churchill, a successful duo.

ROMMEL COUNTERATTACKS

Following the disaster which befell the Italian forces in North Africa, the Germans took the decision to become involved in that theatre and came to the aid of their allies. Of course, this was neither for altruistic reasons nor a yearning for fresh conquests, especially considering the perspective of war in the East in 1941, and the huge demand for resources this meant, but Hitler could not afford a total collapse of the Italians anywhere, as that would have put the southern flank at risk from a British naval attack. Italy would therefore receive the minimum of aid necessary to stabilize its position. On the basis of these premises, on the 11th January it was initially planned to send the so-called *Sperrverband Lybien* force to North Africa, with a 30-tank company. By the 5th February there were already plans to deploy a division, the 5. *Leichtes*, with the 5. *Panzerregiment*. The man chosen to command the German forces in North Africa was Rommel, who had already distinguished himself in France commanding the 7. *Panzerdivision*. With the arrival of another division, the 15. *Panzerdivision*, with the 8. *Panzerregiment,* a General Staff was created to lead what was from then to be called the *Deutsches Afrikakorps* (DAK). On the 10th February, the General Staff ordered the start of the *Sonnenblume* Operation.

On the 14th February, the first German ground units arrived at Tripoli, the 39. *Panzerjäger Abteilung* and the 3. *Aufklärungs Abteilung*, followed by three 8.8 cm batteries of the I./*Flak Regiment* 33. The infantry would arrive later in the month, and the tanks of the 5. *Panzerregiment*, between the 8th and 10th March. During the first half of February the *Luftwaffe* had already started to build an air base near Tripoli. There, on the 12th February, the man who was to change the desert war decisively, *General* Erwin Rommel, arrived on an Heinkel He 111. Although nominally under Italian command, the German forces would operate as a unit, never to be split up along the front. Should the orders given by the new Italian commander, Maresciallo Gariboldi, compromise the security of an operation or of his own troops, Rommel had instructions to appeal to his own superiors in Germany. *Fliegerkorps* X, the air element of the African forces, would remain under Göring's command.

Mechanization was vital for desert operations, and the Afrika Korps was initially much better equipped than their Italian allies after the necessary adaptations of the equipment. (Bundesarchiv)

Initial orders, both from Hitler and from von Brauchitsch, were not to start any offensive action until all of the armour had been completely unloaded. But Rommel was conscious that, despite the defensive mission entrusted to him, an aggressive attitude was necessary, particularly after the Beda Fomm disaster of the 7th February. It seemed that nothing would stop the British from reaching Tripoli along the coast and, as a matter of fact, units of the *Long Range Desert Group* were carrying out aggressive patrols inside Tripolitania, perhaps as the prelude to a larger offensive. However, the situation for the British was not so promising, as they were completely exhausted after the amazing advance they had made and were hurriedly taking defensive measures with the scarce equipment available to them, for their attention and resources were moving to Greece.

The original German plan only contemplated stopping the British from achieving total domination of North

A 20-mm anti-aircraft Flak gun in the port of Tripoli, a key point for the arrival of the Afrika Korps and subsequent supplies. (Bundesarchiv).

Africa but, as the German forces advanced on four successive nights with hardly any opposition beyond Sirte on the 21st March, they decided to advance on Marsa-el-Brega. In any case, a push on Libya was never considered before the arrival of the whole *15. Panzerdivision*, in May.

The war in the desert

Rommel was conscious of the peculiarities of the desert war or, at least, that this would be very different from the European theatre. His

The Vickers Mk VI light tanks were useful as reconnaissance vehicles, but were too often used as cruiser tanks, paying a high price.
Illustration: Julio López Caeiro.

troops had no African experience at all, something the British had plenty of. Rommel could only count on Italian advice, which was hardly a reassurance. They would have to learn as they went along. The desert war was, and is, something totally different from other theatres of operations. North Africa, in general, was dry uncultivated land peppered with the fertile plantations of the Italian settlers along the coastal strip, around the few centres of population. Water was concentrated in the rare millennium-old wells, visited by nomadic tribes. The climate changed a lot, with an alternation of periods of calm and violent sandstorms. Thermal oscilla-

tion was brutal, with torrid days and freezing nights.

Communications were very poor and limited movement a lot. There was really only one coastal road which had been built by the Italians, with a number of tracks going inland, very heterogeneous and of doubtful logistic value. The presence of certain geographic irregularities would condition military operations, like the Halfaya pass, the cliffs on the Egyptian border, the Qattara Depression and the seas of quick sands. The small number of ports, like Sollum, Bardia and Tobruk, would gain vital importance for supplies.

Logistics, as in every war, was fundamental but also had its peculiarities. Movement along the coastal road was easy but at risk from air raids, as there was no place to seek cover. Supplies for units operating only a few kilometres inland became a nightmare, as they had to resort to off-road or tracked vehicles, with desert-hardened drivers. Driving was torture, tracks disappeared under sandstorms and navigation required special abilities. Regarding combat, the situation was no better, as,

The *Panzer III* became the main German tank in the first campaigns in North Africa, proving once again its reliability and adaptability to any situation.

apart from the extreme climate that made everything difficult, something so basic as distance ranging varied a lot when compared to the European theatre. Tank gunners and anti-tank gun crews had to learn elementary things, like the thermal effect on a sandy surface that caused very deceiving effects, such as mirages. Besides, there was the omnipresent dust, uneven ground, the effect of the extreme temperatures on guns and mechanisms, etc. Vehicle maintenance itself required a huge effort, as sand became an engine's worst enemy. Tanks needed to be overhauled after doing half the mileage covered in Europe. The Germans had a lot to learn and would have to do so as they fought an enemy that was experienced in the desert war, and whose navy was the master of the Mediterranean and had so far only experienced victory.

The British Forces

After having defeated the Italians, the British had left only minimum forces in Cyrenaica and had concentrated on the Greek theatre. Morale was very high. After a ten-week campaign that had started with the assault on the Italian fortified camp at Nibeiwa and finished at Beda Fomm, results had exceeded any expectations. Two divisions had covered over 800 kilometres, destroyed ten Italian divisions, captured over 130,000 prisoners, over 380 tanks and armoured vehicles and 845 guns, at a cost of a little over 500 killed and 1,370 wounded. The Italian 5ª *Squadra,* with 380 aircraft at the beginning of the campaign, had also ceased to exist. It was not only a question of equipment or the quality of their troops, but also the mediocre level of the Italian intermediate commands and of the extremely

poor ability of the high command, which was totally inept for the desert war in the face of a modern enemy.

British armoured forces were quite battered at the end of the campaign, as the slow Matilda and cruiser tanks had sustained endless mechanical problems that had decimated their ranks. The 7th Armoured Division had been sent to Egypt for a rest and to repair their worn-out tanks. There were only the *3rd Hussars* left behind, with 63 Mk VIB's, many of them requiring repairs. On the 22nd February, the 6th Royal Tank Regiment (6th RTR) arrived at Tobruk, without tanks or vehicles, and started to equip with captured Italian M. 13s. These tanks were slow and uncomfortable when compa-

The first German armoured units to arrive lost no time and drove along the coast road to their first objectives. The huge Sahara desert was a very different scene from their previous experience. (Bundesarchiv).

Early in 1942, three *StuG* III ausf D's took part in the battle of Gazala and the capture of Tobruk.

Illustration: Luis Fresno Crespo.

red to cruiser tanks, but had an effective 47 mm gun. On the 18th March, A Squadron left for the border with fifteen M.13's, of which only nine were operational by the end of the journey. On the 13th March, the only unit equipped with cruiser tanks, the 5th RTR, was sent to the border, but many of the tanks suffered breakdowns along the way. On the 31st March, only twenty-five Mk IVAs were fully operational. Overall, the British armoured units that were to confront Rommel on the 31st were as follows;

General Staff of the 3rd Armoured Brigade: 3 Mk VI's
3rd Hussars: 26 Mk VI's and 12 M.13's
5th RTR: 25 Mk IVA's
6th RTR: 36 M.13's (at Beda Fomm)

There were other, perhaps more serious problems. Anti-tank gun crews were badly needed; some of the guns themselves were over 20 years old. New tanks arrived at a desperately slow rate. A very obscure aspect of the desert war was the behaviour of the ANZAC troops, who, although terrific shock troops, were a cause of continuous trouble for the British command. Fights and acts of indiscipline were not uncommon. But there was much worse, several dozen Italian prisoners were butchered (bayoneted to death after surrendering) following the fall of Tobruk, looting in coastal towns that had been captured and the rape of the women of the Italian

settlers... all of which remained unpunished, for fear of causing a revolt. Only Montgomery, one year later, facing a generalized uprising by Australian troops that had sustained heavy losses at the hands of the Folgore, finally adopted a serious and resolute attitude, taking exemplary steps to re-establish discipline and avoid the repetition of atrocities.

Supplies became an obsession for the British command, as with the arrival of the Luftwaffe, operating from Sicily and Tripoli, they began to have serious problems in receiving them. Benghazi, because of its vulnerability, could not be made into an advanced supply base and so it was Tobruk that was chosen. But this vital port was also within range of the Luftwaffe and anti-aircraft defence was never fully up to strength. Air mining operations off the approaches to the port became constant and caused serious losses to Allied convoys. The Luftwaffe was to prove that, although few in numbers, it was a far superior adversary compared to the Regia Aeronautica.

The offensive starts

On the 14th, Rommel ordered several Italian units to leave for Sirte at once. After his first reconnaissance flight, Mussolini gave him the command over all units at the front. Italian troops were followed by German reconnaissance and anti-tank units. On the 16th, the Axis forces occupied Sirte. However, the first contact with the British was not until the 28th, at Nofilia.

After occupying El Agheila on the 24th, Rommel decided to advance along the via Balbia, on the 31st, although this was against orders from Berlin, which expected no offensive action, no matter how limited, until late May. For the attack on Marsa-el-Brega, planned by Rommel for the very 31st March, the Germans enjoyed the support of the Italian Ariete division, with 46 M.13 and over 100 L.3 tanks, and the Brescia infantry division that could only move six companies at once for lack of trucks. The German forces available were 55 light tanks (*Panzer I's* and *II's*), 130 medium tanks (*Panzer III's* and *IV's*), 111 anti-tank guns, including an 8.8 cm battalion, and a recon-

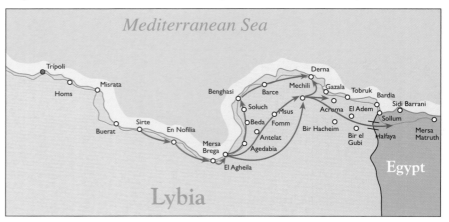

German mechanized units driving across the barren Libyan desert. Upon their arrival, 5 cm anti-tank guns like one seen here were masterfully used in combination with tanks. (Bundesarchiv)

naissance unit equipped with twenty-seven armoured cars (*Sdkfz* 222s, *Sdkfz* 234s,...). Besides this there were three infantry battalions. Italian units contributed 109 anti-tank and 72 field artillery guns.

By the end of the day, he had taken Marsa-el-Brega and Bir-es-Suera, capturing several dozen prisoners and driving back a badly coordinated counterattack by several light tanks. The British command was totally puzzled by German aggressiveness. Wavell himself, a most orthodox man, did not expect a German offensive before May, according to traditional military doctrine. The action at Marsa-el-Brega is a typical example of a tank attack at that stage of the war, and will be described next.

The battle of Marsa-el-Brega

The 6. Kompanie of the 5. *Panzerregiment*, reinforced by elements of the 8. Kompanie and a company of the 605. *Panzerjäger-Abteilung*, went beyond El Agheila and split up into two groups that advanced in parallel along the via Balbia in the following order, a reconnaissance section, an 8.8 cm gun, a *Panzejäger* I section, the command car, the 6. *Kompanie* and the *Panzerjäger Kompanie*.

The Panzer II, although in theory to be used as a reconnaissance vehicle, was too often used as a medium tank.

Illustration: Julio López Caeiro

At 08:00, Mk IVA tanks of the King's Dragoon Guards were seen at kilometre 3 of the via Balbia, and came under fire from the 88's and the Panzer III's. Despite the ferocity of the German fire, only one of the light tanks had the turret jammed by a hit and all of them withdrew about six kilometres, again to be fought back by the German advance. As they arrived at the crossroad to Marsa-el Brega, the Germans found British units deployed there. A light tank was destroyed by the 4.7 cm gun of a *Panzerjäger* I, and the tanks bombarded the British positions. Shortly afterwards, the British abandoned them and retreated. At no time did they try to defend their exposed positions, and withdrew to a defence line in the rearguard, called Aaron.

The column continued with its push, with an engineer group lea-

ding to destroy the mines laid by the British, supported by a section of *Panzer III's*. Several kilometres after Marsa-el-Brega, they bumped into the British defensive line and came under the fire of the British field artillery. The *Panzer III's* advanced and started a duel with the cruiser tanks of the 5th RTR, several of which were knocked out. Despite that, protected by an anti-tank ditch, the British infantry stuck to their positions. Thus, half an hour later, a *Stuka* squadron attacked the positions, although they also bombed several German units by mistake, causing two casualties. In the evening, the German artillery began to bombard the positions at Marsa-el-Brega and through the night the engineers, under cover of machine-gun fire, cleared the minefield, thus permitting the push of the tanks at

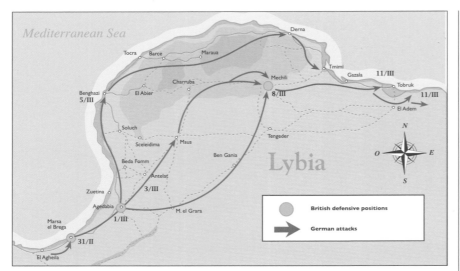

The flashing advance by the Cyrenaica was carried out through three axes attack and ended at the overwhelming Micheli´s victory

dawn, which attacked from two directions. They took the town without difficulty, as the enemy had left it that night with the 23 tanks still operational. The latter continued with their retreat, with the 3rd Hussars in the rearguard, and several cruiser tanks abandoned due to breakdowns.

On the 1st, German units continued their push along the via Balbia for about another 30 kilometres, until they encountered enemy units on both sides of the road. The British tanks had continued their retreat throughout the day at an extremely slow pace due to constant breakdowns, in three parallel columns, the 3rd Hussars on the right, the 1st Royal Horse Artillery in the middle and the 5th RTR on the left. The Italo-German

units advanced meeting very little opposition, carrying out repeated outflanking operations and requesting artillery support as soon as they came up against any opposition. German reconnaissance units maintained a stream of continuous information on British movements.

Shortly after five in the evening, the Axis tanks hunted down the British column, who initially mistook them for elements of the 6th RTR, equipped with Italian M.13 tanks. This confusion was due to the fact that several squadrons in this regiment had previously given support to the Hussars and the latter were afraid of firing on their fellows. However, several cruiser tanks took positions hiding their hulls and prepared for combat. The Italo-German units, around sixty vehicles, occupied a front of about three kilometres and were advancing with the tanks covering the trucks. At about

British A13 and A9 Cruiser tanks in the camouflage schemes of the first North African campaigns.

Illustration: Julio López Caeiro.

three kilometres from the enemy vehicles, they split up into two, forming a crescent formation. At that distance, the British were still sceptical about their identity and, although orders were given to fire at 800 metres, when the enemy was already at less than 2,000 metres, orders were still given to confirm identity before firing.

At 17:32, the first *Panzer III's* of the II. *Abteilung/Panzerregiment* 5, with the setting sun at their backs that obstructed the enemy's view, they fired on the Mk IVA cruiser tanks of C squadron of the *3rd Hussars* from about 1,300 metres. One of the cruiser tanks started to burn at once, although the crew managed to abandon it. The British began to fire back but at such distance and with the sun in their faces, it was not very effective. As they came closer, the Panzer III's scored new hits, despite the fact that the targets had their hulls hidden, and little else than their turrets jutted out. At 800 metres distance, one of the cruiser tanks got a hit on a *Panzer III* and knocked it out, but the crew managed to get out. The German tanks kept on firing from a distance that was very favourable for them. Another

Panzerkampfwagen IV Ausf F1, of the 8. *Pz.Rgt.*, 15. *Panzerdivision*, Tobruk, November 1941.

Illustration: Julio López Caeiro.

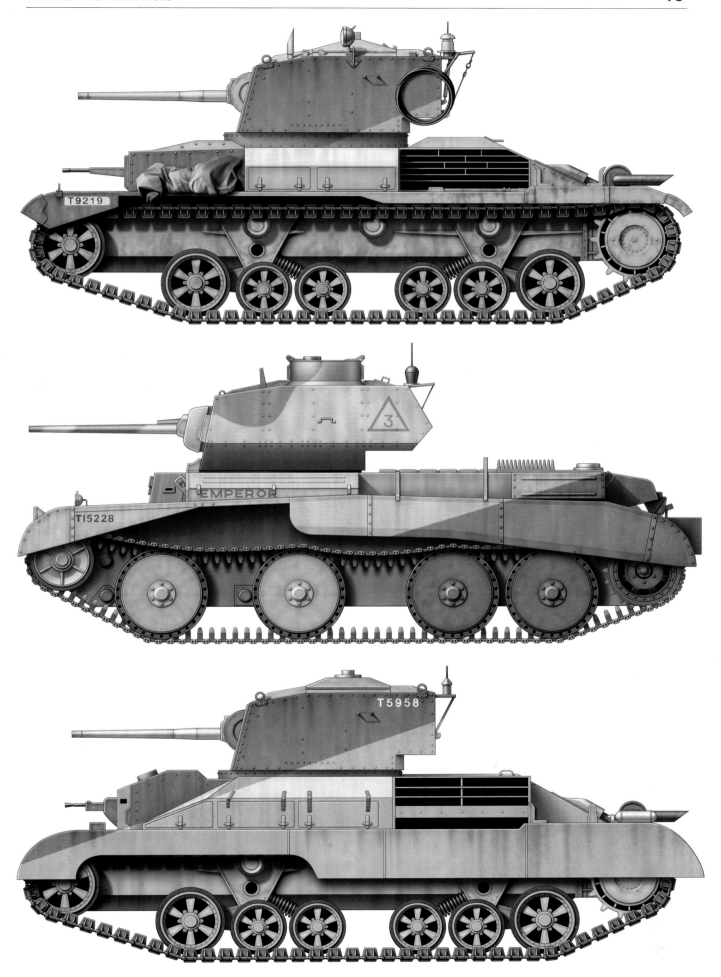

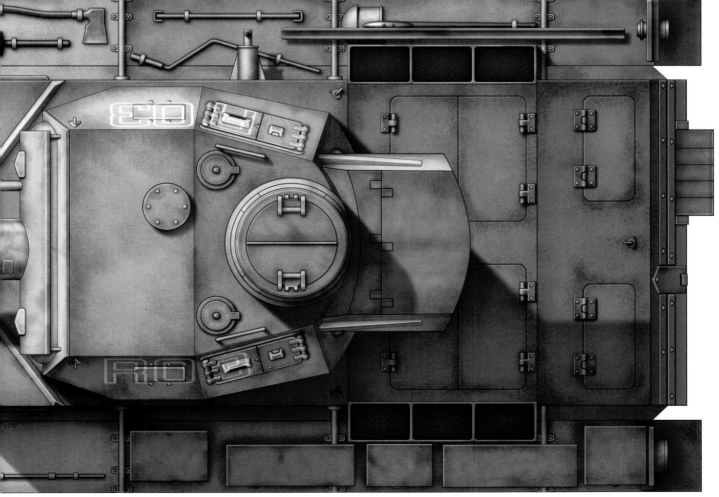

Panzerkampfwagen III

The *Panzer* III was designed in the mid-thirties as an intermediate step between the light (the *Panzer* II) and medium (the future *Panzer* IV, armed with a 7.5 cm gun) tanks, as it became pretty clear that a tank with light armour and armed with a 2 cm gun would be unsuitable for tank-to-tank confrontation on the battlefield of the future. The new tank, in Guderian's opinion, should be armed with a 5 cm gun but the *Heereswaffenamt* chose the 3.7 cm gun for standardization. Guderian accepted reluctantly, on condition that the turret was wide enough to take a larger calibre weapon when it was required. The new tank, called the *Panzerkampfwagen* III (Sd. Kfz. 141), had a similar look to the heavier *Panzer* IV. It would have a three-man turret (commander, gunner and loader), with a further two in the hull (driver and radio-operator). *Daimler Benz* started production of the A model in 1936. Armed with a 3.7 cm Kwk L/46.5 gun and two machine-guns, its armour had a maximum thickness of 15 mm and its *Maybach* 108 TR engine gave it a top speed of 32 kph. Both this first model and its B, C and D successors were produced in small numbers and were phased out of the frontline in 1940, as they had very poor characteristics given the requirements of combat.

The *Ausf* E model was the first to be produced in large numbers and had been much improved. It had armour up to 30 mm thick, a more powerful (*Maybach* HL 120 TR) engine, a new gear box and six-wheel suspension, which increased top speed to 40 kph. Weight had increased to 19.5 tons. After initial experience in combat, it soon became evident that Guderian was right and the 5 cm gun was necessary. Mass production of the latter would take time and the first units of the *Ausf* F model still rolled off the production line with the 3.7 cm gun.

The *Ausf* H, of which 308 units were built, had supplementary armour of 30 mm at the front, a redesigned turret and a stowage bin on the top. Its new armour rendered it virtually invulnerable to the Allied anti-tank guns then in service. The *Ausf* J was built in larger numbers than any other (2,616 units until July 1942), and the new armour (up to 50 mm) had already been integrated. It was initially armed with the 5 cm Kwk L/42 gun, and carried 84 shells, which, from late 1941, were replaced in the last 1,000 units with the L/60, which was much more efficient against tanks, on Hitler's personal insistence. Weight reached 21.5 metric tons and range was about 150 kilometres. Frontal armour on the *Ausf* L was supplemented with a 20 mm spaced shield and many were initially fitted with *Schürzen* (skirt armour), as protection against hollow-charge shells.

Despite all these considerable improvements, it was obvious that it was no longer on a par with combat needs by mid-1942 and that its role had been fully assumed by the *Panzer* IV. The last model produced, the *Ausf* N (663 units), was armed with a 7.5 cm Kwk L/24 gun for infantry support, thicker armour and a weight of 23 tons. The role of the *Panzer* III had changed radically since the by then distant 1936.

Production totalled 15,350 *Panzer* III chassis up to 1945, which gives an idea of the effectiveness of the design. With no special individual features, its main virtue was a balanced design, along with a notable capability to take a large number of improvements. It formed the core of the Panzerwaffe in the *Blitzkrieg*. No other tank, except the *Panzer* IV, still few in numbers in 1940, would have allowed the Germans such rapid penetrations and spectacular advances. Mechanical reliability was very high, crews enjoyed a reasonable degree of comfort with the state-of-the-art equipment and its capability in the anti-tank role remained quite high until 1942. In North Africa, it maintained its superiority until the appearance of the *Sherman* and the *Churchill*. Some units even took part in the Normandy campaign, and during Operation *Market-Garden* several *Panzer* III *Ausf* L's fought effectively in the streets of Arnhem. Adoption of the 5 cm L/60 gun allowed it to confront the early T-34 and *Sherman* models with a high degree of success. Armour up to 50 mm thick at the front afforded suitable protection in normal combat conditions on the battlefields well into 1942. The use of a three-man turret conferred it a tactical flexibility that German tank commanders exploited very well. In any case, its finest hour was in the spectacular advances of 1940 and 1941 on the Western Front and during Operation *Barbarossa*, and in North Africa throughout 1942, where it prevailed in tank-to-tank combat.

Many versions of this extraordinary tank were designed, a command type, a flame-thrower tank, an artillery observation vehicle, an engineers' tank and a recovery vehicle. However, the most successful designs were the assault guns and the self-propelled artillery. Perhaps the most famous variant was the *Sturmgeschütz* III, over 9,000 of which were built. In its different versions, it mounted different guns, from the 7.5 cm L/24 to the 10.5 cm L/28, and its armour was increased to 80 mm at the front. Because of its importance, this type is dealt with in detail elsewhere in this book. Very specific versions were built, in very limited numbers, armed with many different weapons such as the 15 cm SiG. 33 infantry howitzer. This use of the tank in its different versions to the end of the war is an acknowledgement of the excellence of the design.

In May 1942, forty French Lorraine vehicles were transformed into the *Sdkfz 135/1 15cm sFH13/1 (Sf) Geschützwagen Lorraine Schlepper*, fitted with the 15-cm FH 13 howitzer, to be sent to North Africa.

Illustration: Julio López Caeiro.

three cruiser tanks began to burn, but this time the crews could not abandon them. Another tank took a hit in the turret that wrecked the gun. Given this amount of fire, retreat was ordered but a further two tanks were hit and knocked out as they left their original positions. One more of the cruiser tanks, totally disoriented, advanced towards the enemy and was smashed by accurate German fire. In total, the British lost seven tanks and suffered twenty-four casualties (five of them officers). The surviving vehicles retreated for over three kilometres to a new position, to continue shortly afterwards their retreat, according to the original plan. That day, three M.13s and five Mk VIs were immobilized to mechanical breakdown and were left behind. The Germans had lost three tanks in the fighting and regrouped in the newly conquered position, before carrying on with their pursuit.

The British forces had been expelled from a relatively strong defensive position by scarce German forces. They had won their first victory in the desert, despite their inexperience in this theatre, against an enemy that had made themselves respected in France and the British were now in open

Panzer III tanks and a Horch car driving along a desolate strip in Cyrenaica.

retreat. The road to Cyrenaica was open to Rommel and his *Afrika Korps*.

The push to the east

The British retreat continued on the 3rd April, their units left Antelat. By the end of the day, the 3rd Armoured Brigade had a total of eighteen Mk VI's, fifteen Mk VI cruisers and twenty-six M.13's. For Rommel, this was a day for reorganization and distribution of supplies, as communication lines with Tripoli were beginning to stretch and fuel and spares took longer to reach the front. Besides this, he also had a confrontation with his nominal superior, Gariboldi, who ordered him to stop. A radio message from the OKH, giving Rommel total freedom for tactical action, put an end to the problem. Reconnaissance units, which were actually advancing, were meeting numerous abandoned *Commonwealth* vehicles.

Rommel, once again contradicting traditional doctrine that advised the concentrated use of the forces available, used three axis of advance from Marsa-el-Brega. One along the coastal road, to Benghazi and Derna; a second one, to Msus and Mechili and the third one, making a detour inside the desert and converging on Mechili too. Each combat group (*Kampfgruppe*) was a self-sufficient unit and was made up of tanks, anti-tank guns and infantry, capable of almost any type of action, except an assault on a solid defensive position.

On the 4th and the 5th the race continued, the British retreating hurriedly and abandoning broken down vehicles with the Germans

hot on their heels. That day, several pursuing tanks had breakdowns of different degrees of seriousness as they penetrated a minefield. In the same way, it seemed that only off-road vehicles were suitable to keep the pace of the advance. German reconnaissance units penetrated Benghazi, without the slightest resistance. A British fuel convoy for the 3rd Armoured Brigade was destroyed by the *Luftwaffe*. The M.13s of the 6th RTR were in such a poor state that the nine in best condition were ordered to take the fuel from the rest and continue. The others were abandoned and destroyed. The Germans detached a force made up of two tank companies, an artillery battery and a *Panzerjäger* company towards Msus. This group was joined by a machinegun battalion and an M.13 battalion, with 40 tanks (belonging to the Ariete), and was called the *Gruppe* Olbrich, after the *Oberstleutnant* in command.

On the 6th, mechanical problems and lack of fuel began to take their toll on the Italo-German units. Several tanks remained immobilized waiting for the arrival of the mechanics, due to refrigeration problems in the new conditions of the desert that they had to con-

Popularly known as the Diana, nine half-tracks were transformed to take the Soviet 76.2 mm anti-tank gun, of which large numbers were captured. They played an important role in the battles of Gazala in May-June 1942.

Illustration: Julio López Caeiro.

front and the *Gruppe* Olbrich stopped about 20 km east of Msus at noon. The objective was to approach Mechili to attack it on the following day, but all the units were quite slow. For the British, the situation was no better. The 6th RTR had abandoned all of their M.13 tanks and the 3rd Armoured Brigade had only two M.13s, fourteen Mk VIB's and eight Mk IVA cruisers. The exhausted crews feared the arrival of the Germans, and even fired on their own units arriving from an unexpected direction.

The following day, the Italo-Germans managed to circle Mechili at dusk and attack at dawn. In view of an impending attack on Mechili, the British tried to reinforce their garrison but, because of the type of ground, the only feasible way for the tanks to arrive was by making a detour along the road to Derna, to refuel and take the only road that offered some security to the tanks. The retreat to Derna, then on at once to Tobruk, continued with a string of breakdowns, in such a way that only seven cruiser tanks of the 5th RTR arrived. Four of them fought with German units after leaving the town and were destroyed. Only two of the total of 55 cruiser tanks of the 5th RTR that had left Tobruk returned. Nine were lost to enemy fire and the rest to mechanic breakdowns.

The battle of El Mechili
El Mechili was the main caravan junction of Cyrenaica, with an old fort, surrounded by trenches and

fire pits for anti-tank guns. In order to try and catch the British troops in retreat, Rommel detached four mixed columns in pursuit, three of which converged on El Mechili. This position was defended by the division General Staff of the 2nd Armoured Division, the Indian 3rd Motor Brigade, a battery of the *Royal Horse Artillery* and an Australian anti-tank unit. Rommel himself directed the circling manoeuvre from his *Storch*, which coincided with an attempt by the Allied forces to abandon the position and reach Tobruk.

To the north was a tank unit, with eight *Panzer III's* (*Kampfgruppe* Schwerin). In the east was the Fabris column (III/8º *Bersaglieri* and several artillery sections). The rest of the *bersaglieri* battalion, about 300 men (Montemurro column) deployed south and, in the east, the General Staff of the 5. Leichtes Division.

After 05:30, the Indians carried out four successive attacks to try and break the siege from different directions, but each was repulsed one after the other. In the last, at nine in the morning, Fabris's *bersaglieri* pushed the Indians onto Montemurro's 75/27 guns, which smashed them. After these failures, the British commander, General Gambier-Parry, surrendered with 1,700 men and over 500 vehicles to Italian Colonel Montemurro. *Kampfgruppe* Olbrich did not arrive in time to take part in the attack.

Knocked out A13 Cruiser tank. The picture was taken in 1942, but the Valentines had no better luck than their predecessors. (Bundesarchiv)

After this success, the fourth column, made up of the 8. Maschinengewehr Bataillon, commanded by *Oberstleutnant* Ponath, rushed along the via Balbia to Derna, and was extraordinarily lucky, as it captured Neame, Combe and O'Connor, thus beheading the *Commonwealth* forces in North Africa. The Australians retreated from Begasi to Tobruk, leaving behind the remains of the 2nd Armoured Division on their way. Rommel, from his Storch, watched the push of his units through the desert, putting pressure on those he judged too slow. As a matter of fact, he finally dismissed General Streich, replacing him with Prittwitz, previously the commander of the recently arrived 15. *Panzerdivision*. One of the three British *Mammoth* command cars captured became Rommel's car, a real icon of the war in the desert.

On the 10th, the spearhead of the 15. *Panzerdivision* arrived at Mechili, where it joined the rest of the Italo-German forces. Rommel was convinced that the British were defeated and that Tobruk would fall at once. Therefore, he sent the few available elements of the 15. *Panzerdivision*, the weakened 5. *Leichtes Division* and the Italian *Brescia* and *Ariete* commanded by Prittwitz, who headed hurriedly to Tobruk. On the 11th, the 5. *Leichtes Division* had completed the siege of Tobruk. Apart from an important port, it was an obstacle on the via Balbia, forcing a detour of over 50 kilometres. At the time, the two German divisions needed 24,000 tonnes of supplies monthly, the *Luftwaffe*, 9,000, and the Italians, 45,000. A port like Tobruk was vital to continue the offensive, as it was the only one with the capacity to handle that much traffic between Tripoli and Alexandria.

Tobruk: the end of the beginning

Tobruk had an amazing defensive system by the standards of the desert war, inherited from the Italians. A semicircle of defences started on the coast, thirteen kilometres east of the town, to end fifteen kilometres to the west. They consisted of a series of concrete emplacements that were hardly visible above ground, with a total perimeter of about fifty kilometres. They were surrounded by double lines of barbed wire and an anti-tank ditch six metres wide and over three metres deep, partially completed. Besides this, there were numerous minefields, particularly at the places where the ditch was incomplete. The land progressively rose to the sea, affording the defenders a wide command of all of the surrounding land that afforded no protection at all to the attacker. Defences were organized in independent strongholds, surrounded by barbed wire, in two lines five hundred metres apart from each other. About three kilometres behind this, a third line had been built, also surrounded by barbed wire, minefields and an anti-tank ditch. New minefields were set between both main lines. Each stronghold had a minimum of two or three machine-guns, an anti-tank gun and a mortar, positioned in concrete emplacements communicated by deep trenches. Each had about ten to fifteen riflemen. At the rear was the powerful field artillery, equipped with four 25-pounder regiments, an 18-pounder regiment and twelve 4.5-inch howitzers.

There were four Australian infantry brigades (no. 18 of the 7th Division, and nos. 20, 24 and 26, of the 9th Division) inside the perimeter, and the remains of the 3rd Armoured Brigade, with twenty-six cruiser tanks, four Matilda IIs and fifteen light Mk VIb's. Anti-aircraft defences were concentrated around the port, with a total of sixteen heavy and 59 light guns. Out of the total of thirteen infantry battalions, seven were deployed in the advanced fortified points, and a motorized infantry brigade was kept as a mobile reserve in the rearguard, distributed at the three crossroads inside the perimeter, at Adem, Pilastrino and Derna. It also had twenty-four anti-tank self-propelled guns. A final reserve force, equipped with *Bren carriers* and light tanks, was intended to counter likely parachute and amphibious landings. The garrison amounted to 36,000 men, mostly battle-hardened Australians commanded by two aggressive and resolute generals, Lavarack and Morshead. Finally, a landing strip inside the perimeter allowed the *Hurricane-equipped* no. 73 *Squadron* to operate.

The first engagements around the perimeter started on the 11th. For several days, there were sporadic confrontations with the Australian patrols, an unpleasant surprise for the Germans, as the retreats had finished and a war for defensive positions started for which they were not yet ready. *Prittwitz* himself was killed in one of these first skirmishes. Rommel was impatient and acted rashly. An ill-conceived attack carried out by a group of tanks of the 5. *Pan-*

zerregiment was stopped dead by the anti-tank guns and a timid attempt of the *Brescia* hardly managed to make it beyond the start line. To make things worse, the British were gathering a force at the Halfaya pass, a position that would become famous in the next few months, commanded by *Brigadier* Cott, to break the more than likely future siege of Tobruk. At once, they started to harass the III. *Aufklarüngs-Abteilung*, commanded by *Obertsleutnant* von Herff, which had been deploying at Bardia from the 11th.

The first serious attack took place between the 14th and the 17th and ended with a German defeat. Rommel launched the still weakened 5. Leichtes Division and the *Ariete* using the tactics that had earned him many victories in France, a solid phalanx of tanks and infantry, advancing in a crescent, firing their guns in motion, supported by the artillery, attacking on a very narrow front. The defenders were fully conscious of the objective of the attack and stood firm, hitting back on their opponent's flanks. The Germans lost seventeen tanks for no gain. An isolated attempt by the *Ariete* on the 16th also ended in a costly fiasco. The only achievement in this phase was the capture of the Halfaya pass by von Herff's battalion and a recently arrived motorized infantry battalion that managed to expel Cott's force.

The German General Staff was conscious of the real situation of the *Afrika Korps* and the Italians, with their overextended supply lines, disproportionate fuel require-ments that were impossible to meet and a large part of the vehicles badly in need of repairs and maintenance. Apart from this, many of the units had still not had time to acclimatize to the desert, which decreased their operational effectiveness. To re-establish some order, the High Command sent von Paulus, chief of the General Staff, to evaluate the situation on the spot and make an objective report. He was determined to direct Rommel back onto the orthodox path.

Rommel's first counterattack had finished and it was time to expect a British counter-offensive, as they were not ready to leave Tobruk. A new phase of the desert war had begun.

Conclusions

During Rommel's rapid offensive, the British 2nd Armoured Division had lost a total of forty-nine cruisers, forty-seven light tanks and all of their M.13's. Only ten of the cruiser tanks were lost in combat, the rest were due to mechanical problems or lack of fuel. The worst of it was that the enemy had lost only three tanks in exchange.

The initial retreat had been carried out according to plan but, as would become common during the war, it was rigidly and passively developed, with a purely defensive purpose, giving up any attempt at counterattack or ambush, where, given the poor mechanical reliability of the tanks, the British had little to lose.

The fighting on the 2nd April clearly demonstrated the valour of the British crews, who faced a superior

Only twelve of the *15 cm sIG33 auf Fahrgestell Panzerkampfwagen II* (Sf) were built, and took part in all of the operations from their arrival in Africa in early 1942 until the spring of 1943. None returned to Europe.
Illustration: Julio López Caeiro.

enemy, but also their tactical rigidity, as tanks were not allowed to manoeuvre without permission from immediate superiors, neither individually nor as sections or squadrons, regardless of the circumstances, which caused unnecessary and disproportionate casualties.

With the attack at Marsa-el-Brega, the Germans carried out a remarkable example of combined action between different arms. They acted as a perfectly synchronized team to face the enemy defences without unnecessary risk by charging blindly ahead. The *Kampfgruppe* were very well balanced and were quite able to confront anything the British could send against them, except for a fortress, like Tobruk.

On the 2nd April, however, the II *Abteilung* did not show much originality with a frontal charge when, although facing a weak enemy, they should have fixed them and carried out an outflanking manoeuvre. This resulted in the unnecessary loss of three tanks, two *Panzer* III's and a *Panzer* IV.

Perhaps the Germans' only serious error in this phase of the campaign was not to make a suitable evaluation of the movements of the British, as Rommel thought that they were in open retreat in the face of the Italo-German advance, whereas they actually had never intended to maintain such advanced positions with so few forces. Staying there meant risking being outflanked and annihilated, as they had done to the Italians a few weeks earlier. However, the necessary outflanking manoeuvres took a toll on the German tanks. The 5. *Panzerregiment* was decimated not by the enemy but by breakdowns. The high-speed push over broken ground along many kilometres, necessary, on the other hand, for the outflanking manoeuvres, proved to be a more devastating foe than the British two-pounder guns.

As a result, when the regiment was in front of Tobruk, it had been noticeably reduced after an advance of some 700 kilometres, and less than half its tanks remained operational. Twelve of the twenty-five *Panzer I's*, two of the 3 *Kl.Pz.Bef.Wg.'s*, nineteen of the forty-five *Panzer II's*, forty-four of the sixty-five *Panzer III's* and six of the seventeen *Panzer IV's* were non-operational, waiting for repairs, a total of 83 of the initial 155 tanks. The most common breakdown was caused by sand in the oil circuits, because of the inefficiency of the filters, and 58 engines had to be changed. The suspension system was another element that suffered a lot, and had to be replaced in 65 tanks. Breakdowns in braking circuits were frequent, as they were in turret ball bearings and transmissions. The desert was a theatre that required an enormous effort by the maintenance crews.

Rommel's aggressiveness, even recklessness, is a very controversial matter. He openly disobeyed his orders and carried out an attack by the book with the scarce units available to him. However, it is fairly certain that even if he had won an amazing tactical success, this success would probably have cost him the campaign. With his spectacular push, the British retained many units in Africa that were intended for Greece. Because of the extraordinary difficulties that they had to re-embark the troops after the Greek fiasco, it is probable that many would have been lost in Europe and would not have fought the *Afrika Korps*. Had he waited for the whole of the 15. *Panzerdivision*, Rommel would have enjoyed an enormous tactical superiority that would have allowed him to keep up a sustained offensive. But the other side of the mat-

The M3 *Honey*, as it was known to the British, was a mediocre light tank, fast but with weak armour and a totally obsolete main armament. When it was used as a medium tank, it suffered very heavy losses. (Bundesarchiv)
Illustration: Julio López Caeiro

ter is that Rommel had learned that a resolute attack with armoured units, even with scarce forces, often caused panic among the enemy and a messy retreat that ended in chaos and defeat if pressure was maintained, no matter how weak this was. This system had worked very well in France and, initially, it seemed to work with the British too. But the British retreat in North Africa was not the French debacle. The abandonment of an unsustainable position was mistaken by Rommel for a hasty retreat and it was in front of Tobruk where, at last, he grasped the intentions and the real situation of the British.

ROMMEL

Erwin Rommel was born on 15 November 1891 in Heidenheim an der Brentz, Württemberg. His father was a schoolteacher and his mother the daughter of a politician of some fame in the Länder. He joined the army in 1910 as an officer cadet in the 124. Infanterie Regiment. He attended the military school in Danzig in 1911, where he met the woman who was to become his wife; they married in 1916. Their only son, Manfred, was born in 1928.

He fought with his regiment in the First World War, being noted for his valour and recklessness.

He was wounded in hand-to-hand combat in September 1914. He was awarded the Iron Cross First Class in 1915, and in October was posted to an Alpen (mountain) unit to receive training in that type of warfare. Late in 1917 he was posted to the Carpathian front. He served outstandingly at the battle of Caporetto, for which he received the coveted "*Pour le Mérite*", the highest decoration of the German Army in the Great War, and was promoted to captain.

After the armistice, he commanded a security unit until 1921, when he took command of an infantry regiment. He was an infantry instructor in Dresden and in 1929 wrote his famous book «**Infantry Attacks**», where he described his experiences in the Great War. In 1938, now with the rank of lieutenant colonel, he was posted as to the Potsdam Academy Military, and later appointed director of the Wiener Neustadt Military Academy. In those years he met Hitler, who appreciated his heterodoxy and enjoyed discussing new military ideas with him.

In September 1939 he was promoted to *Major General* and was given the command of Hitler's bodyguard during the Polish campaign. When the campaign was over, Hitler entrusted him with a *Panzerdivision*, the 7th, despite his inexperience with armoured units. It was a to be a proof of his opportunistic attitude and his ability to exploit opportunities. In those months he went through a curious change, as he shifted from a defender of the infantry to a diehard champion of the *Panzerdivisionen*.

On 10 May 1940, the 7. *Panzerdivision* was part of Hoth's Corps and played a notable role in the race to the sea through France. He broke through the Somme front between Abbeville and Amiens and later propaganda would call his unit the *"ghost division"*, as no one knew where it was (including the German General Staff). Although he experienced a temporary setback at Arras, his speed and capability in penetrating and disrupting the enemy rearguard became legendary. Rommel soon stood out for his command ability on the frontline and the speed of his advances. He gave a lot of importance to maintaining contact with his men, and often cut off communications with his superiors to continue operating independently.

In January 1941 he was promoted to *lieutenant general* and a month later was given the command of the *Deutches Afrika Korps*, sent to support the Italians in North Africa. He arrived in Tripoli on the 12th February. When he

arrived, he found an appalling panorama, as the Italian forces were totally demoralized, so he decided to disobey his orders and attacked at once with the limited number of units he had. He only stopped before Tobruk, which took a long time to capture (June 1942). During that time, his enemies nicknamed him *"The Desert Fox"*, because of his astuteness and ability to combine the different arms and lead the British into repeated anti-tank ambushes. At 50, he was promoted to field marshal, the youngest in the German army.

The war in North Africa became a succession of offensives and counter-offensives, where Rommel, always very short on supplies and materiel, often had the initiative against an enemy very superior in numbers, and was only stopped at El Alamein, when British superiority was overwhelming. He carried out a model retreat under pressure, as far as Tunis, where he entrenched himself. Seriously ill with amoebaean dysentery, he frequently had to abandon the battlefield to get treatment. In 1943 he returned to Germany, never to see Africa again. After several temporary postings, he was appointed chief of Army Group B in France, under von Rundstedt's command. He devoted himself to the task of reinforcing coastal defences, as he was conscious that, given Allied control of the air, the next battle would be won on the beaches.

He was wounded in an air attack on 17 July 1944, and could not take an active part in the 20th July plot to kill Hitler, although he was very conscious that the war was lost and was party to the elimination of the *Führer*. Because of his popularity, he was given the option to kill himself to avoid the scandal and save his family, this he did by taking poison on the 14th October. Officially, it was stated that he had died of his wounds and was buried a hero.

As a whole, Rommel was a notable commander, above all an excellent tactician, although with a limited strategic vision. His command method became legendary and was later copied by many armies. Always concerned about his men's well being, he was also preoccupied with his prisoners and, as a matter of fact, was one of the few German commanders, with or without reason, not involved in war crimes. However, in Africa his main concerns were his soldiers, too often scorning his Italian allies. He was highly respected by his enemies, who admired his chivalrous behaviour and respected his skill and determination. His independent attitude regarding his superiors led him to make good use of opportunities, but also created serious problems in the operations of the General Staff. Despite all this, he has a very important place among the tank commanders of history. The fact that so many have tried to emulate him is perhaps his greatest tribute.

Rommel with his General Staff in the desert.

BARBAROSSA 1941: THE ENCIRCLEMENT OF MINSK

Unternehmen «Barbarrosa»

Following the signing of the Russo-German non-aggression pact in 1939, Hitler's hands were initially left free to deal with the coming campaign on the Western Front. However, events occurred that soon made it clear that this unatural alliance would not last indefinately. Already, in June 1940, in the middle of the battle for France, Stalin had occupied the Baltic Republics of Estonia, Latvia and Lithuania. When Hitler had earlier accepted that the three Baltic Republics stayed within the Soviet sphere of influence, he had certainly never contemplated their military occupation. Nevertheless, the German High Command saw this act as a logical preventative measure on the part of the Russians in case of any German aggression following victory in the West. Too make matters worse, at the end of that same month, Stalin sent an ultimatum to Rumania, demanding it immediately hand over Bessarabia and northern Bukovina. In 24 hours, Soviet troops had invaded both territories. This was a far more aggressive move which left the Ploesti oilfields, vital for the German war economy, within reach of the Soviets. The plan for the invasion of the Soviet Union began to take form throughout the second half of 1940, it was clear that sooner or later the two powers would clash, and that Stalin had already begun taking advantage of any oppertunities that presented themselves to favour the Soviet position.

In Directive number 21, Published on 18th December 1940, Hitler specified the strategic objectives of an eventual attack on the Soviet Union. In this Directive, Hitler made it very clear that the most important centres of armaments production were in the Ukraine, Moscow and Leningrad. Moscow was also the nation's political and administrative centre, as well as being a vital communications hub int the rigid, centralised Soviet system. The entire Area of Operations was divided into two halves by the Pripet Marshes. The road network in the southern sector was very bad, and, while it was slightly better in the north, by western standards only the Warsaw-Moscow axis had communications that could be considered at all adequate.

The Directive clearly stated that: "*German forces must be prepared to crush Soviet Russia in a rapid campaign, before finishing the war against Great Britain. A particularly powerful force must attack from War-*

The German Infantry made marches of up to 70 kilometres a day in order to keep up with the armoured units in the first weeks of Barbarossa. (Bundesarchiv)

saw towards Moscow. Of the three Army Groups proposed, Army Group North is to focus on Leningrad, and Army Group South on Kiev; in this last mentioned, one Army is to advance from Labun, another from Lvov and another from Rumania. The overall objective is the Volga and the Archangel region. The forces will include 105 infantry and 32 armoured and motorized divisions, of which two contingents will be of primary importance at the beginning of the second wave"... "*The main body of the Soviet Army in western Russia must be destroyed in audacious operations, driving in four deep wedges with tanks, impeding the withdrawl of battle-worthy enemy forces into the wide open spaces of Russia*".

This then, was the essence of Barbarossa, the codename for the operation, consisting of a deep penetration into Soviet territory, in order to destroy the majority of the enemy's forces through gigantic encirclements on the frontier before they were able to withdraw into the interior. To achieve this, the aggressive use of armoured formations was vital, these units having the task of

The armoured divisions advanced at great speed, and without regard for their exposed flanks once they had broken through the enemy's front, their main objective being to encircle as large a number of enemy forces as possible. (Colección Javier del Campo)

rupturing the defences in only a few hours and advancing dozens of miles into the Russian interior, leaving the infantry to advance at their own pace to complete the encirclements. It was vital to destroy the enemy's forces in European Russia within a matter of weeks. The overall strategic objective was to reach a virtual line between Archangel and the mouth of the Volga, including Moscow. Once this had been achieved, the Luftwaffe would be charged with neutralising any Soviet attempt to reorganise armaments production in the east. Hitler designated 15th May for the start of the attack, but events in the Balkans caused the start of operations to be put back five weeks. Finally, on 6th June, Keitel detailed the timetable for operations. On 22nd June, at 0330 hours, German troops would begin the greatest military operation in history.

The three attacking Army Groups (*Heeres-Gruppe*) would be made up differently. Army Group North, under the command of Ritter von Leeb, contained Armies XVI and XVIII, as well as Panzergruppe 4, (under Hoepner) with a total of 18 infantry divisions, three armoured divisions and three motorized divisions. Army Group north would attack from East Prussia, through the three Baltic republics, towards Leningrad, and It was to have the support of 1,070 aircraft. Army Group centre was the most powerful of the three, and was placed under the command of von Bock. It was formed by Armies IV (under von Kluge) and IX (under Strauss), with a total of 24 infantry divisions. It was also assigned two Panzergruppen, the 2nd and 3rd, commanded respectively by Guderian, the grand theoritician of armoured warfare, architect of the victory at Sedan, and Hoth. Between them, they had seven armoured and seven motorised divisions. They were tasked with attacking towards Minsk and Smolensk, along the road to Moscow. There were 1,670 aircraft in support. Finally, there was Army Group South, commanded by von Runstedt, which was composed of Armies VI, XI and XVII, the 2nd and 3rd Rumanian armies and Kleist's *Panzergruppe* 1, totalling 23 infantry divisions, five armoured divisions, and three motorized divisions. Their objective was Kiev and the Dnieper. Army Group South had 1,300 aircraft in support. The general reserve was made up of 24 divisions, of which two were *Panzers* (the 2nd and the 5th) and one motorized.

Heeres-Gruppe Mitte (Army Group Centre), which was the strongest of the three Army Groups, had Moscow as its objective, and was divided into two parts. In the north, the Panzer

A total of 772 *Panzerkampfwagen 38(t)'s* took part in Barbarossa. Their mechanical reliability made them indispensable for the deep penetrations that were required.

Illustration: Julio López Caeiro.

A *Panzerkamfswagen I Ausf B* of *14.Panzer-Division*. Although then obsolete, a considerable number of these tanks took part in the initial phases of Operation *«Barbarossa»*.

Illustration: Luis Fresno Crespo.

divisions were grouped together in Hoth's *Panzergruppe* 3, and consisted of the 7th, 12th, 19th and 20th Panzer divisions, as well as the 14th, 18th and 20th motorized divisions. In the south, Guderian's *Panzergruppe 2* was made up of the 3rd, 4th, 10th, 17th and 18th *Panzer divisions*, and also included the *«Gross Deutschland»* regiment.

This force was to confront the Soviet forces defending the Western Military District, and which was composed, from north to south, of the 3rd, 10th and 4th Armies, commanded by Generals Kusnetzov, Golubiev and Korobkov respectively. Overall command of the District had fallen on General Pavlov. The sector of attack extended from Vilnius to Brest-Litovsk, where the Pripet marshes began, an area totally inappropriate for a war of movement.

The *Panzer* division of 1941 (nineteen of which took part in *«Barbarossa»*) was very different to the one which had participated in the Polish campaign, almost two years earlier. The German Army had a total of twenty-one Panzer divisions in 1941, a year earlier it had only deployed ten. However, the increase had only been attained by considerably reducing the number of effectives in each division. During the French campaign, a division contained two tank regiments, each with about 160 vehicles. For the invasion of Russia, this was halved to one regiment of tanks per division. Of the 17,000 men who,

at least on paper, made up the strength of a *Panzer* division, only 2,600 were tank crews. This reduction was based on the increase in quality which had been achieved, two thirds of the tanks now being *panzer*

Panzergrenadiers with a *Panzer 35(t)* neutralizing a Soviet defensive position. (Bundesarchiv).

The *Sturmgeschütz III* gave the infantry considerable firepower, although its effectiveness against tanks was limited, due to its short gun 7.5 cm (L/24) gun. The one illustrated is a *StuG III* Ausf belonging to the *2nd Battalion, StuG.Abt.203*.
Illustration: Luis Fresno Crespo.

III's and *IV's*, which were superior to the *Panzer II's* and above all, *Panzer I's*, which had previously formed the nucleus of the divisions in Poland and France. Furthermore, Hitler was convinced that, confronted with the geographical immensity of Russia, the increase in the number of divisions was necessary in order to be able to penetrate in depth, any loss in firepower being compensated by Soviet inferiority in material. However, this reduction in strength was to worsen one of the defects present in the *Panzer* divisions, namely, the fact that the majority of its vehicles were not armoured, and lacked the mobility of its tanks. The new *Panzer* divisions had approximately 300 tracked vehicles, the rest, around 3000, were wheeled. This deprived the Division as a whole of the revolutionary mobility of its tanks. In the West, where there was an excellent road network in existence, this had not posed a problem, but in Russia, it was to be decisive.

On 22nd June 1941, the strength of the *Panzerwaffe* on the eastern front was as follows: 181 *Panzer I's* (mainly in engineer units), 106 *Panzer 35 (t)'s*, 746 *Panzer II's*, 772 *Panzer 38(t)'s*, 965 *Panzer III's* (the majority mounting the short-barrelled 5 cm gun), 439 *Panzer IV's* (most being models D or F1) and 230 *Panzer III* Befehlswagens. A total of 3,439 tanks, excluding assault guns and tank hunters (*Sturmgeschütz* and *Panzerjäger*) formed in independent units, or captured tanks (such as the French SOMUA S35), which were

used in security missions in the rearguard areas. A typical *Panzer* division included a *Panzer* regiment, with two *Abteilungen* (battalions). In theory, the number of tanks per division was 7 *Panzer III Befehlswagens*, 45 *Panzer II's*, 68 *Panzer III's* and 28 *Panzer IV's*, making a total of 148 tanks. In spite of the increased capability of the newer tanks compared to those used in the campaign in the west, the German High Command tried to equip each division with a further bat-

talion, which would give, theoretically, a total strength of 218 tanks, equivalant to the 7.Panzer-Division in 1940. However, given the scarcity of available tanks, only the 3rd, 5th, 9th, 16th, 18th, 19th and 20th *Panzer* divisions were strengthened. Three divisions (the 6th, 7th and 8th) were reinforced with an independent battalion, others meanwhile, received an additional light company to each existing battalion.

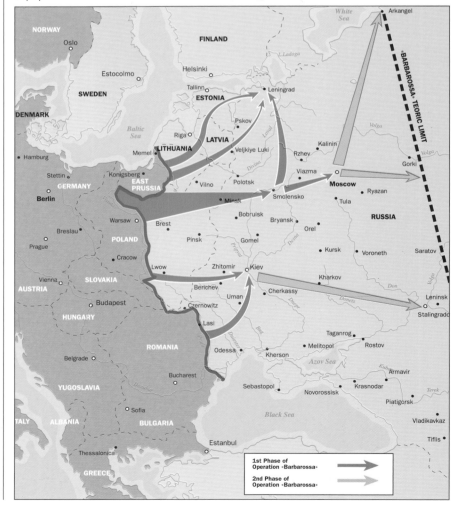

The immense wide open spaces of Russia presented a novelty for the Panzerwaffe. Allowing them to carry out large-scale operations of encirclement, but this made things difficult for the slower moving infantry, and was a logistics nightmare. (Bundesarchiv).

That victory in Russia depended on the *Panzer* divisions was clear to everyone, but, what was not so obvious was the way in which they were to be best employed. Some members of the German High Command wanted to destroy the Soviet forces in a decisive battle, in a classic encirclement, following the theories of Clausewitz, Moltke and Schlieffen. This was based on the supposed necessity of defeating the enemy before penetrating too far into the Soviet Union, which carried its own considerable risk. To achieve this, the tanks would have to co-operate with the infantry, penetrating quickly on the enemy's flanks, encircling him and allowing the slower moving infantry to finish the task.

Proponents of the *Panzerwaffe*, with Guderian at the head, had different ideas. Essentially, they wanted the Panzers to penetrate as deeply and as quickly possible following the breakthrough, following the pattern established in France. Guderian was convinced that as both his and Hoth's group were primarily heading for Moscow, they should not be detained by secondary objectives. First, they had to reach the Dnieper as soon as posible in order to dislocate the Soviet defensive system, and then continue east at all speed. The infantry divisions were tasked with

The BT-7 was one of the most numerous Soviet tanks in service in 1941, but was outclassed by the *Panzers*.
Illustration: Julio López Caeiro

completing and consolidating the encirclement of Soviet forces that had been bypassed, so as to prevent them from escaping and complete their destruction.

The intervention of Hitler, which on other occasions had proved to be more audacious, tipped the balance in favour of the more orthodox approach, denying the *Panzerwaffe* the possibility of trying for a decisive victory. In retrospect, it is possible that this could have been the only way to have defeated the immense Soviet Union, but prudence, and the fear of over-exposing the *Panzer* divisions, prevailed.

Soviet Armoured Units.

In 1941 the Red Army was in the process of reorganising following Stalin's devastating purges, which had resulted in the eradication of the best officers, including possibly their best tank commander, Tukha-

chevsky, not to mention the disasterous result of the war with Finland. It is not possible to establish the exact composition of Soviet armoured units at the start of the war, given their diversity and heterogenous nature. There were brigades, divisions and corps in existence. The basic unit could be considered to have been the armoured brigade. Following the 1938 directives, an armoured Brigade consisted of four battalions of 54 tanks (T-26's or BT-5's), and six artillery tractors, with a 76.2 mm gun, as well as a battalion of infantry, a Recce group, and a small logistics unit. A heavy tank brigade contained 156 T-28 or T-35 tanks.

In November 1939, the armoured corps were replaced by armoured divisions, eight of which were formed in 1940, and a further seven in the first half of 1941. The total strength of an armoured division was 258 BT-

Panzer II's, obsolete as a combat vehicle by 1941, were mainly relegated to the role of a reconnaissance vehicle, and although they had not been designed for this, they performed the task adequately. (Bundesarchiv)

out. Only a third of the crews were operational. Of the 13,500 outdated tanks (T-26's and BT's), only around 3,650 were operational. To these figures it is necessary to add the 967 T-34's and 508 KV-1's and KV-2's which had only just left the factories at the beginning of the year and been hurried to the front with their crews barely trained to face the *Wehrmacht's* 3,500 tanks.

The new models of Soviet tanks were to revolutionise armoured warfare. The KV-1, with a weight of 45 tons, was able to reach a maxi-

5's or BT-7's, 17 T-37's or T-40's, 98 artillery pieces or mortars of a calibre above 50 mm, and 11,650 men. It was foreseen that from 1941, the BT's would be replaced with the new, formidable T-34, which was beginning to come off the production line. Following the defeat of France, the armoured division was transformed to include 413 tanks, 91 armoured vehicles and 58 artillery pieces, and 11,343 men, making it a much more powerful unit, although at the same time more complicated to manage. The higher level unit to the division was the mechanized corps, with a theoretical strength of 1,000 tanks, a formidable force on paper, equal to three or four *Panzer* divisions. There were nine machanized corps and two independent armoured divisions deployed at the beginning of 1941. Shortly after, in February, it was decided to create a total of 21 new corps during that same year which would need to be equipped with 20,000 tanks. Therefore, in theory, on 22nd June 1941, the Soviets would confront the Germans with 29 mechanized corps, made up of 61 armoured and 31 motorized divisions.

Not withstanding these extraordinary figures, these units were at a considerable reduced state of readiness, to the extent that, on 22nd of June, 29% of the tanks were in need of major repairs and 44% needed at least minor work carrying

Soviet losses amongst these models were catastrophic. Thousands of tanks were destroyed in the first weeks of the campaign, such as this BT-7. (Javier del Campo).

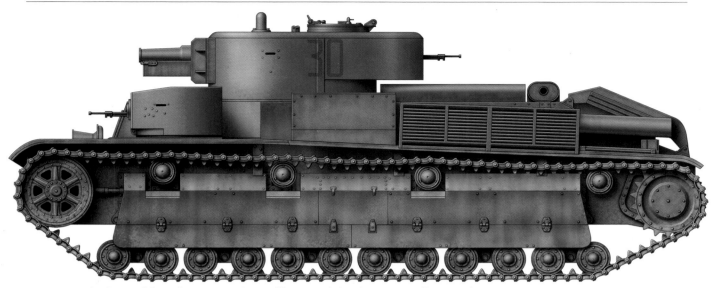

mum speed of over 20 mph, exceptional for that time. Its 75 mm armour made it almost invulnerable to the anti-tank guns in existence at that stage of the war, while its 76·2 mm main armament could destroy any of its contemporaries at the normal combat ranges of the period, and at the same time, it was also effective against infantry. The KV-1 was produced at the Kirov factory in Leningrad and in Cheliabinsk. It made its debut on 11th February 1940, when six of them were used against Finnish positions on the Karelia isthmus.

The revolutionary T-34 was the masterpiece of the engineer Koshkin (who died in September 1940). It was initially produced in the Komintern factory at Kharkov from January 1940 onwards. It embodied the perfect between firing power, mobility and protection and surpassed all the tanks of the world at the time, retaining this position until the appearance of the formidable German tank in 1943. It was armed with the same 76.2 mm cannon as the KV-1, protected with armour up to 60 mm thick at the front. It was able to tilt to 60º, which greatly increased its efficiency. With a maximum speed of 50 km per hour, its high power to weight ratio (18 hp per tonne) and its wide caterpillar tracks provided it with an unprecedented mobility, in the most adverse of conditions. Nevertheless, it was far from being the perfect tank, as it had defects, such as the two-man tower, which gave it a considerable disadvantage in battle. By way of evidence of its good design, it has been used in a wide range of conflicts and in the most diverse operational conditions, up to the end of the 20th Century.

The Soviet plan was completely conditioned by the restructuring their forces were undergoing, especially the armoured units. Furthermore, it is patently obvious that to a large extent the German plan caught them completely off-guard. In fact, the more than 1,200 miles of front between the Baltic and the mouth of the Danube were defended by only forty infantry and two cavalry divisions with express orders to maintain positions, supported by unfinished fortifications. Behind this weak first line of defence was the second line with the armoured units, at least sixty kilometres behind the front line. Of those units making up this second line of defence, the better quality ones were expected to be in position in 72 to 96 hours following the announcement of a general mobilization. On 22nd June, a general mobilization had not been declared. This was in some part due to Stalin's deliberate policy not to provoke the Germans, as he wanted time to complete the slow process of reorganizing the Red Army. It would appear to be quite clear that Stalin was not expecting war in 1941, and that he was preparing for an offensive in 1942. In June of 1941, in spite of its deficiencies, the Red Army had 170 infantry divisions, 32 cavalry divisions and 78 armoured brigades. If the *Wehrmacht's* original plan was successful, 140 would be destroyed, but that would still leave 70 intact.

The T-28 was one of the monsterous multi-turreted tanks which had been designed in the nineteen thirties and turned out to be a disappointment. Its powerful armament, at least on paper (76.2 mm main gun and four machine guns), could not compensate for its weak armour, lack of speed and poor mechanical reliability.

Illustration: Julio López Caeiro.

Drang nach Osten

At 0330 on Sunday 22nd June 1941, German artillery began an accurate bombardment of Soviet positions along more than 2,000 kilometres of front. At the same time the *Luftwaffe* began what was up to that time, the largest air offensive in history, with unprecedented success. On the first day alone, the Russians admitted to losing more than 1,200 aircraft (800 of them on the ground). The Germans claimed more than 1,800 enemy aircraft destroyed for the loss of 35 of their own planes. Strategic surprise was complete, both at small unit and command level, including the commanders of army corps.

Heeres Gruppe Mitte (Army Group Centre) had been given the task of breaking through the Soviet Central Front and advancing towards Minsk, then to surround the city and destroy the encircled Russian units . It was then to continue on to Smolensk. Guderian commanded one of the *Panzer* Groups, and the first really important obstacle he faced was the river Bug and the fortress of Brest-Litovsk, which he had conquered in 1939, but had been handed over to the Russians under the terms of the Russo-German non-aggression pact.

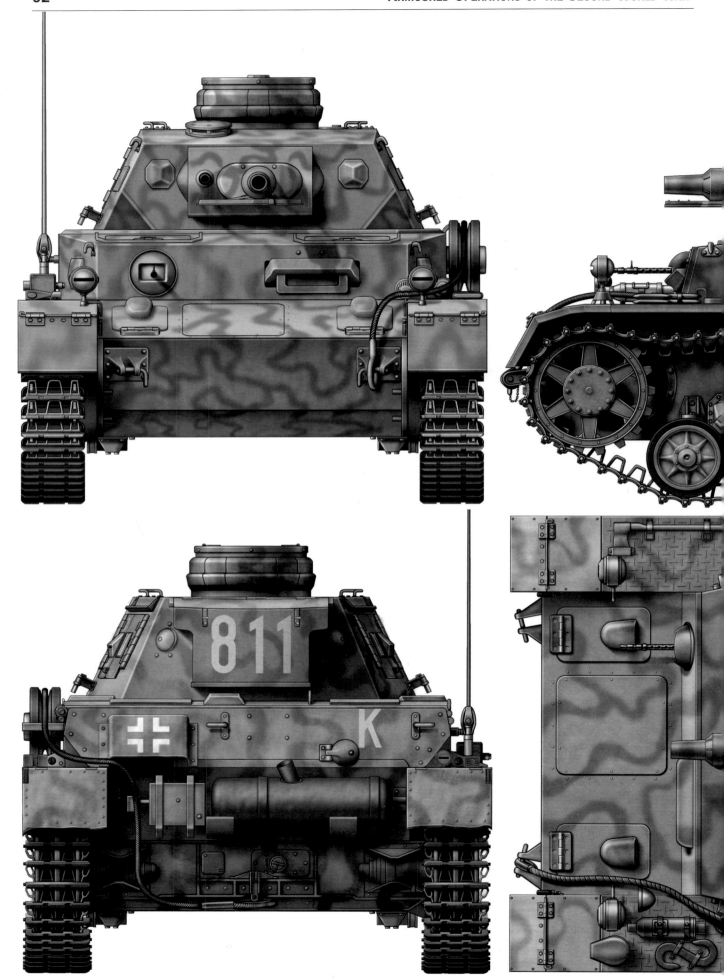

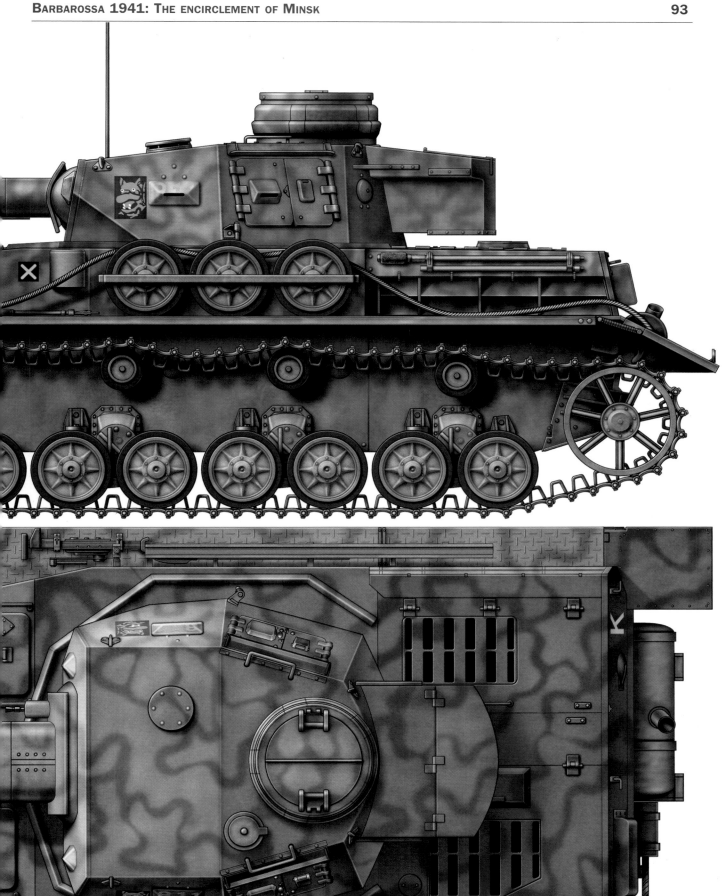

Panzerkampfwagen IV

The origins of the *Panzer IV* can be traced back to 1934, when three companies, MAN, Krupp and Rheinmetall-Borsig, began work on an infantry support tank weighing 24 metric tons, in accordance with the specifications laid down by the Army. After 18 months of development, the Krupp VK2001/K design was chosen as the one best meeting the requirements. However, during the time that had elapsed since the beginning of the Project, the specifications had changed, especially those concerning the drive chain, so Krupp then adapted the design, reaching a compromise with the *Heereswafenamt*, as the need to start production was becoming urgent.

The new tank was reminiscent of the *Panzer III*, but with eight pairs of wheels instead of six. The model A was driven by a 12 cylinder 250 hp Maybach engine, with a six speed gear box, with five forward gears and one reverse. The spacious three-man turret housed a 7.5 cm L/24 and co-axial 7.92 mm machine gun. The tank's armament was completed by another macine gun in the hull next to the driver. At the rear of the turret was a large cupola for the tank commander. Two hatches at the sides allowed access for the gunner and loader. The turret could be turned both manually and, when necessary, by an advanced auxiliary generator. Armour on the first model was 14.5 mm thick on the hull and 20 mm on the turret. The tank only weighed 17.4 metric tons and maximum speed was almost 35 kph. The first model was soon improved on by successive models, and a 350 hp engine was fitted, bringing maxium speed up to 40 kph, despite the tank's armour being increased to 30 mm and its overall weight to 20 metric tons.

Models C and D saw combat in Poland, where they were soon shown to be vulnerable to anti-tank weapons. The result of this was the introduction of the model E, which incorporated significant improvements based on combat experience. Armour was increased to 50 mm at the front of the turret, and extra plates, 20 mm thick on the sides and 30 mm thick at the front of the hull, were added . The model F, which appeared in the Spring of 1941, was an important step forward over previous models. Weighing more than 22 metric tons, its frontal armour was 50 mm thick, and the tracks had been widened to spread the weight better. The turret hatches were now made of double sheets of steel, and there was a large stowage bin at the rear of the turret for storing equipment.

The Russian campaign brought the *Panzer IV* up against the formidable Soviet T 34 and KV series tanks, which were invulnerable to the guns mounted on the German tanks at that time. Following several proposals, it was decided that the size of the *Panzer IV's* turret would permit it to be fitted with the 7.5 cm KwK 40 L/43, which fired an armoured piercing projectile that, with a muzzle velocity of 800 mps, was capable of penetrating 90 mm of 30º armour at 1000 metres. Finally, the German tanks would be able to stand up to their Soviet counterparts. The new model was designated the F2, and entered service at the beginning of 1942. However, the tank's armour continued to be its weak point. The next model, the G, had its armour increased slightly and mounted the new 75 mm L/48, with an improved muzzle-break as well as a faster muzzle velocity, making it more effective against enemy tanks. All these continual upgrades to the tank overloaded the suspension to its limit. The model H, which entered service in March 1943, represented the maximum development of the *Panzer IV*. With frontal armour of 80 mm, as well as on the skirt armour to protect it from hollow charges, it weighed 25 metric tons. More than three thousand tanks of this model were built, making it the warhorse of the *Panzerwaffe*. The last model, the J, had no improvements to speak of, but rather adaptations made to accommodate the necessities of service at the front, for example, the electrical system controlling the turret movement was taken out in order to fit a 200 litre auxiliary fuel tank, increasing range at a time when greater movement was becoming indispensible on the Eastern Front to enable a mobile defence.

The *Panzer IV's* magnificent chassis was used in the development of a great number of vehicles, among them being a command tank, an artillery forward-observation vehicle, munitions carrier, a tank-hunter, an anti-aircraft version, self-propelled artillery and a recovery vehicle. Among the tank-hunters was the *Sturmgeschütz IV*, armed with the 7.5 cm L/48, as well as the various models of the *Panzerjäger IV*, also armed with the L/48, and the formidable L/70, which was also mountede on the *Panther*. Only a very limited number of the *Nashorn*, armed with the 8.8 cm L/71, were built. A particularly effective type of assault gun was the *Brummbär*, which was armed with the 15 cm L/12. The *Hummel* was also a notable self-propelled gun, with its 15 cm armament. Among the anti-aircraft vehicles, which were subject to extraordinary development in the final stages of the war, due to the ever increasing threat from Allied fighter-bombers, was the *Möbelwagen*, armed with a 20 mm *Flakvierling* or 37 mm cannon, the *Wirbelwind*, again with a 20 mm *Flakvierling*, or the *Ostwind*, with a 37 mm gun. The war's most formidable anti-aircraft tank, the *Kugelblitz*, was armed with two 30 mm cannon in an enclosed turret, with a rate of fire of 900 rpm, but only a dozen were made in 1945. This design was not surpassed until the nineteen-sixties.

The *Panzer IV*, all said and done, was a magnificent tank, whose most notable characteristic, perhaps, was its enormous capacity for evolution. It went from being conceived as an infantry support tank to becoming a medium tank that was to carry the weight of the fighting on all fronts to the end of the war. It was the only tank on all sides that saw action in all theatres of the war, with the exception of Norway, fullfilling its role dutifully, often in highly adverse conditions. Although not as *glamerous* as its older siblings, the *Tiger* and *Panther*, without it, many of the legendary exploits of the *Panzerwaffe* would never have been accomplished. Its great versatility and reliability made the development of many variants possible, many of which were very successful. The last *Panzer IV's* to enter combat were sold to Spain, later ending up in Syrian hands. In 1967, they showed they were still useful, causing problems for the modern Israeli *Centurions*.

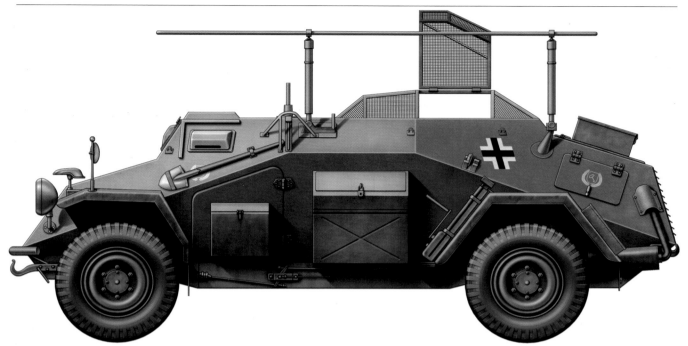

The *Kleiner Panzerfunkwagen Sdkfz. 261*, made an effiective communications vehicle, and became very successful. The vehicle entered service in the spring of 1941 and continued in service to the end of the war.
Illustration: Julio López Caeiro.

Contrary to the frontal assault he had made when he had taken Brest-Litovsk in 1939, this time Guderian decided to surround the city with his tanks, and leave the assault on the city itself, as well as the walled citadel, to the 45.*Infanterie-Division*. A group of 3.*Panzer-Division* sappers, made a surprise move against one of the main bridges over the Bug, south of Brest-Litovsk,capturing it intact. At 0445 hours, the tanks of 18.*Panzer-Division*, some of them fitted with deep wading equipment (developed for Operation Sealion, the invasion of Britain), a kind of *snorkel*, crossed the Bug river near Pratulin. A total of four platoons of *Panzer III's* and *IV's* had been fitted out in this way, which allowed them to advance along streams and rivers to a maximum depth of ten metres. Apart from the *snorkel*, special adhesives were used to seal the joins, while the turret ring was kept watertight by the use of rubber tubes which were inflated from the inside, and which were able to stand the pressure of two atmospheres at a depth of ten metres. Eighty amphibious tanks were used for the Bug crossing, commanded by Major Strachwitz. They had hardly finished crossing the river when they were in action with Russian tanks

German infantry supported by a *StuG III* assault gun: a deadly combination in 1941. (Colección Javier del Campo)

that were harassing the infantry. Several BA-10 armoured vehicles were knocked out from a range of 800 metres, the rest retreating under fire. The infantry and assault engineers had crossed the river in inflatible dinghies, and now contro-lled the bank on the other side, with the support of the tanks, they began building a pontoon bridge. The first pontoon bridge to be completed in the sector was finished at nine o'clock in Drohiczyn, north of Brest-Litovsk. The Bug crossing went ahe-ad according to plan, all the bridges being captured intact and with all crossing points established without suffering any setbacks, something exceptional for an operation of this magnitude.

Once a bridgehead had been established, the armoured units

raced at all speed across the Polish plain. At the end of the day they had penetrated 60 kilometres into Soviet controlled territory. But not all the units advanced so swiftly. The 3.*Pan-zer-Division*, commanded by Model, found themselves confronted by swampy terrain that had not been properly identified. By that evening, the Division had only advanced around twenty kilometres, instead of the eighty they had planned, and given the nature of the terrain, their axis of advanced was diverted north in order to maintain the pace of the advance. In other sectors the Soviets put up considerable resis-tance, such as that met by the *Pan-zer Regiment* 25, which ran into a strong concentration of anti-tank guns in Olita, and following an impe-tuous attack, found itself with half its vehicles out of action

The battle for Brest-Litovsk

The Brest-Litovsk fortress was defended by the 44th and 84th Infantry Regiments, and what happened there is representative of the type of fighting experienced on the Eastern Front at that time. The medieval citadel had been constructed on four small islands in the Bug river, with the most modern fortifications concentrated on the northern island. Following an hour of intense artillery bombardment by the 98th Artillery regiment which included 210 mm pieces) and the 4th Rocket Launcher Regiment (which launched 2,880 rockets in half an hour) the attack began as planned. The 3rd Company of the 135th Regiment attacked the bridge giving access to the south-western island. The audacious assault, support by an engineer unit, captured the bridge and disactivated the demolition charges placed by the Russians. The 3rd Battalion of the 135th Regiment, supported by several half-tracks and armoured vehicles, took the south-western island (where the barracks were located) without any difficulty, and the 1st Battalion of the 130th Regiment did the same with the south-eastern island, while the 3rd Battalion surrounded the citadel, and the 1st Battalion of the 135th Regiment prepared to assault the northern island. When the men of the 135th set foot on the central island, the location of the officers mess and an old church, resistance stiffened, and progress slowed. Soon after, the Germans found themselves facing a fierce Russian counter-attack, led by men who in some cases were armed with sabres and knives. However, the attack was repulsed with heavy losses, but the defenders mettle was beginning to show. By the end of the day the citadel's defenders were completely cut off in the middle of the German tide, but they refused to surrender, paying a high price, but in the process causing more than 300 German casualties.

The citadel was set in a formidable position, surrounded by the river, and its strong walls were protected by ditches and small glacis. The walls had been reinforced with casemates, turrets, gun-ports, and numerous artillery positions for 45 and 76.2 mm pieces, which had been well camoufaged. Resistance was such that the attackers had to be joined by a battery of *Sturm-geschütze* mounting short 7.5 cm guns, in order to attack the bunkers with direct fire, but this did not turn out to be very effective against such solid fortifications. At the end of the day, a company of the 3rd Battalion was pinned down in the old church under intense fire from the defenders

The 133rd Regiment was next in joining the attack. During the days that followed, fighting for control of the fortress continued unabated, the Germans finally committing three whole regiments to the assault. There were intensive air attacks on the 29th, first by Junkers Ju 87's carrying 500 kg bombs and then, later that day, by a group of Junkers Ju 88 medium bombers, their 1,800 kg bombs devastating the citadel's ancient walls. At the end of these air attacks, more than 400 Russian soldiers surrendered, but it was not the end. Small groups of the 44th Rifle Regiment refused to surrender, holing up in cellars, from where they continued to resist for almost a month. However, the citadel was officially declared to have been taken on the 30th. The struggle for the Brest-Litovsk citadel had cost the Germans 482 killed and more than 1,000 wounded, 5% of the losses incurred in the first week of fighting on the Eastern Front. Soviet losses were, however, much higher, with more than 3,000 killed and 7,000 taken prisoner.

Triumph of the Blitzkrieg

Events on the rest of the Eastern Front were to develop differently. Taken completely by surprise and without coordination and lacking initiative, the Soviet units were destroyed one after the other. In the best of cases, they were able to withdraw twenty kilometres and redeploy into something resembling a defensive line, but were unable to halt the advance of the *Panzer* Divisions. The units making up the second line of defence, some sixty kilometres to the rear, were to suffer a similar fate. During the days that followed, Russian forces launched a series of disorganized counter-attacks along the front, without gaining any significant results, but suffering enormous losses in return. At best, an isolated division was able to hold up the German advance for perhaps 36-48 hours. Nevertheless, at the end of the day, Hoth's units had opened an enormous breach, some 100 kilometres across, between the two Soviet military districts facing them, anihilating three infantry divisions in the process.

On the second day, the right wing of the *Panzers* had reached Kobryn, a town more than seventy kilometres to the east of Brest-Litovsk, while the left wing had taken the important railway junction at Grodno. The original front line which had been determined by the partition of Poland two years earlier, had left a salient in the Soviet line, called the "Byalistok Salient". This was to be the first great battle of encirclement carried out by the Germans. The two wings converged on Slonim, more than 160 kilometres behind enemy lines. However, due

A *Panzerkampfwagen IV Ausf D*, of *7.Panzer-Division* crossing a stream on the river bed, the bridge havivg been blown up by retreating Russian troops. (Bundesarchiv)

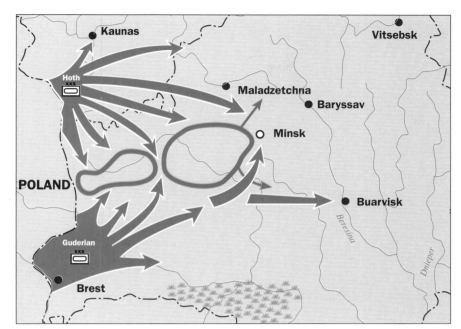

to the slow pace of the infantry units, they were unable to close the trap, with almost half the Russian troops managing to escape. The Germans were clearly able to outmanoeuvre the Russians, but they were not superior to them in fighting spirit. Contrary to the Western Front, Russian units, once surrounded, refused to surrender, continuing to fight on fiercely.

The greatest success of the second day was that of 3.*Panzer-Division*, which entered Kobryn at eleven that morning. The town had just been evacuated by the Staff of the Russian 4th Army. At this moment a battalion of T-26's made a counter-attack, which was easily repulsed. 36 T-26's were left burning, with the Germans incurring no losses. The Division immediately went on the attack, and had reached Szczara by nightfall, having destroyed 107 Soviet tanks and armoured vehicles during the course of that day. They had penetrated 150 kilometres in the Soviet lines in two days. They were beginning to close the trap around Byalistok. The Russian commanders became aware of the danger and attempted a breakout towards Slonim, managing to get through the line where the encircling Panzers were thin on the grond. This event made Hitler uneasy, so he ordered the *Panzer* Divisions to halt in order to give the infantry time to catch up with them. This was one more of series of indecisions which were to cost the Panzers the opportunity to gain a decisive victory.

Panzer Gruppe 3, for its part, had also advanced swiftly in its sector. On the 24th, the 7.*Panzer-Division* reached Vilnius, the capital of Lithuania, and the following day, *Panzer Regiment 25* led the advance to the Minsk-Moscow highway, which they cut at the end of the day, some 20 kilometres to the north-west of Minsk.

With almost the entire Western Military District encircled in the Byalistok pocket, it was now time for the infantry to tighten the noose and eliminate the pocket. The infantry of both the 4.*Armee* and 9.*Armee* were making forced marches of up to 70 kilometres a day along rough tracks and in sweltering heat in order to link up with the tanks. While von Bock wanted to continue the advance in order to maintain the pressure on the Soviets, the Staff, with Hitler at the head, wanted to avoid risks, so they ordered the tanks to halt in order to consolidate the encirclement. The Soviets made desperate attempts to break out, especially in 17.*Panzer-Division's* sector, who were hardly able to hold their positions. The Army Group was reorganised on the 25th, and 2.*Armee* were left with the responsibility of destroying the pocket, while 4. and 9.*Armees* continued their advance in the direction of Minsk and Smolensk. On the 26th, Soviet counter-attacks and attempts at a break out were becoming more and more uncoordinated, with the encircled troops showing ever more signs of being demoralized. The number of

prisoners being taken was increasing by the hour. The German Staff calmed down and ordered the advance to continue without delay.

The Soviets tried to concentrat several divisions in the Minsk sector to counter-attack, but the Germans arrived in the areas where they were concentrating before they were ready. On the 26th, the 12. and *20. Panzer-Divisions* moved on the Byelorussian capital from the north, while the 17.*Panzer-Division* approached from the south. The next day, 20.*Panzer-Division*, supported by 17.*Panzer-Division*, entered the city, gaining control in less than 24 hours. On the same day, Sluzk, which was 300 kilometres from the frontier, fell to a furious assault by 3.*Panzer-Division*. The Minsk pocket had been closed, trapping four Soviet armies, a total of half a million men, which was an unparalleled event in military history. However, the tanks did not stop there, and the advance continued at all speed. The Germans had to reach Beresina and after that, the Dnieper, on their way to the first great strategic aim of the campaign, Smolensk.

The inevitable Soviet attempts at a breakout took place, and one of the divisions facing a critical situation was the 29th Motorized. Like the other German units, they were exceedingly extended in order to cover a very large sector. The Division's 15th Infantry Regiment in particuler, came under repeated Soviet attacks of an unprecented scale. As was to become the norm on the Eastern Front, they faced repeated charges by waves of Russian infantry, who advanced in close order with bayonets fixed, in an attempt to get to close quarters and overwhelm the thin line of German infantry. The whole thing seemed like something from another period of history. Rank after rank of Russian infantry mown down by German fire, but on they came without respite. Even an armoured train was brought into the fray, supported by several T-26 tanks, which were soon knocked out by the German anti-tank guns. A charge made by two squadrons of cavalry, sabres flashing, suffered a similar fate. The German line held. The Soviet attacks were swept away with enormous losses, and the attempted break-out failed.

Panzer II with winged -serpent emblem. This emblem was used in Russia by the *II.Abteilung* of *Panzer Regiment 3, 2.Panzer-Division.*

Illustration: Julio López Caeiro.

During the night of 26th June, General Nehring, commanding *18th Panzer Division*, was searching for a site for his General Headquarters when he approached Radziwill Castle, a position he believed had been consolidated. At that moment, in the pale twilight, two T–26's surged over a bridge and flung themselves at his command half-track. Reacting swiftly, the half-track made for cover while a *Panzer III* that was following identified the Soviet tanks and opened fire, quickly destroying them both with three rounds from its 5 cm gun. This was one of many isolated incidents that took place during the first phases of the campaign, and is indicative of the circumstances in which the armoured units operated when they were exploiting a breakthrough. Surprises and confusion were inevitable, but it was necessary to be able to react swiftly and confront such changing situations on the battlefield.

On 30th June, the ninth day of the invasion, *Panzer Regiment* 6 reached the Beresina river, near Bobruisk, 150 kilometres southeast of Minsk, and seventy kilometres from the Dnieper. In November 1812, the Beresina had been the scene of a massacre of Napoleon's *Grande Armée*, but this time events would be reversed. The Stavka was aware of the danger and organized new units around Smolensk, bringing reserves from central Russia. Specifically, they tried to create a defensive line between Vitebsk and Orsha, using the 16th, 24th and 28th Armies. While the infantry divisions and a few motorized units of

3.*Panzer-Gruppe* were closing the trap around Minsk and the smaller Byalistok, the 2.*Panzer-Gruppe* continued its advance east, south of Minsk. Before long, the advance into Russia was to become a logistics nightmare. In the central sector, there were only two roads worthy of the name, from Brest-Litovsk to Bobruysk and to Minsk. The 27,000 vehicles of the *Panzer-Gruppe* and the 60,000 men of the infantry divisions following them all had to travel along these two roads. To this it was necessary to add the vital flow of supplies, carried in convoys that were very vulnerable to attack from the Soviet forces remaining in the pocket, or which had simply been bypassed by the German armoured units.

While 3. and 4.*Panzer-Divisions* were crossing the Beresina at Bobruysk, the 1st Cavalry Division had penetrated the Pripet Marshes. To protect its exposed flank, the *XLVI Armee Korps*, 10.*Panzer-Division*, 60.*Infanterie-Division (mot.)* and *SS «Das Reich»* continued south, at the same time three more infantry divisions were joining the encirclement at Slonim. On 1st July, eighty kilometres north of Bobruysk, the 18.*Panzer-Division*, after covering 90 kilometres of enemy territory, established a bridgehead on the east bank of the Beresina, at Borisov. This had not been done without a hard fight in the face of constant and determined Soviet counter-attacks, but the Panzer Division's firepower and tactical mastery, along with the Soviets neglecting to blow the bridge, had

won the day. On the night of the 2nd/3rd July, the 10.*Panzer-Division* established another bridgehead between the previously mentioned locations. The great river Dnieper would be the next obstacle.

The encirclements around the pockets were becoming ever tighter, although when the fighting reached the forested areas, the Russian soldiers again demonstrated their tenacity, fighting ability and prowess in the art of setting an ambush, with German losses increasing as a result. One of the bloodiest battles of this type took place in the Bialowiza forest, involving the 78th Infantry Division and the depleted Soviet 4th Tank Division, which had taken refuge in the enormous forest. In two days of fighting the Russians lost 600 killed and more than 1,200 taken prisoner, and the Germans 114 killed and 125 wounded. However, despite the casualties, the outcome was irreversible, and the Russians began to crumble. The soldiers of the 12th, 89th and 103rd killed their political commissairs and surrendered en masse to the Germans.

However, once again the trap could not be completely closed, and a decisive victory evaded the Germans by a small margin. Worse still was the rain, and with it came an enemy far worse than the Red Army, the dreaded *rasputitsa*, the mud. The *Stavka* gained precious time to reorganize their forces and send them into battle, even if they were disorganized and uncoordinated. On the 28th, Yeremenko was appointed commander of the Western Military District, his first order was very precise, defend the Beresina line. In July he would be replaced by Timoshenko, remaining, together with Budenny, as a subordinate. Meanwhile, the German High Command continued to have doubts, fears and hesitations, and could not agree on a decisive advance on Mosow. First of all, they considered sending the *Panzers* north, to support the offensive against Leningrad, leaving the infantry to advance on the Russian capital. Later, they brought both *Panzer Gruppen* together under the command of von Kluge, for the advance on the Dnieper, while they contemplated the destruction of the pockets.

On 2nd July, the Byalistok pocket was finally overrun, resulting in the

annihilation of two Soviet armies. The last pockets of resistance were eliminated three days later. Soviet losses were huge and had no comparison up to that point. Of an initial force of 32 infantry, 8 armoured and three cavalry divisions, as well as 6 mechanized brigades, all but 10 of the infantry and 1 of the armoured divisions were completely destroyed. A total of 300,000 prisoners, 2,585 tanks, 1,500 guns and 245 aircraft were captured. An advanced supply dump was set up in Minsk with more than 73,000 tons of supplies of all types, enough for five days of advance.

Having been unable to destroy all the Soviet forces on the frontier, the German High Command planned a new encirclement, the pincers of which would close beyond Smolensk. First, two formidable obstacles had to be dealt with, the so-called Stalin line and the Dnieper. Both would be overcome in a few days, and the encirclement at Smolensk would bring another 300,000 prisoners, although again the Germans would fail to achieve the total annihilation of the enemy, who would slip through the armoured units. Furthermore, the *18. Panzer-Division* would have the disagreeable surprise of finding itself the first unit in the central sector to encounter the new models of Soviet tanks, the T-34 and the KV-1 and KV-2, which had already made an appearance in the north and south.

Moscow was less than 300 kilometres away. The *blitzkrieg* had demonstrated its potential. Once more a breakthrough had been made, and the encirclement of an unparalleled number of forces in military history completed, although, even this would be dwarfed by what was to come in the Ukraine a few weeks later. The *Panzer* Divisions had penetrated deep into enemy territory and completely dislocated the Soviet defensive system, giving them a master class in tactics and mobility. However, they had not been able to achieve the much sought after decisive victory. The High Command, Hitler the first among them, felt fearful and lacked confidence in the rapid advance of the Panzers, and were not prepared to place their faith in an all-out armoured advance to achieve final victory, hence they ordered inopportune halts in the Panzer's advance (as they had done in France), as they searched for an impossible compromise between the new tactics and classic doctrine. Nevertheless, victory was still possible if they could exploit the opportunities the disorganized Red Army was presenting the *Wehrmacht*.

The *Panzer III*, in its various versions, was the most common German tank during Operation «*Barbarossa*». This example belonged to the *11.Panzer-Division*, and was armed with a 5 cm L/42 gun.

Illustration: Julio López Caeiro

HASSO VON MANTEUFFEL

Born in Potsdam in 1897, to a Prussian family with a long military tradition. He entered a military school at the age of eleven, and three years later he went to a military academy in Berlin. In 1916, at the age of 18, he joined the Army, serving on both the Eastern and Western Fronts during the Great War.

Following the Armistice, he was a member of the *Freikorps*, until entering the *Reischwehr* in 1919, joining a cavalry regiment. Manteuffel was an excellent rider and took part in numerous competitions in various equestrian sports and winning several awards. In 1936 he was promoted to Major and posted to the Staff of the *2.Panzer-Division*. The following year he joined the *Kommando* der *Panzertruppe*, under the command of Guderian. Just before the start of World War Two he was posted to an Armoured Warfare school, and so did not take part in the first campaigns.

In May of 1941 he requested, and was given, command of the *II.Abteilung* of *Jäger Regiment 7*, quite an accomplishment for an officer of his age. A few months later, he took command of *Panzergrenadier Regiment 6*, of the *6.Panzer-Division*, participating in the initial phases of Barbarossa with this unit. Manteuffel stood out for his daring and command style. His unit closed the Vyazma pocket in October 1941, repulsing many Soviet attempts to break out. In December he led a daring attack against a bridge and a power station in the outskirts of Moscow, for which he recei-

ved the Knight's Cross and was promoted to Colonel.

In 1942, his unit was sent to France to reorganize, and then, in 1943, he served briefly in North Africa commanding a mixed, *ad hoc* unit, until he became seriously ill and was evacuated to Germany in April of that year. On 1st May he was promoted to the rank of *Generalmajor*.

In August he took over command of *7.Panzer-Division*, taking part in the fierce fighting which followed the battle of Kursk. In the course of this, his Division reconquered Zhitomir in a night attack, an action for which he received the Oak Leaves to his Knight's Cross. In December 1943 he was promoted to *Generalleutnant* and was given command of the Army's elite *"Grossdeutschland"* Division, and took part in many battles on the Eastern Front. In September 1944, now with the rank of *General der Panzertruppe*, he took command of the *5.Panzerarmee* on the Western Front. His first action in this command was Operation «Nordwind», in Lorraine, where his units suffered the full might of the air power and artillery of the Western Allies, a very different experience to the fighting on the Russian Front. Later he took part in the Ardennes offensive, making a significant advance, although failing to reach his final objectives.

In February 1945, he was again posted to the Eastern Front, this time in command of *3.Panzerarmee*, until he surrendered to the British in Mecklenburg. After the war, he was a member of the German parliment until 1957. He died aged 81.

HERMANN HOTH

Born in Neuruppin in 1885, son of a Health officer, he joined the army as a cadet in 1904. Hoth served as a company and later battalion commander during the Great War, ending the war as a Captain. Following the armistice, he served as a Staff officer in the *Reischwehr*. In 1934, then a *Major General*, he took command of the 18th Infantry Division. In 1938 he was promoted to *General der Infanterie*.

During the Polish campaign he commanded the *XV Armeekorps (motorized)*, forming part of von Rei-

chenau's 10.*Armee*. Still as commander of this unit, he also took part in the breakthrough at Sedan in May 1940, and took Brest on 16th June. At the end of the French campaign, now a *Generaloberst*, he took command of *Panzergruppe 3*, which was converted into *3.Panzerarmee* for Operation Barbarossa. Together with Guderian, he carried the weight of the offensive on the Central Front, leading some outstanding breakthroughs in the front and penetrating deep onto Soviet territory. He recieved the Knight's Cross in July.

In October he took command of the 17th Army in the Ukraine, taking part in the hard fighting that winter to stop the Soviet counter-offensive. In June 1942, commanding 4.*Panzerarmee*, he was involved in the offensive on the Don, and later, under Manstein's orders, in the failed attempt to break through to Stalingrad. He was then immediately drawn into the operations around Kharkov, in the Ukraine, where, acting very efficiently, he destroyed those Soviet forces which had ventured too far, demonstrating his mastery of mobile warfare.

That summer, he took part in Operation Zitadelle, forming, together with *Armee-Abteilung Kempf*, part of the German lower pincer. Although he shared Manstein's pessimism on the final result of the operation, given the delay in the start of the operation and the enemy forces present, he acted with great resolve, and was on the point of achieving the breakthrough. Following the battle, his disagreements with Hitler led to him being retired from service in 1943. The Allies sentenced him to fifteen years in prison at the end of the war, although he was released in 1954. He died in 1971.

Hoth was one of the most brilliant tank commanders of World War Two, receiving the recognition of both friend and foe alike. He understood perfectly the potential of armoured units and was a master of mobile operations, combining the different arms and showing an extraordinary capability to concentrate his forces at the right point at the decisive moment. At times he obtained results out of proportion to the means available to him and the prevailing circumstances.

KRASNOGRAD

The Red Army launched operation Uranus on 19th November 1942. Its aim was to encircle the German 6.Armee in Stalingrad. Hitler gave Manstein responsibility for carrying out a rescue operation, but with insufficient forces. To make the situation worse, on 16th December the Red Army unleashed operation «Little Saturn» against the Italian 8th Army, located further north, causing the front to collapse. If the Soviets could take Rostov, it would deliver a mortal blow to the Germans. Following Manstein's failed attempt to break through to Stalingrad, the fate of the German 6.Armee was sealed. However, an even greater danger hung over the Germans, as the Soviet offensive threatened to cut off the German troops in the Caucuses and destroy them. If this were to happen, the whole southern front would collapse and possibly the entire Eastern Front with it, and nothing would be able to stop the Red Army advancing into Germany itself. In fact, the original intention of the Stavka was to launch operation Saturn directly against Rostov, but they had to change their plans when faced with

the attack towards the Stalingrad pocket by 4.Panzerarmee in the middle of December.

The Panzer divisions were exhausted, in fact the 17th and 23rd divisions each had only 30 tanks operational during Manstein's rescue attempt. In spite of this, they were able to make some headway, causing, as had become the norm, heavy losses among the Soviet forces. The last desperate attempt on 22nd of December was cancelled due to the increasing opposition from the Russian defence, which was concentrating more and more material to face the German advance which, at its high point, consisted of no more than 60 Panzer III's and IV's.

The Red Army of the winter of 1942 had changed a lot compared to the previous year. It had begun to recover from the enourmous losses it had suffered and was also creating a new cadre of officers and NCOs who had begun to understand the principles of the ´battle in depth´. Furthermore, the armoured units were given greater mobility and were equipped with the best tank of that time, the T-34.

The Panzerkapfwagen IV Ausf G, which had recently arrived on the battlefield in January 1943, gave the Wehrmacht a qualitative advantage which it had not had at the beginning of the campaign. (Bundesarchiv)

The Great Soviet Offensive

Following three days of hard fighting, operation «Little Saturn» had opened an enormous 50 km breach in the German front, and into which poured four armoured and one mechanized corps with Tatsinskaia and Morosovsk as their objectives. One example of what the new Russian commanders had learned was the incursion made by General Badanov's 24th Armoured Corps. After penetrating 200 km in five days, they arrived at their objective on Christmas Eve, the large air base and communications centre at Tatsinskaia (the Russians were beginning to use Blitzkrieg tactics, although not yet to the ability of the Germans: In 1941, Mansteins Group had covered the 250 km between Tilsit and Dvinsk in four days). The German garrison at Tatsinskaia, although forewarned and on alert, was very small, with only one Infantry Company, an 88 mm and six 20 mm AA guns. On New Years Day three of

The Russian infantry were not known for their sophisticated tactics, but their great tenacity and numerical advantage compensated for this on many occasions.

Badanov's armoured brigades attacked their objectives, the Railway station, the town itself and the air base, spreading terror and destruction in a few minutes. More than 40 aircraft were completely destroyed, a hard blow for the exhausted *Luftwaffe*. However, despite this, the disaster could have been much worse, as 130 aircraft managed to take off under Soviet fire and land safely at other airfields. The Russians were at the limits of their supplies, both fuel and munitions, so, after completing their mission, they began to withdraw. Reacting with typical swiftness, Balck's *11.Panzer-Division* arrived north of the airfield in the early hours of the morning and, although well below strength, immediately attacked the Soviet forces. The majority of the Russian force had by now withdrawn and only 39 T-34's and 19 T-70's remained. Despite receiving some supplies on the 26th, Badanov's situation was desperate, and on the 27th he was completely surrounded. On the 29th the survivors made a breakout towards the north, managing to reach the Russian lines, but having suffered grevious losses.

The Germans were able to reform their lines following this incursion, and in another example of their ability to improvise, created a makeshift unit, *Armee Abteilung Fretter-Pico*, consisting of the 298th Infantry Division and what was left of various Italian units. This would later be reinforced by the 304th and 355th Divisions. Nevertheless, the defensive line remained weak and very extended. 109 divisions and 11 tank regiments faced little more

During «*Operation Uranus*», German material losses were high.

Soviet KV-1 heavy tank. It would be substituted in this role in 1944, by the IS-I and IS-II. Illustration: Julio López Caeiro.

than 10 German divisions, but when the forces beseiging Stalingrad became available, the situation would become 18 to 1 in favour of the Russians. In the later confused fighting that took place in January, the veteran German infantry divisions proved their worth against the Soviet tanks. To give an example of this, the 336th division destroyed a total of 92 tanks in a period of five days. At the same time reinforcements began slowly arriving from the west, among them *II.SS-Panzerkorps*, commanded by Paul Hausser, and recently reformed in France.

On 29th December the Stavka issued the order to attack in the south to encircle *Heeres Gruppe A*. To do this it would attack along two main axis, one by the Black Sea Group towards Krasnodar, and the other by the Southern Front (the former Stalingrad Front, renamed on 1st January 1943), through Salsa. Both advances were to converge on Tikoretsk. The tough and long drawn out resistente of the 6.Armee in Stalingrad was absorbing an enourmous quantity of Russian material, preventing it from being used on the Central Front. On 4th January the Stavka ordered the Black Sea Group to attack towards Rostov, to cut off Heeres Gruppe A, and the Southern Front to carry out a pincer movement. The right flank

The 45 mm AT guns, while obsolete in 1943, still made up an important proportion of the Soviet anti-tank arsenal. At this time it was unusual to find them as well equipped as those in the photograph.

was made up of the 5th Tank Army, 2nd Guards Army and the 5th Army, while the left flank consisted of the 28th and 51st Armies.

During January 1943, a huge Soviet offensive took place along the entire front from Orel to the Black Sea, with the final objective of cutting off and destroying von Kleist's Army in the Caucuses. The most dangerous operation from the German point of view was codenamed Svezda, and was aimed directly at Rostov.

The bottleneck around Rostov was the most vulnerable point in the German deployment, and Manstein concentrated his efforts there to keep an escape route open. To do this it would be necessary to keep Hoth's *4.Panzerarmee* intact, while von Mackensen's *1.Panzerarmee* withdrew under pressure in order to keep the route of retreat open. The *Stavka's* overall objective was to

cause the front to collapse and advance as far west as possible, before the onset of the thaw and the appearance of the *rasputitsa*, (the feared mud) which would impede any further advance. Stalin was very ambitious and planned a series of successive pincer attacks to destroy not only *Heeres Gruppe A*, but also *Heeres Gruppe Don* and *Heeres Gruppe B*. The whole of the Ukraine would fall and the war on the Eastern Front would be decided in 1943.

On 12th January General Golikov launched a massive offensive between Voronez and Vorochilograd, surrounding and trapping thirteen divisions, most of them Italian and Hungarian, as well as *24.Panzerkorps*. Apart from opening a 200 km breach in the front, the Axis suffered 90,000 casualties and lost almost 200 tanks and armoured vehicles. Immediately following this the Soviets attempted to encircle the

Armoured half-track with 37 mm AA gun struggling against the *rasputitsa*. The Germans used automatic AA guns against the Russian infantry with devestating effect. (Colección Javier del Campo).

German *2. Armee* in the Voronez sector, attacking with four armies, but most of the German forces managed to escape the trap. However, the breach was now enormous, between Kursk and Kupiansk, 250 km to the south, only five weak German divisions held the front. Stalin saw an oppertunity to recover the Ukraine and destroy 75 German divisions in the process, if the Red Army were capable of advancing towards the Donezt and Kharkov. Skatchok was overseeing the operation.

A dramatic race was underway between the Germans retreating from the Caucuses and the Red Army trying to prevent their withdrawl and destroy them. On 27th January, Hitler, under the insistance of Manstein, finally gave the order for *1.Panzerarmee* to withdraw towards Rostov to support the general withdrawl and prevent the fall of that city. The task was herculian, 1.Panzerarmee was in Terek, some 600 km from Rostov, and salvation. The whole of *Heeres Gruppe A*, 800,000 men, was in danger of sharing the same fate as Von Paulus´ 6.Armee in Stalingrad. On day seven, some Russian tank units were already only a few dozen kilometers from the city. At a place called Manoutskaia, where the Don and Manitch rivers converge, Yermenko's forces were able to establish a bridgehead to the south of the river, from where they were able

to threaten *1.Panzerarmee's* retreat. This force consisted of a group of tanks and infantry commanded by Colonel Yegorov (initially eight T-34's and three T-70's supported by around 200 troops transported in armoured vehicles). These had taken the location in a raid and had been reinforced by a Brigade two days later. In a few hours they had established a defensive perimeter and had dug in their tanks in well camouflaged positions.

On 22nd January, Manstein sent the *11.Panzer-Division*, under Balck, along with elements of the 16th Motorized division to destroy this bridgehead. The battle for the vital location of Manoutskaia began on the 25th January. It had just been fortified and formed the centre of the Soviet deployment. The first German attack fell under the fire of

the dug-in tanks which had remained hidden until the last moment and was repulsed, though with little loss, only two *Panzer IV's* which had been surprised by around a dozen entrenched T34s.

A second attack was completely successful. A diversionary attack made from the north of the village by several half-tracks under the cover of smoke, forced the Russian tanks to abandon their original positions in order to meet this new threat. Meanwhile, tanks of *Panzer Regiment 15*, choosing a point of attack completely unexpected by the Russians (the same as that from which they had been earlier repulsed), broke through the defences around

The T-70 was the main Soviet light tank in 1943, and remained in service until the end of the war.

Illustration: Luis Fresno Crespo.

The SU-76, armed with a 76.2 mm gun, remained in service until the end of the war. As well as serving as field artillery, it was also to prove useful in urban combat.
Illustration: Julio López Caeiro.

Manoutskaia from the Russian rear-guard area, annihilating the Soviet troops in a classic combined tank-artillery-panzergrenadier action. The Russians lost 20 tanks and 600 infantry, while the Germans suffered only one man killed and fourteen wounded. The threat to Rostov had been, at least momentarily, averted.

At the end of January, the eight *Panzer* divisions of *Heeres Gruppe* mustered only 170 tanks (*Panzer III's* and *IV's*) and *28 StuG III's* between them, little more than the theoretical strength of a single *Panzer Division*. By the end of January the repeated counter attacks were able to gain sufficient time for the troops in the Caucuses to get through the Rostov corridor and therefore stabilize the front. However, it could not be forgotten that 6.Armee had been annihilated and part of the 2.Armee had suffered a similar fate. The Italians, Hungarians and Rumanians had each lost an army. At this stage of the war such losses were impossible to replace. At the end of an almost month-long march from Terek, the last units of *1. Panzerarmee* crossed the Don on 8th of February, blowing the bridges behind them. *4.Panzerarmee*, for its part, had managed to retreat from the outskirts of Stalingrad to the north coast of the Azov Sea, where they had set up a

defensive line (Gothic Line) at the base of the Taiman peninsula, encompassing Krasnodar, for the rest of *Heeres Gruppe A*. This scenario was to witness a dramatic Soviet combined operation in an attempt to isolate the German forces on the Taiman peninsula, which finally succeeded, at a high price, in establishing a bridgehead at Novorossiysk.

Meanwhile on the Soviet side, the South-East Front received the order to begin «*Operation Skatchok*» from the 29th January. The 6th Army reached the Donetz ready to continue south-west, and the following day

the 1st Guards Army would do the same towards Barvenkovo. A few hours later Popov's mobile units were to advance between the two armies through the open breach and arrive in Mariupol, on the Azov Sea, cutting off *Heeres Gruppe Don*.

Although this was a golden strategic opportunity to capitalize on the success at Stalingrad, the Stavka overlooked certain aspects. The coordination of Soviet tank units left a lot to be desired, and their lines of communication were too extended

German infantry, especially that of the Waffen SS, were well equipped for the winter by the end of 1942. (ECPA).

(they were already more than 300 km from their original bases), even more so given the chronic shortage of trucks (they only had 1,300 trucks, plus 380 tankers capable of transporting 900 tons of fuel, instead of the 2,000 needed). Secondly, the Russian reserves were exhausted and the attacks had to be carried out without depth, denying themselves the capability for manoeuvre. Thirdly, the Russian commanders were only thinking in the pursuit of a beaten enemy. Even the usually prudent Vassilievski let himself become infected with the *Stavka's* optimism.

Dramatic fighting took place during the first days of February as the Germans attempted to stop the Soviet offensive, and in which the heavily worn down Panzer divisions (the *7.Panzer-Division* had 30 tanks and 11 *StuG III's*, while the *11.Panzer-Division* had only 29 tanks) made the Russians pay a high price for the ground they recaptured. The 320th Infantry Division also came under a lot of pressure, inflicting severe casualties on the Soviets during their withdrawl. Elsewhere, the 298th became cut off by the rapid Soviet advance, eventually being virtually annihilated after several days of combat. However, the 320th, after an odyssy of several weeks, was able to reach its own lines and was saved,

thanks to a risky and dramatic action by a combat group under the command of Peiper.

On the Voronez Front, along the Donetz, the determined resistance of *Leibstandarte*, *SS regiment Deutschland (Das Reich)* and *Grossdeutshland* stabilized the sector. They had to stop Ribalko's 1st Tank Army, one of the most outstanding Soviet tank commanders who best understood how to employ armoured forces. Although they were able to cross the Donetz at various points, and penetrate twenty or more kilometres west, they were eventually stopped by the determined, elastic German defence. Nevertheless, Manstein was concious of the fact he needed to withdraw the SS divisions from the battle of attrition to the east of Kharkov, against Hitler's orders, which had expressly sent them there with the mission of defending the city. The *SS-Panzerkorps* was vital for the counter attack with

A Sd.Kfz 262 on a muddy track. To maintain the flow of supplies under these conditions was a herculean task. (ECPA)

German defensive lines were often based around machine gun posts which swept a wide field of fire. Two or three such posts, in the right conditions, could repulse an attack from an entire battalion of Soviet infantry.

and reserve it for a future counter attack. Nevertheless, Hitler was categorical in regard to holding Kharkov at all cost.

On the 8th the Red Army attacked Rostov, but it was too late, the Germans having completed their withdrawl. The Russian advance continued over the next few days, heading southwest, although steadily slowing. It was only with the capture of Bielgorod on the 9th February that gave new impetous to the Soviet advance.

The city of Kharkov, defended by *II.SS-Panzerkorps*, was almost completely encircled between the 12th and 14th February. Hitler once more ordered that the city be defended to the death, but as German commander, Hausser decided to contravene the *Führer's* orders and evacuated the city on the 16th, saving his units from destruction. In fact, the evacuation had actually begun on the night of 9th/10th February. Surrounded by overwhelming numbers of Soviet forces, (the odds were 4:1, rising to 8:1 in certain sectors) the city was lost and had Hausser not taken the decision to withdraw, the only two *Panzer* Divisions in condition to carry out a counter attack would have been destroyed (the *3.SS.Panzergrenadier-Divison «Totenkopf»* had still not been completely formed).

which Manstein intended to restabilise the situation in the Ukraine.

During the first week of February, and despite the enormous losses incurred at the hands of the skillful German defence, the Russians established various bridgeheads over the Donetz, and began to find breaches in the weak and increasingly thin German deployment. Ribalko launched an attack on the 3rd along two axis. On one of these, the 160th Rifle Division was brought to a halt on the frozen Donetz at the hands of two companies of the *LAH*, armed with the new MG42, demonstrating the efficiency of the new weapon. At another point in the sector occupied by the *1.SS.Panzer-Division LAH*, the anti-aircraft battalion destroyed various T-34's

from a range of four kilometres, forcing the other Russian tanks to withdraw. The three divisions of *II SS-Panzerkorps* were placed under strong pressure by Ribalko's units, which attempted to infiltrate their defences time and time again, despite heavy losses. The situation around Kharkov was becoming more and more untenable for the Germans.

On 6th February, following a tense meeting with Hitler, von Kluge obtained authorisation to evacuate the Rzev salient, in order to finally begin the formation of a reserve. In the same meeting, Manstein was also able to get permission for the withdrawl from the Donetz bend to the Mius line. Furthermore, at the same time he was able to withdraw Hoth's *4.Panzerarmee*,

PzKpfw IV Ausf G of *1.SS-Panzer-Grenadier. Division «Leibstandarte SS Adolf Hitler»*, during the capture of Kharkov, February 1943.

Illustration: Julio López Caeiro

mans, who found themselves up against a tank which was superior to their *Pan-*
examined some captured T-34's in order to establish the prerequisites for any
er, the designers, apart from pride, argued against this possibility, owing to the
th a weight of around 35 metric tons, 60 mm thick armour and a maximum spe-
ke the T-34, the MAN, the one finally chosen (against the wishes of Hitler), pre-

7.5 cm L/70 KwK 42 extended over the front of the chassis. The engine was a
which kept it stable over all types of terrain, and thus converted it into a magni-

weighed 43 metric tons (although it was considered a medium tank). The distri-
gunner to his right. Behind them was the combat room, with the turret area and
eplaced with periscopes).In front of him was the loader on the right and the gun-

ment was a formidable weapon, almost six metres in length. It was capable of
the T-34 and *Sherman*, under adequate combat conditions could be destroyed
was located at the rear of the tank, and gave it a speed of 45 kph, and a ran-

ull was 80 mm thick, sloping at 55º, while the sides had 40 mm. The turret front
invulnerable to any gun in service at more than 500 metres, whereas the Pan-
y solid build quality were also notable features.

to combat, and it suffered frequent breakdowns in the engines cooling system.

ellent combination of mobility, armour and firepower, the three fundamental pre-
more than compensated for by its great virtues. It came closest in similarity to
d and feared weapon, capable of upsetting the balance in any scenario, as hap-

rret, and this eased production. A total of 600 *Ausf D*, 1,788 *Ausf A* and 3,740
e *Panther II*, of which there is a prototype in the USA, and the *Ausf F*, an excep-
with a rangefinder and infrared for nightfighting. This model exhibited all the typi-
G's that entered into combat in 1945.

ervation versions, one of the most outstanding was the recovery model, the *Ber-*
the heavy tanks.

s designated, used an *Ausf A* chasis and was armed with the excellent 8.8 cm
and sloped forward at an angle of 55º. The *Saukopf*-type mantel was 100 mm
ain armament was designed to hit targets at a range of 2,500 metres. A total of

elian, a very advanced design equipped with two 37 mm *Flak 43* cannon, moun-
s turret was used as encasements, mainly in the Gothic and Hitler lines in Italy,

«Wiking» and the 333rd Infantry Division attacked the town, where 4th Guards Tank Corps was deployed. This Russian unit hardly had enough munitions and fuel for its T-34's, and even worse for them, a column containing supplies was intercepted and destroyed by the *17.Panzer-Division* at Alexandrovka. Only a few elements of the 13th Tank Brigade managed to escape and reach the Russian lines on the 24th. Meanwhile, on the 20th, as «LSSAH» covered the flank, setting up strong positions in Krasnograd, «Totenkopf» and «Das Reich» advanced towards Novo-Moskovsk and Pavlograd. Vatutín ignored these events and

information on German movements, instead ordering the advance to continue, even requesting that more units be sent to enable the advance to continue, despite having hardly any fuel for his tanks.

The situation rapidly deteriorated. On the 20th, after fierce fighting, the *2.SS.Panzergrenadier-Division «Das Reich»* attacked and destroyed the Soviet 6th Infantry Division. Two days later, Pavlograd was recaptured by «Das Reich» and «Totenkopf», destroying 35th Guards Division in the process. The Stavka began to become alarmed, ordering the 69th Army and Golikov's

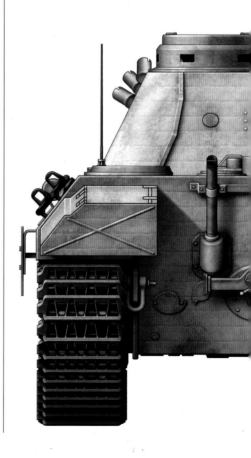

Panzerkampfwagen V Panther

The appearance of the T-34 during the first days of Operation Barbarossa was an unpleasant surprise for the Ger zer IV, then the most powerful tank in service with the *Wehrmacht*. At the end of November 1941, a group of expert future tank which would have to confront it. First thoughts were that the best idea would be to simply copy it. Howev difficulty in mass producing the aluminium engine in the Soviet tank. Instead of this, they opted for a new design, wi ed of 55 kph. The two choices of design were from Daimler-Benz and MAN. While the Daimler Benz was too much li sented a totally different concept.

It had a a higher, wider hull than the T-34, and its turret was positioned further back, but even so, the new, long Maybach HL 210 and the running gear consisted of double torsion bars with large interleaved wheels on eight axels, ficent gun platform.

In its definitive version, the new tank, which was designated the Sdfkz 171, *Panzerkampfwagen V Panther Ausf D,* bution of the crew was typical of the time. At the front of the vehicle sat the driver with the radio operator/machinej three men. The commander was positioned at the back and to the left; beneath a cupola with six vision blocks (later ner on the left.

Apart from its main gun, the tank also mounted a 7.92 mm co-axial machine gun. The 7.5 cm L/70 main arma perforating 140 mm of armour at 1000 metres, although thanks to its excellent optics, its most frequent targets, at twice that range. The magazine held seventy-nine 7.5 cm rounds. The engine, a 700 HP V 12 Maybach HL 230, ge of 200 km.

Along with its main armament and engine, a third impressive feature of the tank was its armour. The front of the h was 110 mm, and the mantel 100 mm. Therefore, although the sides were the weak point, the front of the tank wa ther's main armament could knock out its rivals from over 1000 metres. Its capacity to resist mines and its general

However, its operational debut at Kursk was not outstanding due to the haste with which it had been ushered in

Once these defects had been ironed out, the Panther became the best tank of the Second World War, with its exc requisites for a tank. Its main defects were weak lateral armour and complex maintenance. Nevertheless, these wer the modern concept of the MBT *(Main battle tank)*. In the hands of a well trained crew the Panther was a determine pened on numerous occasions on the Eastern Front.

In its later versions, the A and G, some specific features were improved, such as the downwards trap under the tu *Ausf G* (the last model to enter service) were produced. At the end of the war two new versions had been planned, th tional model with reinforced armour and a smaller turret, capable of eventually mounting an 8.8 cm L/71, equipped cal features of western tanks of the nineteen-fifties. In fact the night vision equipment was installed in several *Ausf*

Several variants of this formidable tank were produced. Apart from the more common Command and Artillery Obs *gepanther*, of which 350 were built. This version was, along with the rare *Bergetiger*, the only one capable of towing

The tank hunter version was to become the most successful of its type during the war. The *Jadgpanther,* as it wa L/71, which also equipped the *Tiger II*. Weighing in at 46 metric tons, its frontal armour had a thickness of 80 mm thick. It had a crew of five men and a maximum speed of 46 kph. With its advanced target adquisition system, its m 382 units came off the production line, and they wreaked havoc wherever they engaged in the fighting.

Among the variants which hardly entered in service, it is worth mentioning the anti-aircraft version, designated *Ko* ted in an enclosed armoured turret, and with a very modern aiming system. A special *ad hoc* set up of the *Panther* as well as some sectors of the *West wall* in 1944.

---

from two directions, the *Waffen SS* from the north-east and *XLVIII Panzerkorps* from the south, while Popov's group would be attacked from the east by *XL Panzerkorps*. Manstein intended to use all available armoured units for the counterattack, seven divisions with 225 tanks and *StuG III's*, supported by several units of Panzergrenadiers (6th, 7th, 11th, 17th, 2.SS «*Das Reich*», 3.SS «*Totenkopf*» and *5.SS* «*Wiking*»), while *1.SS* «*Leibstandarte*» acted as a covering force to the north. Two infantry divisions, the 15th and 333th were to accompany the armoured forces in order to block any

Soviet movements and reduce any pockets created during the counterattack.

One of the most dramatic and decisive operations of the Second World War was about to begin.

While the *7.Panzer-Division* surrounded Krasnoarmeiskoie, the *5.SS.Panzergrenadier-Division*

German infantry advancing through typical snow-covered countryside on the Russian steppe.

The Soviets consolidated their capture of the city after three days, but they were completely disorganised, giving the Germans more time to reorganize.

The fighting in and around the city had been very costly for the Russians. The speed of the Soviet advance had been progressively slowing down due to increasing losses both in infantry and vehicles, and Golikov's offensive was noticibly falling behind in regard to the initial planned schedule, the 19th January. The attempt to surround Kharkov had completely failed and the Germans had escaped the trap. The Russians had been unable to destroy *Armeeabteilung Lanz* and neither had they cut the open corridors to the south-west.

Hitler was furious with such open disobediance to a direct order, and was ready to relieve as many commanders as he deemed necessary, but when the *Führer* arrived in Zaporojie, the able Manstein convinced him of the reality of the situation and that in actual fact it was the Stavka who had a problem. The *SS-Panzerkorps* was regrouping in the region of Krasnograd, along with *4.Panzerarmee*. At last Manstein had two armoured forces which he could launch against the exposed Soviet 6th Army, which had reached the limit of its logistic capabilities. Furthermore, Manstein had convinced Hitler of the interest in not attacking Kharkov directly, but of first annihilating the

Soviet forces. The city would soon fall after that.

Manstein's counter attack

On 19th February, at the last moment, Manstein revealed his

In 1943 the *II.SS-PANZERKORPS* was equiped with the best armour available to the Germans, such as the *Panzer IV* Ausf G and *Tiger I*.

plans to his officers. Following the reorganisation of his units, the plan was for *4.Panzerarmee* to attack the Soviet 6th Army

ERICH VON MANSTEIN

Erich von Lewinski was born on 24th November 1887 in Berlin. The tenth son of an Artillery General who died in 1906. Soon after his birth he was adopted by his uncle Georg von Manstein, also a General (infantry), who gave him his surname. Both families belonged to the Prussian military aristocracy, and possessed large estates in Prussia. Various members of both families reached the rank of General in their military careers.

At the age of 13, Manstein entered the Cadet School at Plön. In 1906 he joined the *3rd Garderegiment zu Fuss*, and was promoted to Lieutenant in 1907. During the First World War, he saw combat at Namur and the Masurian Lakes, where he was seriously injured. He took part in the battles of the Somme and Verdun as a Staff Captain, as a cavalry officer fighting the Bolsheviks in 1917 and finally, in the *213 Sturm Division* in 1918. During the bloody offensives of 1918, he was profoundly struck by the number of casualties suffered by the infantry in their assaults on fortified positions. Following the armistice, due to his great experience, he participated in all aspects of the reorganisation of the *Reischwehr*.

During the 1930s, Manstein made several visits to the Soviet Union, where he had contact with Russian officers and observed large scale manouvres in the Ukraine and Caucuses. En 1931, as a *Oberstleutnant* he commanded a

Jäger Bataillon in Kolberg. He was promoted to Colonel *(Oberst)* in 1933 and Chief of Staff to General von Witzleben. In 1935 he was appointed Chief of Operations at *Oberkommando des Heeres (OKH)*, and was promoted to General in 1936. During this time, he supported the development of the Panzerwaffe, although he believed the infantry would remain vital on the battlefield, although they would have to be motorized, carried in armoured vehicles to limit casualties and accompanied by assaualt guns, a concept which did not appeal to the High Command. During 1937 and 38, Manstein took part in the preparation of various plans, both offensive and defensive, until he was promoted to *Generalleutnant* in April 1938, and took command of the *18th Infantry Division*. A year late he was appointed as von Leeb's Chief of Staff.

Manstein, with von Runstedt and Blumentritt, planned the invasion of southern Poland in 1939. Following this successful campaign, he then spent his time in Coblenza planning the future invasion of France, placing himself in opposition to the more conservative theories of Halder, who wanted to repeat the Schliffen plan of 1914. His thesis was finally the one accepted and the main attack through the Ardennes broke through the French line at Sedan. The German armoured units surged through the French countryside to the sea, at Abbeville, and the campaign in the west, unlike that of 1914, was decided in a few weeks. Manstein participated in the French campaign as commander of the *XXXVIII Armee Korps*, a

recently created infantry formation, following his replacement at the High Command, a result of his continuous disagreement with the more orthodox theories.

During the initial phases of Operation Barbarossa he commanded the *LVII Armee Korps (motorized)*, making important advances into enema territory, crossing the Dvina on the fifth day, and completely disorganising Soviet defences in the Baltic Republics. Through a brilliant manouvre, he destroyed the Russian 34th Army in the Demiansk sector. In September 1941 he took command of *11.Armee*, with the objective of conquering the Crimea. At first his subordinates treated him with suspicion, and were wary of his apparent arrogance, but he soon gained their confidence, as well as that of the rank and file, with his frequent visits to the front and his operational effectiveness. In November all that remained was to capture the fortress of Sebastopol. Now with the rank of *Generaloberst*, he concentrated on making an assault on the fortress, and used all the means at his disposal to avoid heavy losses amongst his men. The operation was completed in less than a month. Manstein was promoted to *Generalfeldmarschall* on 1st July 1942.

His greatest moment was about to arrive. Although Hitler initially wanted to send him to Leningrad to take that city, in September he had to face a counteroffensive in that sector. Despite achieving great success, destroying large numbers of Soviet units, he lost his son Gero Erich, a leutnant in the *Panzergrenadiers*. Soon after, when "Operation Ura-

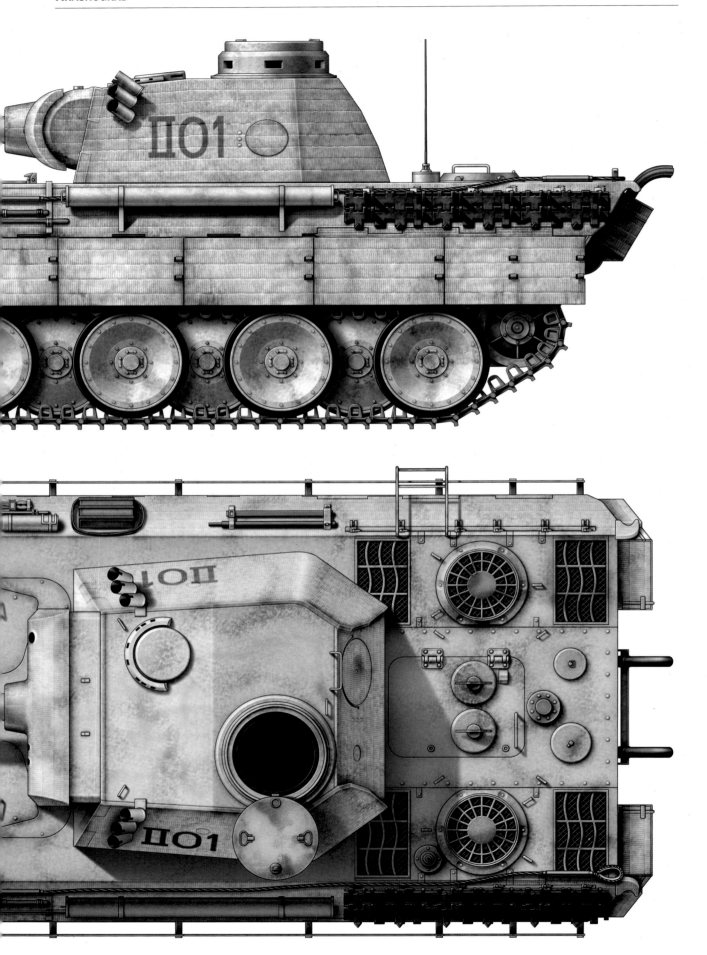

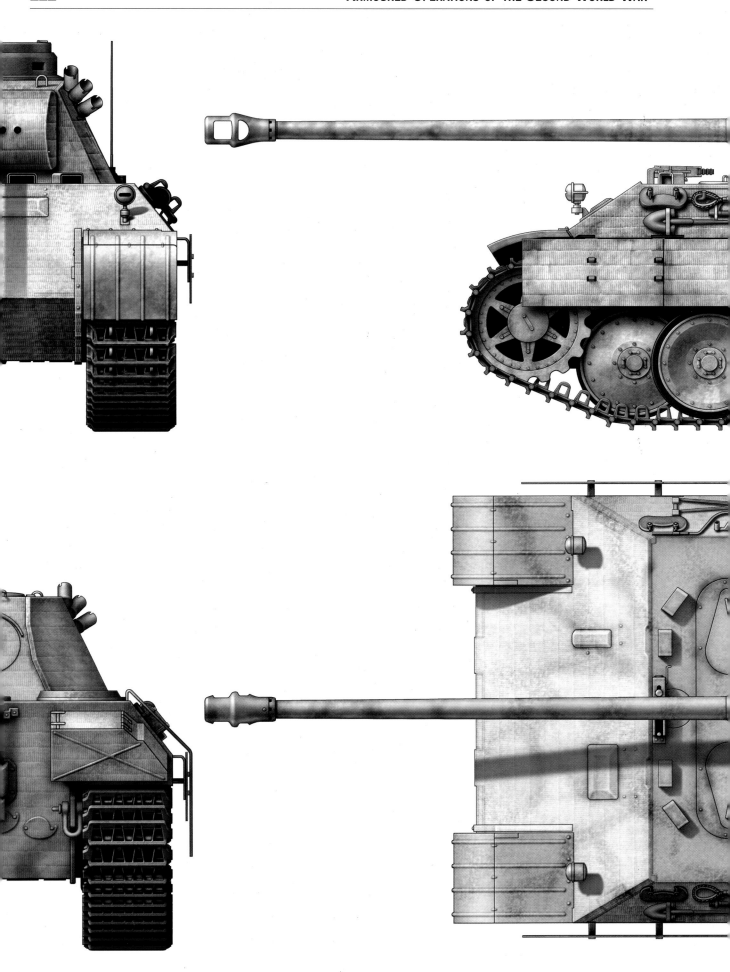

nus" encircled 6.Armee in Stalingrad, Hitler ordered Manstein to carry out an operation (Winter Storm) to break through to the beleagured German troops in the city. With scarce means, he made some progress, until his advance came to a halt some 50 kilometres from his objective, and with Paulus unable to decide on a breakout. Immediately after this, during the great Soviet offensive in the Ukraine, and following strong arguments, he convinced Hitler of the need to withdraw in order to launch a devastating counter-attack. The proceeding counter-attack at Krasnograd and subsequent reconquest of Kharkov has gone down in History as a model for armoured operations, without precedent and difficult to repeat. It was Manstein's masterstroke.

In the summer of 1943, despite criticising the plan, considering it to be the result of a lack of any other option due to delay, he commanded the Southern Front at the battle of Kursk, and came close to a breakthrough. Following this strategic failure, he was to have continued disagreements with Hitler due to the latter's obsession with holding ground, which went against Manstein's ideas of a flexible, elastic defence that would wear down the Red Army, which despite its apparently unlimited numbers, was on several occasions to come close to the abyss. In spite of the difficulties and obstacles, Manstein was still able to achieve some notable successes, such as breaking the encirclement of Tcherkassy in February 1944. Finally, on 30th March, he was replaced by Model. Manstein remained on the reserve until the end of the war, when he was tried and sentenced to twelve years in prison, although he was released in 1953. He was an advisor to the *Bundeswehr*, and his book **«Lost Victories»** recorded most of his wartime experiences. He died in 1973.

From both a strategic and tactical point of view, he was one of the greatest commanders of World War Two. To his solid, intellectual grounding as a staff officer was added his carisma and his resolve to carry out all manner of operations under all kinds of circumstances, with great success.

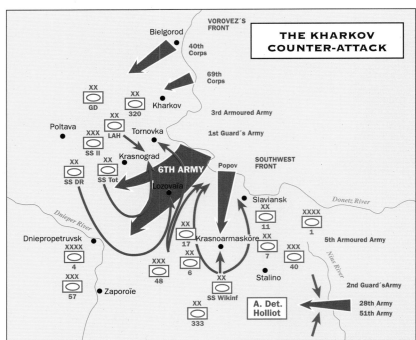

3rd Tank Army to attack Krasnograd in order to support Vatutin. It was too late. The *3.SS.Panzergrenadier-Division «Totenkopf»* penetrated through the open breach in the Soviet defences, cutting off two Infantry divisions. Pereschepino, with its vital bridge, was captured through an audacious attack carried out by the *«Deutschland»* Regiment, which charged directly onto the bridge with its half-tracks, tanks and light vehicles, taking the defending Russian soldiers by surprise and overrunning them. On the 23rd, the 25th Tank Corps was encircled, losing all its tanks, the survivors having to break out on foot.

«LSSAH» advanced against Popov's 3rd Tank Army on 19 February, in the outskirts of Krasnograd. Not far from there at Poltava, in 1709, the powerful Swedish army of Charles XII had been decisively defeated by the Russians under Peter the Great. Perhaps Vatutin dreamed of a similar victory, but this time it was to be different.

The Russian forces deployed in typical fashion, extended over the rolling, show-covered steppe, almost without reconnaissance, in a never-ending column of infantry, tanks and other vehicles. They were at the point of running out of supplies, which had become very scarce since they had crossed the Don. Soviet logistics had never been excellent, but now they were reaching a very dangerously low level.

An extraordinary combat group had been organised in Ziglerowka, in the vicinity Jeremejewska. It contained nothing less than the *III.Abteilung* of *SS Panzergrenadier Regiment 2*, commanded by Jochem Peiper, the *I.Abteilung* of *SS Panzer Regiment 1*, commanded by Max Wünsche, and a reinforced reconnaissance unit, *Aufklärungsabteilung* under Kurt Meyer. There were a total of 30 *Panzer IV F-2's*, four heavy *Tiger I's* and a number of Sd.Kfz 250 and 251 half-tracks carrying *Panzergrenadiers*. Several off-road vehicles including *Schwimmwagens* can also be added to this. Furthermore, there was also powerful artillery support. The frozen ground favoured mobility, and the Germans were soon to demonstrate how tactically advanced they were compared to the Russians.

At 0400 hours on the 20th, Peiper's group, flanked by Meyer's, started off. In a few hours they had attacked the first group of Russians, who were advancing in a huge column across the snowy steppe. Taken by surprise, the Russians had no time to react. The panzergrenadiers charged across the snow

The *II.SS-Panzerkorps*

El II.*SS-Panzerkorps* was officially formed on 9th July 1942, under the command of *SS-Obergruppenführer* Paul Hausser. Following months of hard fighting on the Eastern Front, the three most veteran divisions were withdrawn to France at the end of the year to rest and refit. Each division was converted into a *Panzergrenadier* division, with an added tank battalion and diverse support elements. In reality, each division had an armoured regiment of two battalions, and so were *Panzer* Divisions in all but name. One of the *Panzergranadier* battalions was equipped with armoured half-tracks (Sd.Kfz 250 and 251), and the others, all completely motorizad, used various models of trucks and cars (including the amphibious *Schwimmwagen*). The divisions were also greatly influenced by their own commanders, who organizad and trained them according to their own criterias, at the same time imprinting their personalities on them. *Leibstandarte Adolf Hitler* was commanded by Josef Dietrich, a bavarian and a First World War veteran of the *Stosstruppen*, hardened by street fighting with the Freikorps, and Hitler's former chauffer. Deitrich had served in one of the first German tanks in 1918 and had taken part in several of the rare encounters betwen tanks in the Great War. Das Reich was organised under Paul Hausser, a Prussian Staff officer with a lot of command experience in World War One. *Totenkopf* was under the command of Theodor Eicke, a fervent national socialist and former commandant of Dachau concentration camp. When *Das Reich* returned to Russia in 1943, command was given to *SS Obergruppenführer* Georg Keppler, as Hausser had been made commander of the *Panzerkorps*.

The subordinate officers included some of the most celebrated tank commanders of World War Two, such as Fritz Witt, commander of *SS-Panzergrenadier Regiment 1* and future commander of the *SS Hitlerjugend* Division, Theo Wish, commander of *SS-Panzergrenadier Regiment 2*, whose half-track battalion was under Jochem Peiper, Heinz Westernhagen, who commanded *SS-Sturmgeschützabteilung 1*, and Otto Kum, who commanded the *Der Führer* Regiment. Many of the battalion commanders, like Peiper, achieved great notoriety during the war, two examples are Max Wünsche and Kurt Meyer. History's greatest tank ace, Michael Wittman, belonged to *1.SS.Panzergrenadier-Division «LSSAH»*. One common feature among the officers of *SS-Panzerkorps*, was a quality the Germans called art; a mixture of aggressiveness, contempt for danger and leadership based on personal example, a quality almost exclusive to the German army during the Second World War.

There is no question that in January of 1943, no comparable unit existed in the world that could match this powerful corps, which itself would never again reach the same degree of quality. The Corps grouped together three *Panzer* divisions; *1.SS «Leibstandarte SS Adolf Hitler»*, *2.SS «Das Reich»* and *3.SS «Totenkopf»*. Each division included a Panzer Regiment (two battalions) equipped with the new *Panzer IV Ausf G*, mounting the 7.5 cm L/48, capable of knocking out the T-34 from long range (although there were also numbers of *Panzer III Ausf L* and *Ausf M*, armed with the 5 cm L/60). The divisions were also reinforced with a company of heavy *Tiger I's*, which gave them unequalled firepower when compared to the other *Panzer* divisions, which at this time had an average of 30 *Panzer III's* and IVs. Added to this was a battalion of *Sturmgeschütz* assault guns or *Panzerjäger* tank hunters, equipped with the *Stug III* or *Marder III*, as well as a powerful artillery element and several companies of Nebelwerfers. Initially, the divisions were almost 100% up to strength in regards numbers of effectives and the men were perfectly trained. Many of them were now battle hardened and were well rested. All the company, battalion and regimental commanders had three or four years of combat experience, and understood the principles of surprise, concentration of firepower and the employment of combined arms. Above all, they were masters of the use of firepower combined with mobility. They had been trained to be aggressive, both in attack and defence, and were convinced of their superiority over the enemy. This was to be the first time the three divisions would fight together en masse, and they were to demonstrate all of which they were capable.

aboard the *Schwimmwagens* and half-tracks, firing their machine guns as they moved, mowing down the surprised infantry. The survivors took refuge in nearby Jeremejevka, where they were finished off by fire from the German 20 mm AA guns. Wünsche's tanks attacked another column further away, which included numerous artillery pieces. The column was totally annihilated. Kurt Meyer was awarded his Oak Leaves for this action. At the same time that this was taking place, a company of *Panzer IV's* surged across the centre, covered by another company. The artillery joined the fight at this point, adding to the *pandemonium* of fire and destruction. For the loss of one man killed and half a dozen wounded, Peiper's group destroyed a Russian battalion in a few minutes.

By 15.00 Jeremejewska was in German hands, who then used it as a base to manoeuvre against the Russian columns which unceasingly continued to arrive. Using the undulating terrain as cover, and occupying enfilade positions, hulls hidden from view, one after the other the *Panzer IV's* began destroying any T-34's that came within range. Not only were the Russian tanks targets, 76.2 and 45 mm AT guns were also put out of action by the 7.5 cm L/43 guns of the Panzers, which were outside the effective range of the Soviet anti-tank guns. The *Tiger I's* especially, demonstrated their worth, knocking out the Soviet guns from a range of 2.000 metres or more, a distance which not only made them invulnerable to Soviet projectiles, but also a very difficult target for the Russian 76.2 mm guns to achieve an impact. After the tanks and guns,

The T-34/76 model 42. The final models of the *Panzer IV*, above all the G, were more than capable of overcoming them.
Illustration: Julio López Caeiro.

came the turn of the trucks and Soviet infantry. It was slaughter, and come nightfall, the steppe was strewn with burnt-out tanks and Russian dead. During the following days, the soviet attacks against Jeremejewska were repeated, with the same results. The Germans´mobile defence overcame the T-34's, and from their advantageous firing positions, they were able to destroy them with almost total impunity. Withdrawing to the village to reorganise and refuel, the *Panzer IV's* and *Tigers* returned to destroy the next Soviet column.

On the night of the 20th, Popov, conscious of the danger, and now aware that not only «*LSSAH*», but also elements of

Movement in the mud was very difficult, even for the wide tracks of the *Tiger I*. *Pz.Kpfw. VI Ausf E* of *3.SS-Pz.Gren.Div* «*Totenkopf*», Kharkov, March 1943.
Illustration: Julio López Caeiro

the *7.Panzer-Division* and the *5.SS Panzer Grenadier Division «Wiking»*, were rushing towards him, asked Vatutin, in vain, for permission to withdraw. In fact, Vatutin did not become aware of the seriousness of the situation until three days later.

Meanwhile, unknown to Popov, Hausser had placed the rest of *II.SS-Panzerkorps* in position to the south of the axis of Soviet advance, where a large breach was forming. «Das Reich» and «Totenkopf» advanced against Karitonov's 6th Army, supported by *4.Panzerarmee*. Later continuing north to encircle and destroy Vatutin's entire South-Western Front. In the course of all these attacks, German losses were very low, due to the excellent coordination between the assual force and their supporting artillery, anti-tank guns and close support units (assault guns and AA guns), not to forget the devastating efficiency of the *Stukas*. The superior German firepower overcame the Soviet defences and allowed the assault groups to cose at speed, overunning the Russian positions. In order to carry out these operations it was essential to be able to effectively combine companies and battalions of different units to create specific combat groups for both offensive and defensive operations.

On the morning of the 25th, Wünsche, along with Peiper's bat-

talion, made an aggressive attack on the Russian 350th Division, which was entrenched along a chain of hills on the river Bogotaja. The Panzers charged directly at the enemy line, covered by an effective artillery barrage, and were able to breakthrough without incurring any losses. They then immediately headed for the Russian rearguard, where they found their artillery, which had still not been positioned. The speed of the attack caught the Soviets off guard and all the artillery pieces were put out of action before they could fire a shot. At the same time the *panzergrenadiers* frontally attacked the Russian infantry, the Panzers, now having eliminated the artillery, attacked the Russians from their rear. It was an awful massacre. More than 1,000 corpses covered the snowy ground,and more than fifty guns were either captured or destroyed. Max Wünsche was awarded the Knight's Cross for this action. The Germans had suffered only five killed and fourteen wounded.

Soon after, the *SS Panzerkorps* advanced north over the snow in thick fog. The flow of supplies could not be guaranteed as the only road had not been completely secured, and isolated Soviet units threatened and harassed the supply convoys. The *SS Panzerkorps* and *XL Panzerkorps* took Losovaja on the 27th (*«Das Reich»*, in a combined assault

This officer from *«LSSAH»* takes a moment to light a cigarette during the fighting for Kharkov. *(Bundesarchiv).*

with artillery, *Stukas* and *StuG III's*, destroying the T-34's in the vicinity), then continued north, annihilating any Soviet mobile forces they found and encircled a part of 6th Army. The Russians withdrew to the north in disorder before the German push. The German advance was supported by the Luftwaffe, with more than 1,000 sorties being flown daily. Contrary to the *Luftwaffe*, Russian aircraft had to operate far from their airfields, leaving them at a

The Soviet motorized columns were vital in maintaining the flow of supplies to the armoured units during their rapid advances However, they were vulnerable, and during the battles of the winter of 1942/43, they were decimated by German mobile forces and the *Luftwaffe*.

clear disadvantage. In Barvenkovo, what was left of Popov's group, some 50 tanks, almost without fuel, dug their tanks into defensive positions, relinquishing any mobility they had. The pursuing Germans surrounded their positions and continued their advance.

Ribalko was intending to make one final attempt in the Krasnograd sector with his 3rd Tank Army, when he received orders to redeploy his units to the south, in order to counterattack the *SS Panzerkorps*. Meanwhile, the Germans, who had been made well aware of Soviet movements by their reconnaissance units, detailed a *Kampfgruppe* from *«LSSAH»* to cut off the 3rd Army. The following day, the three SS divisions attacked. There were multiple engagements throughout the day, with the Germans advancing along two axis, overwhelming the Russians and forcing them to retire in disorder, as they pursued them across the snowcovered fields in the outskirts of Alexejevka. A day later, the majority of Ribalko's forces had been encircled in the Kegitschevka-Jeremejevka sector, and were then liquidated in a few days. Das Reich and Totenkopf, having blocked the threat to the bridges over the Dnieper, and brought the advance of 6th Army to a halt, had swing north and joined *«LSSAH»* in the destruction of 3rd Tank Army. *Kharkov* was close. *1.Panzerarmee* was firmly established on the Donetz, and could block any attempt to penetrate south. Popov's group had been virtually destroyed, and attempts by the Red Army to cross the Mius had also been bloodily repulsed. The Soviet 6th Army and 1st Guards Army had been bled white and were in disorder. Worse still, both the Russian soldiers and command, which had sensed they were on the point of a decisive victory, were now on the

Panzerjëger 38(t) Marder III Ausf H of *1.SS-Pz.Gren-Div «LSSAH»*, Kharkov, February 1943.

Ilustración: Luis Fresno Crespo.

retreat and had been completely demoralised by their opponents reaction.

Forever the optimist, Vatutín, finally became aware of the situation and informed the *Stavka*. 1st Guards Army and 6th Army were ordered to withdraw to the other side of the Donetz, while 3rd Tank Army was to counterattack in order to detain the German advance. This was in vain. Two of its three tank corps were encircled on 3rd March, and two days later they ceased to exist. The road to Kharkov was open. On the 28th February, the Germans took stock: They had penetrated more than 120 kilometres along a front of more than 150, capturing or destroying more than 300 tanks, 200 guns inflicting more than 23,000 casualties on the enemy. Manstein announced the new objective, the enemy forces deployed south-east of Kharkov. On 6th March, the *II SS Panzerkorps* broke through the Russian defences, and

Waffen SS panzergrenadiers penetrating into a neighbourhood of Kharkov. The second vehicle is an Engineers' Sd.Kfz 251 carrying bridging equipment. In spite of its specialist mission, the crew are prepared for combat.

advanced north. They reached the suburbs of Kharkov on the 10th, and began encircling the city, forcing the 69th Army to retreat. Further north, *Grossdeutschland* continued eastwards, and *Kampfgruppe Peiper* took Bielgorod on the 18th. Kharkov fell a few days later...

Results

Kharkov had been recaptured and the front re-established. Confi-

dence too, had been recovered. The training, material quality and tactics of the Germans had been shown to be superior to that of the Red Army. Looked at objectively, the counter-offensive had exceeded all reasonable expectations and the Germans had achieved an unprecedented success.

However, victory had come at a cost, and losses in both men and material had been high, above all

Panzergrenadiers of II.SS-Panzerkorps in recently captured Kharkov. They gained control of the city in a few days, showing the experience of Stalingrad had not been in vain.

in *II SS Panzerkorps*. The *Waffen SS* would never again be able to fill its ranks with so many experienced officers and NCOs and motivated, well trained men, such as those who had arrived in Russia in January of 1943. Nevertheless, the losses inflicted on the enemy by *4.Panzerarmee* were above expectations: more than 560 tanks, 1,070 field guns and more than 1,000 anti-tank guns. More than 40,000 Russian soldiers had been killed and over 12,400 captured. The Red Army had come close to delivering the *Wehrmacht* a mortal blow, but an excess of optimism and overconfidence had cost the *Stavka* dearly.

At the end of March 1943, the Russians had lost almost all the territory they had recaptured between November 1942 and February 1943. Added to this, their losses in men and material were so high it was to take several months to replace and reorganise their forces. Manstein's counter-attack had tipped the strategic balance in favour of Germany, and it would remain so until Kursk. During the counter-attack the *Waffen SS. Panzer-Divisions* had been decisive in overwhelming the Soviets and pushing them back eastwards.

Following the battle for Kharkov, *2.SS-Pz.Gren.Div. «Das Reich»* pressed a considerable number of T-34/76s into service.

Illustration: Julio López Caeiro

PROKOROVKA, 1943

5th Guards Army

By the summer of 1943, the Soviets had five tank corps operational, which had been created during the previous months. This had been due, in great part, to anglo-american aid, which had enabled the Red Army to motorize units to a degree that had been previously impossible.

5th Guards Army's commanding officer was Pavel Rotmistrov. Born in 1901, before the war he had been an instructor at the Armoured Warfare Academy. In 1941 he was Chief of Staff of 3rd Mechanized Corps, and commanded the 8th Tank Brigade during the first winter of the war. In April 1942 he took command of 7th Corps, which was decimated at Stalingrad in September of that year. He later had success in December at Kotelnikovo, although he was not able to take Rostov in time to cut the German withdrawl from the Caucasus. Despite this, he was appreciated by Stalin, who gave him command of this elite unit.

5th Guards Army contained 37,000 men organized into two Corps, the 5th Mechanized and

29th Tank Corps, as well as many support units, such as the 6th Anti-Aircraft Division, equipped with sixty-four 37 mm cannon and numerous 12.7 mm machine guns. Its artillery was powerful, with a total of twenty-four 122 mm howitzers and twenty-four *Katyushka* rocket launchers, as well as around twenty 76.2 mm ZIS-3 anti-tank guns. The organisation was completed by an Engineer battalion, three motorized regiments, one motorcycle, another of tanks (with thirty-four T-70's and T-34's) and one of self-propelled guns, with the new ISU-152. Each Corps was made up of four Brigades and various support units.

The 29th Tank Corps was composed of three tank Brigades and one of motorized infantry. There were also three artillery regiments (with thirty-six 120 mm mortars, twenty-four 76.2 mm field guns and twenty-four self-propelled SU-122s), two reconnaissance companies and an anti-aircraft battalion with twelve 85 mm guns, employed as anti-tank weapons.

The 5th Mechanized Corps had three mechanized Brigades, each with a regiment of 48 tanks, a bri-

The *Panzer III*, armed with the L/69 5 cm gun continued to make up a high percentage of the total number of German tanks serving in the middle of 1943, and with its veteren crews was capable of taking on the RussianT-34. (Bundesarchiv)

gade of sixty-five T-34's and a rocket launcher battalion with eight Katyushkas. These two powerful units were reinforced with eight artillery regiments (one with ISU-152s), and three independent corps (the 2nd and 18th Tank Corps and the 2nd Guards Tank Corps). Curiously, the 18th Corps had a regiment equipped with 35 British *Churchill IV* tanks. The 2nd Guards Corps was reinforced with a regiment of 39 T-34's. Reconnaissance units and other armoured vehicles were, however few in number.

On 11th July, on the eve of the battle, Rotmistrov had 70,000 men and almost 900 tanks of varying types (more than 500 were T-34's), to confront Hausser's force of 300.

«The battle of Kursk» has become one of the most legendary and at the same time distorted battles of the Second World War. This chapter will focus on one of the most famous actions of Kursk, the

The SU-122 was one of the earliest Soviet attempts to develop a self-propelled gun for supporting the infantry and neutralising German strong-points, as well as well as having a limited anti-tank capability. It did not prove to be a very successful model and was not built in large numbers.

ying their mobile forces before they could reach fortified positions. As Hitler did not wish to contemplate the idea of ceding ground, an offensive was the only option, and the most obvious place to conduct one was the Kursk salient, which had been created during the Kharkov offensive. The salient seperated *Heeresgruppe «Mitte»* and *Heeregruppe «Süd»*. The initial date set for the offensive was April 1943. The offensive had two objectives, to destroy a large number of Russian units in a classic battle of encirclement, and at the same time to shorten the Front considerably.

But the delays soon began to accumulate, which only favoured the Soviets, to whom the objective was also obvious, and who began to prepare in ernest. Given the magnitude the Russian defences were beginning to take on, Model demanded more resources, which in turn produced more delays. Manstein, Guderian, and von Kluge were all against any delay, as they were convinced that any possibility of success rested on making the attack in April, before the Russians could fortify their defences even further. Hitler decided to put back the attack to June. One of the reasons for this decision was to allow time for enough of the new *Panthers*, in which a lot of hope had been placed, to enter service. Unfortunately, the rush to get them to the Front on time resulted in 200 new tanks going into combat with various "teething troubles" still to be sorted out, as well as the crews being inadequately trained, all of which was to reduce their effectiveness. The day for the start of the attack was finally fixed for 5th July. It was to be the last chance for the *Wehrmacht* to maintain the initiative on the Eastern Front.

Marshal Zhukov had been very aware of the German intentions since April of that year. He was also concious of the German superiority in mobile operations, and therefore believed it paramount to weaken their armoured units before initiating any kind of large-scale coun ter

In spite of the increasing use of radio, the command and control system in Soviet tank formations was based on giving the crews their orders before going into combat, limiting considerably their ability to act independently, as well as overall operational flexibility.

battle of Prokorovka, which, according to generally accepted history, was the greatest tank battle of all time. Nothing could be further from the truth, as *«Operation Goodwood»*, during the Normandy battle in 1944, involved a considerably greater number of tanks, and even this is overshadowed by the great tank battles that occurred during the Yom Kippur war of October 1973.

For the Germans, the battle of Kursk is synonymous with *«Operation Zitadelle»*, while the Soviets understand *«Zitadelle»* as meaning the first, defensive phase (the first German attack), while the offensive

to the north of Kursk on 12th July is known as *«Operation Kutuzov»*, and that in the south on 3rd August as *«Operation Rumiantsev»*. How did this situation occur?

Following the extraordinary victory at Kharkov, which stabilised the southern Front, Manstein outlined the strategic prospects for 1943 to Hitler. There was an urgent need to shorten the Front, since *Heeresgruppe «Süd»* had only thirty weakened divisions to defend more than 700 kilometres. There were two alternatives, either to give up the strategic initiative to the Soviets, so that they would attack towards the Dnieper, allowing for a counterattack against their flanks, or attack first, when the *rasputitsa* had disappeared and the ground was suitable for large-scale operations, with the objective of destro-

T-34/76 model 1943. The high rate of production lead to adaptations, such as the absence of rubber on the wheels.
Illustration: Julio López Caeiro.

offensive. Zhukov had learned from his earlier mistakes. On 21st April, the *Stavka* ordered the construction of stronger fortifications in the Kursk salient, concentrating on anti-tank defences and vast minefields. A total of six defensive lines were built, with a depth of up to 200 kilometres. Nevertheless, Stalin was still worried. His fear was that if the Germans were able to break through at Kursk, they would continue all the way to Moscow. Intelligence reports indicated an offensive was imminent, and both Rokossovski and Zhukov favoured a preventative strike. Finally, on 2nd July, the *Stavka* was informed that the attack would begin between the 3rd and 6th. The dice were rolling.

The Battle of Kursk

When the offensive began, the *Wehrmacht* had not recovered from the losses it had suffered in the bloody winter and spring battles. It also had 1,000 fewer tanks than at the end of the previous year. In the case of the infantry, the situation was even worse. The 400 newly manufactured Panthers, mechanically unreliable as they were, would not be enough to tip the balance. 200 participated in the Kursk offensive, of which 65 were not operational due to mechanical problems. It was not a very promising start for a tank that within a few months was to prove itself to be the best tank of World War Two.

Nor had the *II.SS-Panzerkorps* completely recovered from the losses it had sustained during the third battle of Kharkov, which had

reached the figure of 11,000 irreplacable men. For their offensive, the Germans had concentrated 1,865 medium and heavy tanks, a further 384 outdated tanks (most of them *Panzer IIs* and *Panzer III's* armed with the 5 cm L/42 gun), 533 *Sturmgeschutzes* and *Marders*, and 90 *Ferdinands*. Giving a total of approximately 3,000 tanks of all types.

The *II.SS-Panzerkorps*, which was to be the main protaginist on the German side at the battle of Prokorovka, had been reorganized as follows: «*Leibstanderte Adolf Hitler*» *(LSSAH)* now had a *Panzer.Abteilung* equipped with four companies of medium tanks (*Panzer III's* and *Panzer IV Ausf G's*), and a heavy tank company of fifte-

The SU-76 was a notably successful vehicle that remained in service to the end of the war.
Illustration: Julio López Caeiro.

Pz.Kpfw. III Ausf M belonging to *Pz.Rgt. 3, 2.Pz.Div,* on the outskirts of Khifzky –north of Orel–, August 1943.
Illustration: Julio López Caeiro

en *Tiger I's.* «*Das Reich*», a *Panzer.Abteilung* with two companies of light tanks and two of medium

General Balk, commander of XL *Panzerkorps,* in a Mercedes-Benz Type 1500A. (Bundesarchiv: 101 I-146-2005-48.

tanks, another *Panzer.Abteilung* with a company of light tanks and two companies of T-34's captured that winter, plus a company of *Tiger I's.* Finally, «*Totenkopf*» was equipped with two *Panzer.Abtei-*

lungen, each with one light and two medium tank companies, and a heavy company of fifteen *Tiger I's.* As can be seen, this was nothing like the mythical accounts which spoke of hundreds of *Panthers and Tigers.* The SS divisions did have a sizeable component of panzergrenadiers, from six to eight battalions, which gave them a tremendous shock value, as well as a strong defensive capability. It is worth remembering that the panzergrenadies, apart from their organic anti-tank guns, (four 5 cm Pak 38s per battalion, and the highly effective 7.5 cm Pak 40s) also had a great short range anti-tank capability, and throughout the war demonstrated their ability to stop attacks made by T-34's, overall if the Soviet tanks were not well supported by artillery. Furthermore, casualties among Soviet "tank riders" tended to be horrendous.

Another highly effective element of the *II.SS-Panzerkorps* were its two *Nebelwerfer* regiments, with their 15 and 21 cm tubes. This inaccurate but devastating weapon proved its capabilities when grouped together in sufficient numbers, as was to be the case. Each division had a strength which varied between 20,600 and 24,500 men, which meant they were large, powerful units.

The Soviets, for their part, had more than made up for their earlier losses, producing 6,000 tanks,

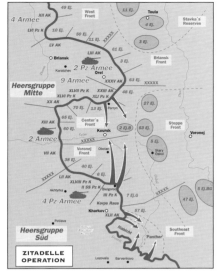

many of them T-34's. For the battle of Kursk, The Red Army had 5,300 tanks, including allied *Churchills*, *Valentines* and M3 *Grants*, in which the Russian crews showed little confidence.

The Red Army was also going through a profound transformation, replacing the enourmous losses it had suffered in the first two years of war, and adapting itself to the new situation on the battlefield. For example, in 1943, a Soviet tank corps had more or less the same number of effectives as a *Panzerdivision*, with around 11,000 men, some 200 T-34's and 50 assault guns, 60 field guns and 8 rocket launchers. A mechanized corps was larger, with 15,000 men, plus 230 tanks of all types and more than 100 artillery pieces and rocket launchers. Russian officers were gaining experience and becoming more professional, they were also starting to copy the German model of mobile operations, although they still had a lot to learn.

The Soviet Defensive System

In order to be able to confront the new German offensive, the *Stavka* had stockpiled an enormous amount of resources. There were 1,910,316 men, 28,304 guns and mortars, 338 *Katyushka* rocket launchers, 5,047 tanks and tank-hunters and 3,120 aircraft. The Soviets were deployed in three Fronts: Central Front was in the north, the Voronez Front in the south and the Steppe Front was in reserve. Infantry divisions had a strength of around 9,000 men, although with a higher proportion of combatants than in a German division, due to their poor logistics. Central Front had 1,647 tanks of all types, the Voronez Front 1,843 tanks and the Steppe Front 1,702.

There was an impressive concentration of artillery, with 60 guns and mortars per kilometre along the sectors alloted to Vatutin's 6th and 7th Guards Armies, and 100 guns and mortars per kilometre in the Central Front. With the help of more than 300,000 civilian workers, up to six successive defensive lines were constructed, in which the defenders would have an advantage of two to one, which takes on major significance when one considers that according to traditional doctrine an attacker should be able to count on a superiority of three to one. The previous two years experience had shown the Russians the potential of any German attack, and therefore they were aware that even these defences could be overcome. To counter this, they deliberately weakened the first lines of defence in order to group together sufficient forces to form a reserve, which they could then use to launch immediate counterattacks. All this was undoubtedly in immitation of German doctrine.

The defences constructed by the Soviets were very elaborate. In the Voronez front alone they dug more than 4,200 kilometres of trenches and prepared 500 anti-tank obstacles in only two months. In the 13th and 48th Army sectors they installed 112 kilometres of barred wire, ten of them electrified. A typical Army Corps had a defensive arrangement 20 kilometres deep, and between 13 and 30 kilometres of front line.In 6th Guards Army's sector, for example, for every 1,500 metres of front, 2,400 anti-tank and 2,700 anti-personnel mines had been laid. In fact, the worst enemy of the German armoured forces was not to be the enemy tanks or artillery, but rather the minefields. 28 anti-tank positions (designated *pakfronts*) defended the sector, each with a minimum of four 45 mm and 76.2 mm guns,

Sturmgeschütz with 8.8 cm PaK 43/2 Elefant, of 2 Kp, Panzerjäger Abteilung 653. Contrary to most accounts, the powerful Ferdinand performed well at Kursk, in spite of its defects. The two units equipped with them destroyed 500 Soviet armoured vehicles and anti-tank guns, for the cost of just over a dozen of their own number throughout operations in the Kursk salient, most of them being immobilised by mines.

Illustration: Julio López Caeiro

Sd.Kfz 250/9. Mounting a 20mm cannon and an MG in a rotating turret, similar to that of the Sd.Kfz 222. This vehicle performed well in a reconnaissance role, although few were made.

Illustration: Julio López Caeiro

(and a maximum of ten), and approximately twenty –seven AT rifles, as well as larger pieces up to 152 mm, or even dug in T-34's. These positions were set up to give a cross fire and support the reserves. This entire deployment was backed up by a powerful artillery support consisting of 1,250 pieces (two thirds of which was made up of 82, 120 and 160 mm mortars) and *Katyushka* rocket launchers.

The deployment of 52nd Guards Division is fairly representative of the Soviet defensive scheme. With more than 9,000 men organized in three regiments, the main body of this force was deployed in the front line, but each battalion was deplo-

yed to a depth of two kilometres. Two regiments deployed in the front line, with two battalions in the first line of trenches and the third battalion in the second line of defence, on average two kilometres behind. The third regiment occupied the third line of defence, some five kilometres to the rear. Advanced posts controlled the approaches out to about five kilometres in front of the the front line, making it difficult for the German reconnaissance patrols. Thirty-six divisional 76.2 mm and 122 mm guns were reinforced with three artillery and two *Katyushka* battalions. The forty-eight 45 mm regimental anti-tank guns were reinforced by another forty-eight 76.2 mm guns, as well as 270 anti-tank rifles. An anti-tank brigade (the 28th), was kept as a divisional reserve. The anti-tank guns were distributed in four *"pakfronts"*, with the majority of the 76.2 mm pieces

kept in reserve. To all of this must be added the 23 T-34's of the 230th Regiment, also in reserve, and the 16 T-60s and T-70's sent out on reconnaissance to observe the enemy's route of advance. However, this organisation was in no way homogenous. For example, the 375th Infantry Division was organised into seven *"pakfronts"*, with a total of Sixty-eight 76.2 mm field guns, twelve 76.2 mm and forty-one 45 mm AT guns, one hundred and thirty-four anti-tank rifles and sixty-one tanks in reserve.

Fifteen to twenty kilometres behind this deployment was another triple line of defence, and behind that was the Steppe Front deployed in another two defensive lines. It could be said that the *Blitzkrieg* was about to find itself confronting a defensive system more like the Hindenburg line of 1918, exceptionally well prepared and reinforced with large numbers of tanks.

However, in spite of this massive deployment, the Guards of the Soviet 52nd Division, above all those who were veterans of Stalingrad, had no illusions about what was to come, they new the strength of the Panzer Divisions, and only hoped to hold up the German advance for as long as they could, before being pulvarized by the *Waffen SS*. More than 60% of the men were new recruits, well indoctrinated and with high morale, but lacking experience.

Russian infantry in hurriedly dug trenches. At Kursk, the defences would be much better prepared.

Panzerkampfwagen IV Ausf G of 3.SS.Pz.Gr

Panzerkampfwagen IV Ausf H of 2.SS.Pz.G Kursk, July 1943

Panzerkampfwagen IV Ausf H of 3.Panzer-D

Three photographs of *Panzer IV Ausf G* and *H* tanks, together with other German armoured vehicles: Top, an ammunition re-supply vehicle built on a *Panzer 38(t)* chassis, centre, a *Panzer III Ausf L* and bottom, a Sdkfz 251/1. (General Administrative Archive and Bundesarchiv)

...ed by M.I. Koshkin, presented a tank designated A 20. This design had Christie-type suspension, was ...partly based on experience from the Spanish Civil War, and soon a new improved prototype was built.

...as 30 mm thick, its main gun was a 76.2 mm L/10 instead of the earlier 45 mm weapon. Mobility ...model came to be called the A 34, and was then subjected to an intensive period of testing. Problems ...d for the first 150 T-34's, as the new tank was by then known. By 1940, the production programme

...ere not as striking as is traditionally thought, because although the Russian tank was superior in res-...ed itself to be superior in other aspects, especially in the design of its turret, engine, gun-sights and ...lopments which would be impossible to carry out on the T-34. Therefore, the Russians made modifi-...end of the year only 115 tanks had been completed, less than 20% of the number originally planned. ...ptation was needed than at first thought. Given the situation, and the enormous requirements of the ...ately for the Russians, the T-34 project went ahead, with production now concentrated in Stalingrad.

...it had its engine and transmission housed at the rear of the tank. It weighed 28 metric tons. The dri-...th a radio). The combat room was in the centre, with the commander and loader squeezed into a flo-...front, sloping at 60°, which was increased on successive models up to 65 mm. The sides also had

...exagonal shape on the final versions. ...nain armament was the L /11, but this was soon replaced by the more powerful F 34 L/41, 5. Rate ...l the final models up to one hundred. Access to many of these was complicated or even dangerous.

...isy. At 450 hp, it gave the tank a power ratio of 18hp/ton, living it a maximum speed of 53 kph. Its

...ar progressed, the Germans introduced new models that equalled or bettered it. Because of this, at ...not enter service. The improvements included the suspension, an increase in the tank's armour, and ...on chosen was an 85 mm D5T L/48.5, an anti-aircraft gun already in service. The hull's armour was

...e new gun and three crew members. It also had a higher rate of fire than the 76.2 mm model, up to ...st. One of the defects of this gun was it lacked high explosive ammunition, only having a fragmenta-...bility.

...he T-34/85 went on to serve with many different countries on four continents, almost up to the pre-

...nd the SU 100, armed with the powerful 100 mm D-10T, which was capable of penetrating 100 mm ...al with some third world countries up to the nineteen-seventies. The SU-122, with its 45 mm of fron-...the beginning of 1943. Some 1,100 being built.

THE SOVIET T-34

Stalin and Molotov attended a meeting in Moscow on 4th May 1938, in which the Komintern factory in Kharkov, manag
protected by sloping armour, and was armed with a 45 mm gun. Many of those present at the meeting raised objections,

This new prototype was designated the A 32 and had five wheels instead of four, only used tracks, and its armour w
tests proved very satisfactory and the armour was soon increased to 45 mm. With a few more minor modifications, the r
with the transmission and suspension led to many more minor modifications, but finally in 1939, production was ordere
was for the manufacture of 600 tanks at two factories (in Kharkov and Stalingrad).

In the summer of 1940, two *Panzer III's* were bought in order to compare them with the T-34, and the initial results w
pect to the three most important features required in a tank, armour, mobility and firepower, the *Panzer III* in fact show
communications. In short, it was a tank with the operational potential to be tactically superior, able to accomodate deve
cations to the design to try and compensate for any defects, but these were not brought into effect immediately. By the
The manufacture of such a new design exceeded the capacity of Soviet industry at that time, and a longer period of ada
Soviet armoured forces, the continuation of T-34 production was closely contested by those in favour of the BT-7. Fortun

The T-34 got over its teething problems and showed itself to be a formidable vehicle. It was a traditional design in that
ver sat at the front of the hull alongside the radio operator/machine gunner (although only command tanks were fitted w
orless turret. Access was through a large forward-opening hatch on the top of the turret. Hull armour was 45 mm at the
sloping armour and were 40 mm thick.

The turret underwent many modifications throughout the war, from being welded on the first model through to a cast

Crew space was very limited. The tank mounted a 76.2 mm main gun and a co-axial machine gun. The first model's
of fire did not exceed more than four shots per minute. The first models carried seventy-seven 76.2 mm projectiles, anc
The maximum thickness of the turret armour was 60 mm.

The V-2-34 12 cylinder diesel engine, with many of its components made of aluminium, was magnificent, although no
wide tracks, up to 55 cm, gave it excellent mobility over rouge terrain. Range was 400 kilometres.

When it first entered combat it made a great impression on the Germans, who had nothing similar. However, as the v
the beginning of 1942, the Soviets began studying improvements that led to a new tank, the T-43, which in the end did
a three-man-turret. At the end of 1943, they decided to re-design the tank, giving it a heavier main armament. The weap
60 mm at the front (up to 75 mm on some models), and 90 mm on the turret. Weight was 32 metric tons.

The main difference between the two versions was in the turret, which was much more spacious in order to house th
ten rounds per minute. From March 1944, the S-53 L/54.6 was installed, with a slightly better performance than the fir
tion round, which was much less effective. It carried 55 rounds. However, the three-man turret gave it much better opera

Almost 26,000 T-34/85s were built up to 1946. The total number of all variants of the T-34 was more than 65,000.
sent day, which is a testament to the design's durability, as well as its reliability and simplicity.

Several tank-hunter versions were built, following the German example, such as the SU-85 (around 2,700 were built) a
of armour at a 60º angle from a range of 1,500 metres, entering service in January 1945, and continued to be operation
tal armour, was armed with the M-30 122 mm howitzer, and had a crew of five. It entered service in limited numbers at

The offensive begins

Soviet intelligence was well informed of German preparations, and the defenders artillery launched a counter-barrage three hours before the start of the attack, which while not causing many casualties, did create disorganisation and cause delay for many units. An attempt at a preventative air strike had a very different outcome, as the Germans had been alerted by their *Freya* radars, and the *Luftwaffe* was able to intercept the Soviet bombers and fighter-bombers without difficulty, preventing them from reaching their targets and causing heavy losses.

In the north, *9.Armee* advanced towards Poniry and Olkovatka, with the *Tiger I's* in the vanguard, and with the *Ferdinands* wreaking havoc amongst the Russians. The first defensive line was breached, with the advance continuing on to the second line, but without being able to make any breaks. The following days saw a battle of attrition, which in Poniry, resembled the Great War. Moreover, Rokossovsky ordered his tanks to be dug in, and prohibited any counter-attack against the Panzers, such was the carnage being caused by the German tanks. On 9th July, with the opposition stiffening, as well as a constant flow of supplies being brought to the defenders, the Germans ceased offensive operations. On the 11th a new attack was launched against Olkovatka, but on the 12th, the Soviets unleashed «*Operation Kutuzov*», a counter-attack from the north, forcing the Germans to call off the offensive and go on to the defensive. They had lost the initiative.

On the southern front, the *4.Panzerarmee* started its attack after a three-hour-delay, due to the Soviet barrage. A *Panther* battalion strayed into a minefield and was knocked out by artillery fire.

Furthermore, many of these new tanks suffered problems with their engine cooling and started to show a tendency to spontaneously catch fire. The

A *Stug III*, mounting a 7.5 cm L/48, together with two other armoured vehicles. In the foreground is one of the rare Sdkfz 262. The *Stug III* tank-hunters maintained their effectiveness to the end of the war, further proof of the worth of the *Panzer III* design, on whose chassis the Stug was built. (Bundesarchiv)

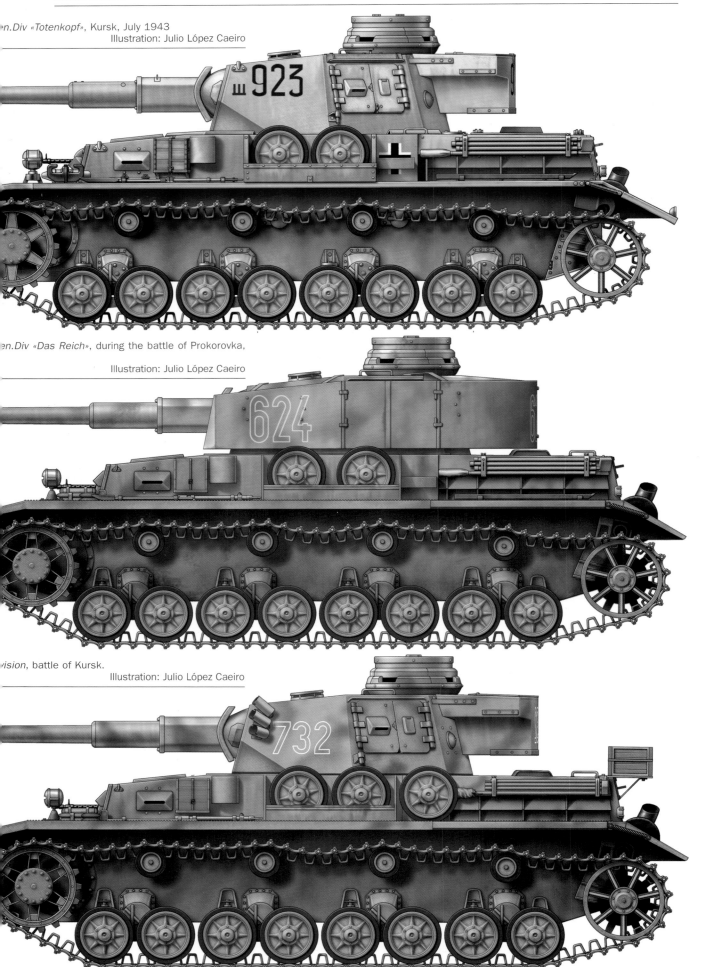

n.Div «Totenkopf», Kursk, July 1943
Illustration: Julio López Caeiro

n.Div «Das Reich», during the battle of Prokorovka,

Illustration: Julio López Caeiro

vision, battle of Kursk.
Illustration: Julio López Caeiro

Mittlerer Schützenpanzerwagen (7.5 cm) Sd.Kfz. 251/9 Ausf. C of 19.Panzer-Division. Belgorod Sector, July 1943
Illustration: Julio López Caeiro

this advance was outstanding given the circumstances, they were still short of the 30 kilometres a day that were foreseen as being necessary in order to close off the Kursk pocket, which had to be done in four days.

During the days that followed, progress was slow, as the *II.SS-Panzerkorps* continued to throw back the repeated Soviet counter-attacks on their exposed right flank. The German advance slowly overcame the Soviet defences, gaining room to maneouvre. On the sixth day, they advanced an average of 8 kilometres, although the *11.Panzer-Division* penetrated ten, breaking through the second Soviet defence line at Doubrova. The II.SS-Panzerkorps penetrated a little further, also breaking through the second line, claiming to have destroyed 150 tanks and guns in the process. The Russians began pouring in more and more reserves to block the route to Oboyan. On the 8th, the 5th Guards Tank Army deployed behind the third defensive line, heading towards Prokorovka. This was the last day that the Germans made any notable progress, against a defence that was being constantly being reinforced in order to replace the heavy losses it was suffering.

2nd Guards Tank Corps, which was readying to attack the exposed German flank, was surprised by the *Luftwaffe*, and for the first time in history, an armoured unit was destroyed from the air. The new Hs 129B, armed with 30 mm cannon, as well as SD-1 and SD-2 fragmentation bombs, supported by Fw 190F fighter bombers, sewed death and destruction amongst the Soviet column, destroying more than 50 tanks and numerous armoured vehicles in less than an hour.

In spite of this spectacular success on the part of the *Luftwaffe*, Soviet aircraft on the southern front were able to fly more missions than the Germans, despite suffering heavy losses. On the second day alone, the Russians flew 1,632 sorties compared to 899 by the Germans.

On the 8th, it was clear to both sides that Oboyan was the key to the battle. Soviet commanders were concious that their main enemy in the sector was the *II.SS-Panzerkorps*, and so they deployed the 69th Army, 5th Guards Tank Army and 2nd Tank Corps behind the third defensive belt to confront it. That day the *XXXVIII.Panzerkorps* advanced about ten kilometres, their maximum advance during the attack. During the days to come they would advance no more than five or six kilometres. *«LSSAH»* was able to penetrate deeper and lost contact with its neighbouring Corps, while *«Das Reich»* advanced about thirteen kilometres, arriving some ten kilometres from the Soviet third line of defence. In the evening its armoured regiment went to the aid of *«LSSAH»*, which had had some of its units overwhelmed in a massive counter-attack

A battery of *Hummels* open fire. The Hummel consisted of a 15 cm gun fitted on a *Panzer IV* chassis, an outstandingly effective combination, which, for the Whermacht, was never made in sufficient numbers.

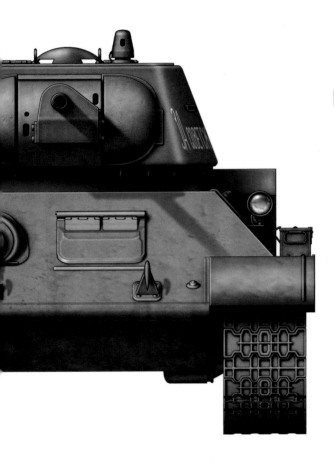

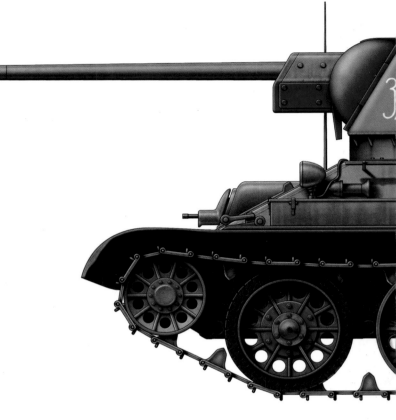

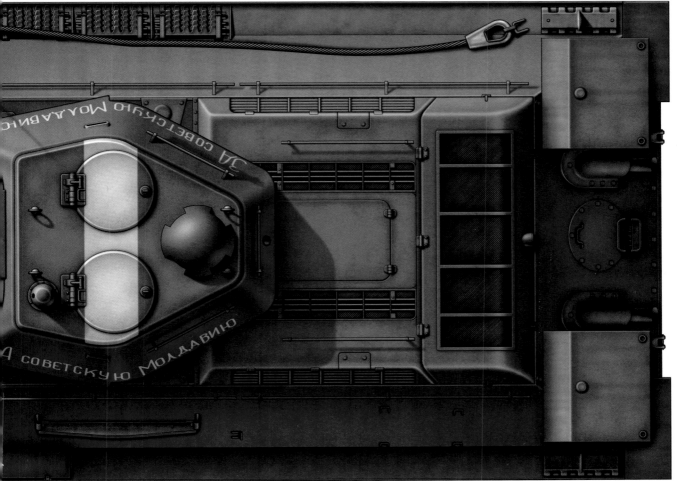

Each *Panzerdivision* had a panzergrenadier battalion mounted in half-tracks. These troops had a formidable degree of mobility and firepower. In the top photo are various Sd.Kfz 251/1, and in the bottom, a Sd.Kfz 251/10, armed with the 3,7 cm anti-tank gun. (Bundesarchiv)

worst losses suffered by the Germans on the southern front were on the first day.

The German attack developed according to a fairly simple plan. A typical tank battalion, of around 50 tanks, deployed itself along a front of more or less 1,200 metres, with two companies at the head, one company forming the second line and another the third line. Each of the two companies forming the vanguard deployed two platoons of five tanks along a 500-metre front, that is to say one tank every 50 metres. Each company deployed its tanks to a depth of 500 metres, so that

the battalion was deployed to a total depth of 1,500 metres. The first line was tasked with attacking the enemy defences, especially the enemy artillery, a task for which the *Tiger* was particularly well equipped. The *Tiger's* 8.8 cm main gun could knock out the Russian field pieces from a range of more than 2,000 metres, well out of the effective range of the Russian guns, as well as their tanks. Contrary to myth, the *Tiger* was very effective at making breakthroughs, and losses were minimal. Most of the tanks lost were put out of action due to mines, and most of these were later recovered and

repaired in either a few hours or days at most. To illustrate this, the *s.Panzer Abteilung 503*, in two days of fighting, suffered the permanent loss of only two of its *Tiger I's*. The unit started the attack with 30 tanks, and 23 remained operational after 48 hours of combat.

As the evening drew near, Vatutin, under strong pressure, ordered the 1st Tank Army to launch a counter-attack to support the second defensive line, but its commanding officer, General Katukov, was very reticent due to his lack of ability in offensive maneouvres. At the same time, the 2nd and 5th Guards Tank Corps were ordered to attack towards Bielgorod. On the first day of the battle, the Waffen SS armoured units had made a breach 20 kilometres wide and fifteen deep in the Soviet defence. During that day, they had destroyed the 375th Infantry Division, and repulsed the continued counter-attacks of the 51st Guards Division and 230th Tank Regiment. Although

made by a large formation of T-34's. In the subsequent fighting, which continued until night fell, almost a hundred Soviet tanks were destroyed. That day, the *II.SS-Panzerkorps* claimed a total of 184 Soviet tanks destroyed, rising to more than 400 over the first four days.

The repeated, tenacious Soviet counter-attacks finally managed to halt the German advance. At the end of the day the Germans found themselves still about 100 kilometres from Kursk. Vatutin received very clear orders from Stalin to hold his ground at all cost. His first decision was to dig in his tanks up to their turrets, so as to convert them into mini-fortresses. Although this measure had some defensive justification, it was completely contrary to the concept of the tank as a weapon of maneouvre. Despite many voices in opposition, who were in favour of using the tanks mobility, Stalin approved the immobilization of 1st Tank Army.

On the 9th, Hoth decided to take advantage of the success of the Waffen SS and move the axis of attack, giving the SS time to reorganise. Therefore, *Armee Abteilung Kempf* not only had to protect the flank of the *SS-Panzerkorps*, but also penetrate the defences to intercept the counter-attacks of the Soviet armoured reserves. Again, *II.SS-Panzerkorps* repulsed several Soviet counter-

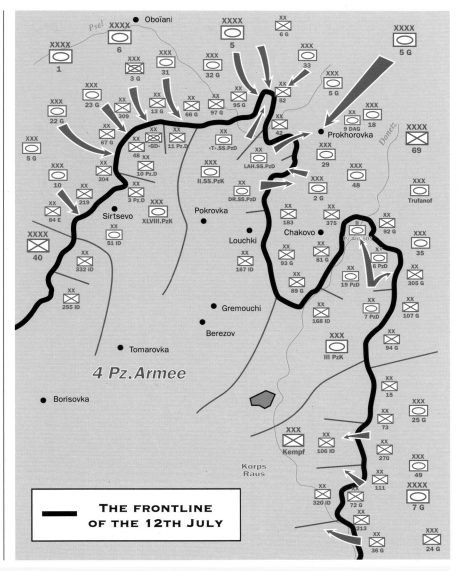

THE FRONTLINE OF THE 12TH JULY

GERMAN ORDER OF BATTLE (SOUTHERN FRONT)

A Total of 50 divisions, 10 of them *Panzer*, 13 recently arrived from France and 7 of dubious quality. 11 of the infantry divisions were of high quality. All together there were 776,907 men, 1,813 tanks and 610 tank-hunters, of these 132 were *Tiger I's*, 208 *Panther Ausf D's* and 90 *Ferdinands*, as well as 7,417 guns and mortars, and 1,830 aircraft.

North: *9. Armee*

West: *2. Armee*

South: *4. Panzerarmee and Armee Abteilung Kempf.*

The *4. Panzerarmee* was the strongest element in the German order of battle:
    52. Armee Korps: 57th, 255th and 332nd Infantry Divisions
    48. Panzerkorps: «Grossdeutschland», 11.*Panzer*, 167th Infantry Division, 3.*Panzer* (reserve),
        SPz Abt 502 (with 14 *Tiger I's*), *Panzer Regiment 39* (with 204 *Panthers*) and *Sturmgeschütz Abt. 911*. Elite units with the mission of making breakthroughs and exploiting them.

II SS Panzerkorps:
    «LSSAH»: 107 tanks (67 *Panzer IV* s and 13 *Tiger I's*), plus 34 *Stug III's*, 20 *Marder III's* and 20 7.5 cm Pak 40 anti-tank guns. 85% of its effectives were in armoured vehicles and half-tracks.
    «Das Reich»: 145 tanks (33 *Panzer IV's*, 12 *Tigers* and 25 T-34's), as well as 10 *Marder III's*. This Division was the strongest in terms of numbers of panzergrenadiers (8 battalions).
    «Totenkopf»: 139 tanks (44 *Panzer IV's* and 10 *Tigers*). This Division was deficient in numbers of 5 cm Pak 38s (5 out of a theoretical strength of 39) and also armoured vehicles (45% of effectives).

The *Waffen SS* had a total of 179 guns, *138 Nebelwerfers* and 450 tanks of all types, including 156 *Panzer IV's*, 117 *Panzer III's*, 95 *StuG III's* and 35 *Tigers*.

Armee Abteilung Kempf: 6th, 7th and 19th Panzer, 168th infantry.

A Sd.Kfz 10 half-track of «Das Reich» passes the remains of a Churchill tank. Numbers of these tanks were sent to the Soviet Union, but were not very appreciated by the Russians, who tended to regard all the anglo-american tanks they received in much the same way. (Bundesarchiv)

attacks, inflicting heavy losses, while «Totenkopf» consolidated a bridgehead north of the river Psel. If Prokorovka fell, it would be possible to surround Oboyan from the east and open the route to Kursk. The battle could still be won. Nevertheless, on the 10th, an event with great strategic implications occurred, the Allied invasion of Sicily, reminding the Germans that a second front had opened up in the Mediterranean theatre. Vatutin was very concious of the importance of Oboyan as a key position, and concentrated all the units he could in an effort to block the route. The hard hit Soviet Air Force received the order to concentrate on mass in that sector. However, in spite of these measures, on the 10th, a Kampfgruppe composed of a Panzergrenadier regiment, a battalion of StuG III's, the «LSSAH» Tiger company, supported by the «LSSAH» divisional artillery and a mortar battalion, broke through the Russian

defences, destroying the remains of the 51st and 42nd Guards Divisions. II.SS-Panzerkorps had bitten into the third defensive belt and was breaking it up, but it was the only unit to have done so.

Faced with this situation, Vatutin reacted by ordering a massive counter-attack with all his units for the 12th, in the Prokorovka sector. To make this attack he had Rotmistrov's 5th Guards Tank Army, which was already in position on the 10th. The counter-attack was to have some ambitious objectives, 1st Tank Army and 6th Guards Army were to attack the left flank of the XLVIII Panzerkorps, while 5th Guards Tank Army and elements of 1st Tank Army had the task of forcing themselves between that unit and the SS-Panzerkorps, then Rotmistrov, together with the rest of 1st Tank Army were to advance south in order to link up with the rest of the Soviet forces,

encircling and destroying the bulk of 4.Panzerarmee.

Manstein ordered Kempf to make one final effort to link up with the SS armoured divisions in Prokorovka. On the 11th, Rotmistrov had already had to send some of his units into combat as a result of the German advance, putting Vatutin's planned counter-attack at risk. On that day, his 2nd Corps lost around 120 vehicles in halting the Waffen SS. On the same day, the «LSSAH» had taken a sovjoce (a type of collective farm) designated "October" and the surrounding heights a few kilometres from Prokorovka, at a cost of a 200 men, but had destroyed 21 tanks and 45 guns in the process. «Das Reich» was involved in hard fighting against the 183rd Rifle Division and the 2nd Tank Corps, while «Totenkopf» was defending its bridgehead north of the Psel and trying to breakthrough the lines of the 95th Infantry Division.

Worse still for the Russians, during the night of 11th-12th July, the 6.Panzer-Division managed to establish a bridgehead over the Donetz following a daring raid. If the following day, the III Panzerkorps were able to link up with II.SS- Panzerkorps in Prokorovka, the Soviet 69th Army would be encircled and destroyed. Furthermore, on the German left flank, «Grossdeutschland» reorganizad during the night, ready

Pz.Kpfw. VI Ausf E Tiger I of 13.Kp tank regiment of 1.SS-Pz.Gren.Div «Leibstandarte Adolf Hitler», march 1943. During the Prokhorovka battle, the 13th company claimed to have destroyed 151 tanks, 85 AT guns and four enemy batteries.
Illustration: Julio López Caeiro

to support the advance of *11.Panzer-Division* towards Oboyan.

So it was then, that this unheard of Russian village came to be the scenario of the collision between to opposing plans, Vatutin's decisive counter-attack and the final German effort to open the route to Oboyan. If the Germans succeeded in making a breakthrough, the way to Kursk would be open, and the Soviets were using up their reserves.

The Battle of Prokorovka.

The Prokorovka battlefield is not simply an immense plain, but rather more undulating, with hills and narrow water courses, which break up the terrain. A cloudy, muggy day with scattered showers greeted the breaking dawn on 12th July. The battle was to consist of numerous individual attacks and counter-attacks over a 20 kilometre arc. As the German advance began, Rotmistrov decided to bring forward his planned attack two hours, employing four corps in two or three waves, and leaving the 260 tanks of 5th Mechanized Corps and 53rd Guards Regiment in reserve. 18th Corps' 190 tanks would confront «Totenkopf» and «LSSAH», which at the same time would be attacked by the 212 tanks of 29th Corps, which had been given the sovjoce «October» as one of its objectives. «Das Reich» was to be attacked by two weakned corps, the 2nd and 3rd Guards, which had

200 tanks between them. Therefore, around 600 Soviet tanks (more than half of them T-34's) were to face 211 German tanks (most of them *Panzer III's* and *Panzer IV's*, and fifteen *tigers*) plus 57 *StuG III's* and about a dozen *Marder IIIs*. Apart from these 600 tanks, Rotmistrov had the support of several Rifle Divisions and a large amount of artillery (the 17th Mortar Brigade alone had one hundred and eight 120 mm tubes).

A little before nine o'clock in the morning, while «LSSAH's» advanced along the valley to the north of the sovjoce, Rotmistrov's tanks received the codeword "Steel" and surged forward to attack. «LSSAH» had been informed by reconnaissance aircraft of what was heading for them, and when they reached the crest of a hill, they could see two brigades of T-70's and T-34's from 29th Corps sweeping towards them, loaded with "tank riders". At the same time, «Totenkopf» faced a similar attack from part of 18th Corps, while «Das Reich» became the target for two tank corps. What happened next was to be repeated throughout the day in the area around Prokorovka.

Badly coordinated, without radios and concious of their technical inferiority, the Russian tankers had been ordered by Rotmistrov to charge at all speed towards the German tanks in order to close the range and be in

a position to fire at the flanks of the *panzers* at almost point blank range, and overcome them with numbers. This was their only possibility of success out in the open. If they could manage to get near the panzers' flanks, overwhelm the anti-tank screen and break the cresent-shaped attack formation known as the *panzerkeil*, then maybe they would be able to cause serious losses amongst the German tanks, something that they had not been able to achieve up to then.

However, things were not to turn out that way. The German anti-tank screen of 7.5 and 5 cm guns, as well as the tank hunters, caused many losses amongst the T-34's and T-70's as soon as they had them in their sights, outside the effective range of the Soviet tanks, which on top of this, were having to fire on the move, minimising their chances of hitting their targets. The *Panzer III* were to prove deadly against the T-70's. The few *Tiger I's* present soon demonstrated their worth, firing from a range of 2,500 metres and scoring repeated hits on target. The panzergrenadiers reaped a deadly harvest among the "tank riders". Only the 31st Tank Brigade managed to get through the German lines and reach a battery of 15 cm howitzers, managing to destroy them before the Soviet tanks were systematically erradicated. The Soviet second wave sufffered a similar fate.

In spite of their appalling casualties, the repeated Russian attacks prevented the *II.SS-Panzerkorps* from continuing its advance, even forcing the Germans to retreat a few kilometres in some sectors. In particular, the attacks made by 2nd and 29th Corps, together with a battalion of SU-122s and a Parachute Brigade, supported by a tremendous artillery barrage, managed to bring the *«LSSAH»* to a halt just a few kiliometres from Prokorovka. *«Totenkopf»*, for its part, had managed to penetrate ten kilometres to the north of the Psel, the greatest extent of the German advance on the 12th. *«Das Reich»* had caused the Soviets serious losses, but was still hardly able to advance, and what is more, it was unable to support *«LSSAH»*.

At the end of the day, the Germans had suffered moderate losses, at most no more than fifteen tanks were completely destroyed, not the mythical three hundred and fifty. Many, it is true, were damaged, but these were repaired. In fact, on the 11th there were 268 tanks operational, and on the thirteenth, two days later, there were still 227 intact. The number of men lost was about 800. The Soviets however, lost more than 250 tanks and a further 400 were either broken down or badly damaged. Rotmistrov's tanks had been massacred, but *II.SS-Panzerkorps* had not achieved its objectives. Neither, for that matter had the other German units succeeded in linking up with the *Waffen SS*, although the bridgehead on the Donetz had been

preserved. At the price of ceasing to exist as an effective unit, 5th Guards Corps had stopped the German advance.

On the 13th, the battle continued in intensity, as the Russians tried to reduce *«Totenkopf's»* bridgehead, and the Germans fought to maintain their positions, and at the same time, *«LSSAH»* in particular, to continue the advance and support their neighbouring units. The Russian defence became ever stronger, with many dug in T-34's and heavy artillery barrages, while the determined counter-attacks continued in such a way that by the end of the day *«Totenkopf»* had given up most of the ground it had won.

On the 14th the fighting moved southwards, where *«Das Reich»* was trying to link up with *III Panzerkorps* in the midst of the Soviet attacks. However, 400 tanks from 4th Guards Tank Corps and the 1st Mechanized Corps took up position behind Rotmistrov's forces, as if they were needed. The battle was decided. It was clear Kursk was beyond the Germans' reach. The Sicily landing had been consolidated, and the Red Army unleashed two offensives on the flanks of the salient, one in the Orel sector and the other at Mius, which were to result in some of the most savage fighting of the whole war.

The Germans had demonstrated an enormous tactical superiority over the Red Army in this phase of the war. They were masters in the art of using tactical groups combing different arms, well suppor-

ted by effective artillery that included *Nebelwerfers* and the *Luftwaffe*, with which they were able to break through the first two Soviet lines of defence. The famous "pakfronts" did not prove to be very effective against the Germans' combined arms tactics. The Red Army was obliged to commit all the reserves of the Voronez and Steppe Fronts to stop Hausser, and these were decimated in the process. In fact, these two Soviet Fronts lost around 1,250 tanks, approximately 50% of their tank force. The infantry divisions performed well, holding the flanks, with only one division giving way.

Nevertheless, if the tactical victory is clear, then so is the strategic victory, and that at least belonged to the Red Army. The massacre at Prokorovka, and the enormous losses suffered by the Russians during the battle, was the price they had to pay for stopping the Germans. They succeeded in wearing the German attack down and the Soviet counter-offensives forced them back. This lead to a change in the strategic balance on the Eastern Front which was to last until the end of the war.

The controversy regarding the casualty figures.

The battle of Prokorovka was one of the crucial moments in the Kursk

A *Wespe* belonging to *«Grossdeutschland»*. Carrying the proven 10.5 cm FH 18 howitzer, this self-propelled artillery piece mounted on the *Panzer II* chassis remained in service until 1945.

Illustration: Julio López Caeiro

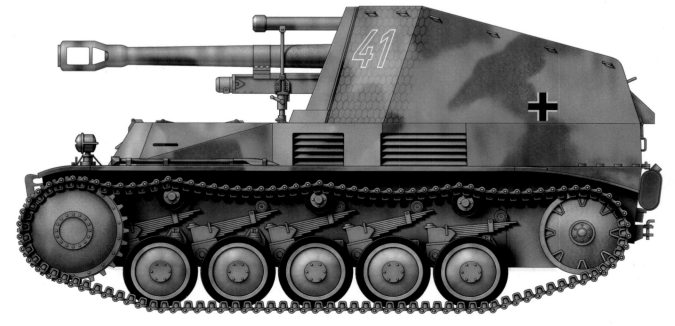

StuG III F/8 of the *StuG. Abt.* of *2.SS-Pz.Gren.Div «Das Reich»*.
Illustration: Julio López Caeiro

campaign, and became something of a myth until recent years. At the hand of well-known authors such as Clark, Ericsson and Jukes, who used sources like Rokossovsky's memoirs, came the idea of two enormous armoured masses charging towards each other under the sun over an immense plain, like some great medieval battle. According to these sources, the more than 600 tanks of *II.SS-Panzerkorps* (with numerous *Tigers* and *Panthers*) fought Rotmistrov's 800 tanks in a decisive battle. Although the T-34's suffered many losses at the beginning, charged on at top speed and managed to get in among the panzers, resulting in an extraordinary melee in which even the *Tigers* were knocked out by the Russian tanks. At the end of the day the Germans lost 350 tanks and the Red Army a few more, and with the Germans in headlong retreat, leaving the Red Army in possession of the battlefield....

The reality was somewhat different. German and Soviet archives released in the last few years that have been studied and published by authors such as Nipe y Glantz, show that events were very different...

During the whole of July the *II.SS- Panzerkorps* lost 8.000 men. In the Kursk offensive alone it lost 100 tanks put out of action, but only 36 were totally destroyed (three of them *Tiger I's*). 8% of its half-tracks were destroyed. *«LSSAH»* had 17 less tanks operational on the 13th than it had had on the 12th; *«Das Reich»*, 14 less, and *«Totenkopf»*, approximately 45 less. The maximum number of tanks put out of action on the 12th can in no case be more than 82, from a total of 211 which had been operational at the start of the day. Nevertheless, in spite of being considerably less than the traditionally accepted figure, it still represents a

high proportion given the total of tanks available.

5th Guards Tank Army had at least 222 T-34's, 89 T-70's, 12 *Churchills* and 11 Su self-propelled guns totally destroyed in three days of fighting. To these figures can be added the many tanks which broke down and were therefore left out of action for days or weeks, as well as the more than 600 guns of varying calibres destroyed and 7,000 men taken prisoner.

In the whole of the Kursk battle, the Red Army lost 1,650 tanks and almost 180,000 men, as well as 460 aircraft, while Germans losses were 70,000 men and 62 aircraft. Their tank losses were a few more than 500, including the Orel salient.

Bottom, is a T-70 light tank armed with a 45 mm gun. This vehicle was all too frequently employed as a medium tank, with inevitably high losses as a result. It had been conceived as a reconnaisssance tank, but made up a significant percentage of Soviet armoured forces in 1943.
Illustration: Julio López Caeiro

PAVEL SEMENOVICH RYBALKO

Was born on 23rd October 1894 into a family of humble origin, in a village in the province of Kharkov, in the Ukraine. After elementary schooling, he worked in a sugar factory until the start of the Great War, in which he served as an infantryman on the Galician front, where he was wounded.

Rybalko enlisted in the Red Guard soon after the start of the October Revolution, and during the first months of the Russian Civil War served as a political officer with the Yuca Partisans against German troops in the Ukraine, and in a short time became commander of his unit. In 1919 he was a political officer on the Turkistan front, and later, helped set up the Bolshevik Government in Bashkir. He met his future wife while combatting a typhus epedemic in the region. In 1920 he was transferred to the 1st Cavalry Army, where he served with future outstanding commanders such as Timoshenko and Budenny. At the end of the Civil War he took command of the 61st Cavalry Regiment, and while with them gained much experience in mobile operations.

Nevertheless he remained concious of the fact that while he had gained a lot of combat experience, he lacked the basic training of an officer, so he immersed himself in self study to make up for this. He was posted to Moscow in 1924, and in 1926, was selected to attend what was then called the Red Army Senior Officers course (later the Frunze Military Academy). He graduated with outstanding results in certain subjects, and was then posted as an advisor to the Mongel Army on the Chinese frontier, and later commanded a regiment of cossack cavalry for three years. Then, he spent another three years at the recently created Frunze Academy, where his thirst for knowledge and military eruditeness made him stand out, something unusual among Soviet officers of the time. In fact, he could be described as an intellectual. After graduating with honours, he worked on the reorganisation of the Soviet armoured force, and studied the theories of Fuller and von Kleist. During Stalin's purges he was mili-

tary attache in Warsaw, although he had little sympathy for the Poles. In 1940 he was Professor of tactics at the tank school in Kazan.

While Rybalko was at Kazan imparting his classes, Operation Barbarossa began, and to his intense frustration and desperation, despite repeated requests, he was refused an active service command. Finally, with the help of his old comrade Yeremenko, he was attached to the Staff of 3rd Tank Army in May 1942, although with some reserve on the part of the High Command.

Rybalko soon became aware of the deficiencies in the Soviet tank arm: lack of cooperation between arms, contempt for the artillery, logistics chaos and misconceptions on the use of the tank as a weapon. Stalin finally decided to appoint him commander of 3rd Tank Army in September 1942, a post he held to the end of the war, and with which he would go down in history.

Six Tank Armies were created during the war, detailed to operate independently, following Guderian's theories. They all served with such distinction that by the end of the war all had received the coveted "Guards" title. 3rd Tank Army was the first to receive this distinction in May 1943.

After reorganizing his unit at the end of 1942, it saw action on the Voronez front at the beginning of 1943, until the recapture of Kharkov on 25th February. However Manstein's counter-attack destroyed most of the Soviet forces in this area and recovered most of the lost territory. Rybalko learned much from these operations, and on several occasions was able to temporarily halt the German advance, using *ad hoc* mobile groups. He was promoted to Lieutenant General at the end of February 1943, and was awarded the Order of Suvorov 1st Class. Rybalko soon drew very relevant conclusions regarding long range armoured operations, night movements and operations over difficult terrain.

Following the reorganization of his worn out and decimated unit, he took part in the battle of Kursk on the central front under the command of Rokossovsky, where he distinguished himself despite chronic logistics shortages. He played a

decisive role in the Ukraine offensive to liberate Kiev at the end of 1943. He carried out a model maneouvre, making a night advance over difficult ground, along two axis, maintaining radio silence, and using deception and the maskirova to mask his advance. After crossing a large minefield, he succeeded in establishing a bridgehead on the western bank of the Dnieper, with Kiev being finally recaptured on the 6th November.

During the first months of 1944, there were many operations to recapture the Ukraine in which 3rd Tank Army acted very effectively as a mobile group, breaking through the German front line and making deep penetrations into enemy territory, culminating in the capture of Lvov on 27th July.

The next big operation in which 3rd Tank Army participated was the advance into Silesia in January 1945, where, after breaking through the German defences on the first day, it succeeded in establishing a bridgehead on the Oder on the 23rd. At the end of the war it took part in the bloody battle for Berlin, as part of Koniev's 1st Ukrainian Front, attacking the city from the south. Its last operation of the war was the conquest of Prague, which was also a model example of a mobile operation over difficult terrain.

At the end of 1945, Rybalko was promoted to Marshall. He was a two times Heroe of the Soviet Union. He died of natural causes on 28th August 1948 while he was working on the remodelling of the Soviet armoured force.

Rybalko was the most distinguished Soviet tank commanders of the Second World War. He understood perfectly the concept of the tank as a weapon for creating a breakthrough, and its capabilities and the possibilities it held. This was in spite of his beginnings as a political officer and his late start in his military education. His personal charisma and his influence over the troops under his command was enormous. He had immense confidence in his own abilities and was hard-working and methodical, showing unlimited resolve in overcoming obstacles, and an extraordinary pragmatism and determination to solve problems himself.

VILLERS BOCAGE 1944: WITTMANN'S MOMENT ARRIVES.

Although Caen was a D-Day objective, the British failure to capture it as planned led to a long struggle to break the resulting stalement. The operation had already been designated *«Perch»* before the invasion. The British 22nd Armoured Brigade, reinforced by the 8th, was to advance via Tilly, towards Villers-Bocage, in order to take the hills in the area of Mont Pincon. However, *«Panzer Lehr»* had brought the British advance to a halt, and Tilly was not taken. A little towards the west, the Americans manager to advance a bit further against the German *352.Infanterie-Division*, which had caused them so many problems at *Omaha* beach, but which was now exhausted after various days of hard fighting, and had not received any reinforcements. Facing the whole of the American V Corps, it was forced to withdraw, leaving a gap between itself and *«Panzer Lehr»*. At last XXX Corps had an opportunity, so its staff developed a plan to penetrate the German lines and attack Caen from the rear.

Dempsey's Second Army had been awaiting favourable circums-

tances to deploy 7th Armoured Division, with the objective of breaking through the German front in the Caen sector, but so far this situation had not arisen, but now the opportunity was to present itself. In the first week of the invasion, XXX Corps was the main element of Second Army west of Caen, and was under the command of Lieutnant-General Gerry Bucknall. His main formations were 7th Armoured Division and the 49th and 50th Infantry Divisions, as well as 8th Armoured Brigade and the 56th Infantry Brigade. The 49th Division was a newly formed unit, and only recently arrived in France, and which Montgomery did not consider ready to take part in an offensive.

On the 11th, Dempsey was aware of the opportunity which had presented itself and unleashed 7th Armoured Division, covering the gap with other units. The Division had to advance along a single road, with 22nd Armoured *Brigade* in the van, followed by the 131st Infantry Brigade. At 1200 on the 12th, Brigadier Hinde, commander of 22nd Armoured Brigade, met with the chief of the Division, Gene-

A *Tiger* I of *«Leibstandarte»* in Normandy. In the difficult Bocage terrain, it was the ideal defensive tank. (Bundesarchiv)

ral Erskine, and received instructions for the attack. His objective was to go round the enemy's flank and take the hills north-east of Villers-Bocage. Hinde was a colourful character, an ameteur naturalist, unworried for his personal safety, and who had been involved in several curious incidents during the desert war due to his hobbies.

The advance was led by the *4th County of London Yeomanry («Sharpshooters»),* commanded by Viscount Arthur Cranley. This unit, a veteran of the desert campaign, had already suffered some losses in the fighting in the bocage for hardly any real gain. They were well aware that the terrain was very different from that they had known so far, and their advance had to be cautious and prudent. The *7th Hussars*, equipped with *Cromwell* tanks, ccovered the flank, while the *11th Hussars* (only the Headquarters and C squadrons) acted as reconnaissance with their *Daimler* armoured cars. Direct support for the *«Sharpshooters»* was provided by A Coy, 1st Battalion, the

A *Cromwell* of 5th RTR, followed by a variety of other armoured vehicles, the first being a *Bren Carrier*. The *Cromwell* was better than the *Sherman* in some aspects, and represented the maximum development of the cruiser concept, until the appearance of the magnificent *Comet*, which arrived too late to see much combat.

A *Stuart* Mk V of 7th *Armoured Division* on the move through typical Norman countryside.

Rifle Brigade, mounted in *White* half-tracks, but without their reconnaissance section.

Following in the wake of the tanks were 1/7th *Queen's Infantry*, 5th *Regiment Royal Horse Artillery* (equipped with 25 pdr *Sextons*), I Coy, 1st Battalion, the *Rifle Brigade*, 5th RTR and 260th AT battery, *Royal Artillery*. This long ponderous column advanced along a single road, as using another would have meant entering too far into the American sector, which in the best of cases would have caused confu-

sion, and in the worst, casualties from friendly fire. The advance began on the evening of the 12th, and by 20.00 they had begun to encounter the first signs of resistance in Livry, when a *Cromwell* was knocked out by an enemy anti-tank gun. The German position, a single PaK 40 with some infantry, was wiped out after two hours of fighting. As night fell, Hinde, anxious avoid the Germans discovering their position, called a halt to the advance until dawn the next day. During the first hours of night, the reconnaissance units made contact with the Americans, as well as the extreme end of *Panzer Lehr's* positions. Meanwhile, the rest of the force camped to the north of Livry in a typical Normandy drizzle.

The advance to Villers-Bocage. 13th June 1944.

The vanguard of the British advance broke through to Livry a little after 0500, they found the village abandoned and continued on towards Briquessard, Tracy and finally, Villers-Bocage. The advance was slow; with the tanks at the head leap-frogging

22ND ARMOURED BRIGADE

- 4th County of London Yeomanry (the «Sharpshooters»)
- 5th Royal Tank Regiment
- 1st Battalion (Motorized) the Rifle Brigade

Attached Units: 7th Hussars
                   11th Hussars
- 1/7th Battalion Queen's Royal Regiment of Infantry,
- 5th Regiment Royal Horse Artillery
- 260th anti-tank battery, Royal Artillery.

forward in short movements. The first tank would move forward to a covered position, stop and observe, looking for enemy activity. If nothing was sighted, then the next tank would move forward, passing the first, which would be providing cover, and then stopping to start the whole process again. At the back of the column, the confusion, impatience and the lack of kowledge regarding the situation at the front made it difficult to maintain discipline on the march. All of this was due to the decision to make the advance along a single road, something which would have grave consequences if serious opposition was encountered.

At 0830, the first vehicles entered Villers-Bocage, to be greeted by the few inhabitants who had not left the previous day, before the commencement of the British artillery bombardment. Some even opened cafés and shops, which were soon filled with British soldiers. Villers-Bocage had around 1,000 inhabitants in 1944; it was a typical Norman market town, located at an important crossroads. The RN 175 ran through the town, linking Vire with Caen, the route passed through the town along two streets,

The *Daimler Mk II*, armed with the 2pdr, with its high road speed it was an excellent reconnaissance vehicle.

Illustration: Julio López Caeiro

The Sherman was the most numerous tank in service with the British Army in 1944.

the rue Pasteur and rue Clemenceau. The British column had to pass in an easterly direction along both, with one street continuing into the other, in order to reach the other side of the town. It took more than half an hour for the head of the column, following the RN 175, to arrive at its initial objective, the top of Hill 213, one and a half kilometres to the east of the town. At 0900, A Squadron reached Hill 213, with its tanks taking up defensive positions along the road. Almost a kilometre behind, A Coy, 1st Battalion the Rifle Brigade, on board their White half-tracks, left the road free for the rest of the

column. They were followed by two 6pdr anti-tank guns and three *Stuart* light tanks. Thirty metres behind them, inside the town, followed the «*Sharpshooters*» Staff, with their commander, Colonel Cranley. Cranley was worried about the lack of adequate reconnaissance and when Hinde arrived, he urged him to go to Hill 213 and check the situation for himself. Cranley arrived at the head of the column in an armoured vehicle to make sure things were going as planned. Hinde turned round and disappeared towards the rearguard

of the column. The next vehicles were four *Cromwells* under Major Carr, two artillery observation tanks and various other armoured vehicles, and behind them, four more *Stuart* reconnaissance tanks. Further behind, on the town's main street, the *Cromwells* of B Squadron were starting to arrive, with a *Firefly* at their head. The tanks halted and the crews dismounted their vehicles in the pleasingly tranquil atmosphere that greeted them.

Wittmann Hour Arrives

On the afternoon of the 12th, a platoon of *schwere SS-Panzer-Abteilung* 101 had just arrived in the area of Villers-Bocage, to support «*Panzer-Lehr*» and help close the breach that had opened in the front. Many of the *Tiger I's* had suffered mechanical problems of some kin, having driven non-stop from the Belgian frontier to Normandy, and only six of the *Tiger I's* had arrived at the front line. Com-

An M5 reconnaissance vehicle overtakes a column of *Sherman* tanks advancing in single file and maintaining a certain distance. Losses amongst reconnaissance tanks tended to be high.

manding the 2nd Company was *Obersturmführer* Michael Wittmann, Eastern Front tank ace, with more than one hundred tanks destroyed to his credit. His own tank, numbered 205, had broken down along the way, and he had boarded another.

At dusk, he had positioned his tanks, well camouflaged, some 200 metres south of the RN 175, in a farm called «*La Ciderie*», on the old Caen road, a little more than a kilometre to the north-east of Villers-Bocage. His presence went unnoticed by the British. 15 kilometres to the east, the ten *Tigers* under Captain Möbius, commander of the 1st company, had also recently arrived and were regrouping, while the 3rd company was still in Falaise, and would not take part in the action.

The commander of a *Tiger I* Ausf E tank inspecting the terrain around the site of his hidden vehicle. (ECPA-France).

On the morning of the 13th, the German crews saw to their surprise how a large column of British armoured vehicles was confidently passing along the road, and informed their chief, who arrived to take stock of the situation himself. Although his orders were to regroup and reinforce the Panzer-Lehr, the sight of the British tanks on Hill 213, with their half-tracks parked along the sides of the road, and with more tanks confidently grouped together on the outskirts of the town and back into the centre, led him to the decision to take advantage of such a golden opportunity.

Wittmann boarded the nearest *Tiger*, but this broke down after a few metres, so he transferred to the next, bearing the number 222. The other four *Tigers* followed behind, instinctively knowing what was to be done.

It was around 09.00 when Sargeant O'Connor, of the 1st section, shouted over the radio: "*for the love of God, move! There's a Tiger advancing, only 50 metres away*". Initially, four Tigers took part in the attack. The first tank destroyed was a Cromwell of A

Squadron, which erupted in a ball of flames. The next was a *Firefly*, which completely blocked the road. Leaving the other *Tigers* to finish off A Squadron on Hill 213, Wittmann directed his tank towards the RN 175, and then turned left on reaching it, and headed for Villers-Bocage. What he saw was an undreamed of opportunity, a long column of armoured vehicles taken completely by surprise, incapable of reacting to the emerging threat. The Tiger's 8.8 cm gun began picking off targets. One after the other, the *White* half-tracks, six pdr anti-tank guns and the *Stuart* tanks were destroyed, impotent before the sudden fury which had fallen on them. The panic stricken British infantry took refuge where they could from the heavy fire from the *Tiger's* machine guns. The British troops inside the town itself were unable to appreciate what was going on, the first sign they had of what was happening was seeing the *Stuarts* blown into the air. One of the *Cromwells* tried to fall back, but without successs. Major Carr saw a *Tiger* from his *Cromwell* and fired, hitting the turret from less than 100 metres, but it was use-

less, given the thickness of the German tank's armour. In the next instant, his tank was "brewed-up". Pushing a destroyed *Stuart* off the road, Wittmann's *Tiger* continued on its way, entering the town along the main street, rue Clemenceau, towards rue Pasteur.

Passing through a column of thick black smoke coming from the incinerated vehicle, the *Tiger* spotted another *Cromwell* about 40 metres away. One hit was enough to see it knocked out. The next tank was destroyed from a range of 20 metres. Wittmann did not see a *Cromwell* that had hurriedly concealed itself in a garden, and passed by, continuing to wreak havoc. The British tank, commanded by Captain Dyas, was unable to fire at the overtaking *Tiger*. The chaos in the British column was absolute, and attempts to control the situation proved futile. Some officers ordered the tanks and other armoured vehicles to scatter in the midst of the confusion, in the hope of escaping the destruction. To make

The commanders of a company of *Tiger I*'s receiving instructions before a mission. A varied collection of uniforms can be seen. (Bundesarchiv)

matters worse radio communication was breaking down, and the only reliable form of communication became by word of mouth. One of the British officers, Lieutenant Pierce, managed to move back along the column and inform various commanders of what was happening. Four *Stuarts* attempted to move off the street, while other tanks started reversing at speed. One of the few *Fireflies*, the only tank, with its 17 pdr gun, able to offer a serious threat to Wittmann, halted on a pavement at the entrance to rue Pasteur, and waited for the German tank.

When B Squadron's commander, *Major* Aird, became aware of what had happened to the reconnaissance units, he became blocked, unable to comprehend the situation clearly. He was soon joined by the C Squadron commander, *Major* McColl, who had the presence of mind and sufficient resolve to take decisions without awaiting orders from above, and began trying to bring the situation under control. Meanwhile, Wittmann continued up and down the street, destroying everything in his path. The turn came for the two artillery observation tanks, a *Sherman* and a *Cromwell*, which tried to turn round. The *Cromwell* had its 75 mm gun, but the *Sherman* had a false wooden one. The *Sherman* was in front of the *Cromwell*, which was almost completely hidden. An 88 mm projectile penetrated the turret and the *Sherman* began to burn. The *Cromwell* tried to escape, and turn round on a nearby property, but became immobilized when one of its tracks stuck. When the crew saw the *Tiger* moving towards them, traversing its gun ready to fire, they abandoned the tank just in time. The 88mm projectile passed cleanly through under the turret of the British tank. While this was happening, Captain Dyas' *Cromwell* had overtaken *Wittmann*, and had got back on the street and was following the *Tiger* at a certain distance, waiting for an opportunity to hit the thinner armour at the rear of the German tank.

Wittmann, for his part, continued on his way around the centre of Villers-Bocage, until a shot fired

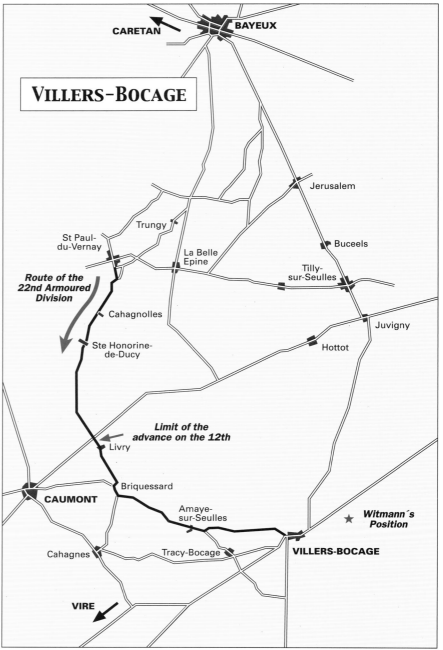

from his front only just missed, hitting a house. The Tiger traversed its turret to meet the new threat, but visibility in the street was very bad due to the smoke and dust. The tank shuddered under a direct impact which, luckily for Wittmann, failed to penetrate its armour. Wittmann finally managed to locate the source of the shot. A Firefly, some 400 metres away half hidden by the smoke, was hugging the sides of the houses. The Tiger's first two shots narrowly missed, hitting the buildings and covering the covering the British tank in rubble, making it even harder for the *Tiger* to see its target. The *Firefly's* 17pdr was capable of destroying the *Tiger*, and Wittmann

had lost the element of surprise. Low on ammunition, he decided to turn round and rejoin his unit, which had stayed to attack the British forces that had been cut off on Hill 213.

On the way back, in the middle of all the smoke and wrecked, flaming vehicles, he ran into Dyas' *Cromwell*, which had been following him. Two 75 mm proyectiles bounced uselessly off the Tiger, which then return ed fired with its 8.8 cm, penetrating the *Cromwell's* turret without difficulty. Dyas, although badly shaken, was fortunate enough to survive the encounter. A little later, after reaching the Tilly crossroads, Wittmann's luck ran

A *Tiger I Ausf E* of «Leibstantandarte» moving along a road in Normandy. The thickness of the foliage of the bocage greatly favoured the camouflaging and hiding of tanks from the ever present danger presented by Allied aircraft, although it restricted movement greatly. (Bundesarchiv)

able to get its engine started and had reached the RN 175, spotting two *Cromwells* near Hill 213, destroying them with two successive shots. It then withdrew to cover, stopping its engine to make the minimun necessary repairs. The other three tanks took up positions around the British and awaited reinforcements. The Germans had no real idea of the nature of the force they were facing, and were without their commander (Wittmann was at this moment making his way back on foot), although the British were also completely disorientated. All they could do was wait for reinforcements to arive from Villers-Bocage.

Meanwhile, in Villers-Bocage, confusion reigned. *Major* Aird found himself in command of the armoured forces there. He supposed the worst had happened and that his best option was to call up the following infantry battalion to come forward and consolidate the position in the town, and then try and make contact with A Squadron, trapped on Hill 213. If he could, he would keep in radio contact with his Colonel and keep him informed of the situation. At 0930 the 1/7th

The British *Firefly*, with its 17pdr gun (equivalent to the German 8.8 cm) was the only Allied tank that seriously threatened the *Tiger I*.
Illustration: Julio López Caeiro.

6pdr guns which had been put in position, managed to hit and immobilize the German tank. Wittmann had no other option than to abandon the vehicle, surrounded by the enemy and almost two kilometres from his own forces. The crew fired at everything within range with all the *Tiger's* weapons in order to cover their retreat, and then they abandoned the tank and headed without further difficulty for their own lines north of the town.

Hardly ten minutes had passed since the Germans opened fire. In the town and along the road, the British had lost thirteen tanks of varying types, as well as seventeen other armoured vehicles and two anti-tank guns.

While all this was happening in Villers-Bocage, the drama was repeated on Hill 213. After losing two tanks in the initial contact, A Squadron had scattered around the position. It had at least seven *Cromwells*, two *Fireflies* and Colonel Cranley's *Dingo*. There was also an artillery observation tank and a disorganised group of infantry from Company A, as well as seven officers and N.C.O's, who had survived the initial mayhem, three *White* half-tracks, two *Dingos* and several motorcycles. However, it was no longer a balanced force.

The Germans began to converge on the hill. As well as the *Tigers*, infantry were also starting to arrive on the scene, and began harassing the British with small arms fire, causing several casualties. The Tiger that had firt taken Wittmann on board, but then broke down, had been

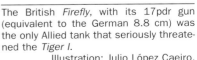

E Tiger I

tank, capable of carrying out a wide variety of missions, it was too vulnerable against determi-
s decided that a heavy tank was needed, capable of penetrating any potential enemy formation

t of 35 metric tons and armed with a 7.5 cm gun. But it soon became evident that this would
nd *Henschel*. Both were armed with the potent 8.8 cm anti-aircraft gun, in its anti-tank version,
cteristics.

inal in its conception, transformed over time into one of the most powerful tank-hunters of the
cm L/71, with a total of 90 entering service. Henschel's new heavy tank was designated the

d the driver and radio operator at the front. The engine was a *Maybach* HL 210, V12, producing
a notable achievement given the fact it weighed 56 metric tons. Range was approximately 200
with the wide tracks, gave it stability on the move and turned it into a solid gun platform. This
advanced and efficient, it required adequate maintenance from specialised personnel, and had

ved from the famous 8.8 cm AA gun, which had by then already demonstrated its lethality as
a defensive position. It carried a total of 92 projectiles, most being easily accessible, again,
nsisted of a co-xial 7.92 mm machine gun, and another of the same calibre in the hull. The
her. One of the *Tiger I's* few defects was the slowness in traversing its turret, a disadvanta-

of armour at the front of the turret, 80 mm at the sides and rear. The top and bottom of the
nich allowed it to receive and absorb impacts that would have seen any other tank blown apart.
4, when the 17pdr, American 90 mm and Soviet 122 mm began to appear in numbers.

hed. Only a few of the elite divisions had them, the rest being concentrated in independent bat-
ad sector in August 1942, without a good deal of succes. In fact, the four tanks that participa-
e appearance at the beginning of 1943 in Tunisia and Italy.

e able to turn the course of a battle. It was not only its main armament which was impressive,
even 76.2 mm projectiles, fourteen 45mm and 57 mm ones and more than 230 from anti-tank
nies with good reason.

ger, or recovery tank, and the curious *Sturmtiger*, a vehicle equipped with an enormous armou-
the Ardennes battle. A command vehicle was also built *(Panzerbefehlswagen)*.

ar Two. Weighing in at 67 metric tons, its armour, sloped like that of the *Panther*, was as much
a road speed of 35 kph, and carried the powerful 8.8 cm L/71, probably the best anti-tank gun
under, manufactured by *Porsche*, the rest were made by *Henschel*. The 489 tanks produced up

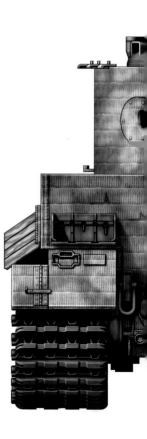

A *Tiger* towing another that has broken down. In order to move the 56 metric ton *Tiger*, it was either necessary to use three 18 ton tractors, or another *Tiger*. This problem was only solved when the *Berganther* and
Bergetiger entered service in limited numbers. (Bundesarchiv)

Panzerkampfwagen VI Ausf

The early campaigns of World War Two showed the German military that although the *Panzer IV* was an excellent ned enemy tanks (such as the *Matilda*) or when assaulting positions with strong anti-tank defences. Therefore, it wa and defeating any enemy tank, either present or future.

Work on a design for a tank that could meet these requirements had already begun in 1937, initially with a weig not meet requirements, and a more powerful tank would be needed. Two companies submitted a design, *Porsche a* capable od penetrating 100 mm of armour at 1,500 metres, and both were protected against a gun of similar chara

In April 1942 the prototypes were reviewed, and the Henschel model was chosen. The Porsche design, more orig war, and about which much erroneous information has been written, the Ferdinand, or Elephant, armed with the 8.8 Tiger I, and some 1,350 had been built by the end of the war.

The new tank had the typical structure of the time, with the engine at the rear, the combat room in the centre an 650 hp, (an HL 230 of 700 hp in the final models) giving it a road speed of 37-38 kph and 20 kph cross country, kilometres. The running gear had its wheels interleaved in a way similar to the Sdkfz 251 half-track, which together also spread the distribution of weight. The transmission was one of the weak points, as although it was technically to be driven with care. The same can also be said for the steering.

One of the most outstanding features was the main armament. The tank mpunted a 8.8 cm KwK 36 L/56, der an anti-tank weapon. The maximum angle of elevation was 17°, and angle of depression 6.5°, very important in very important in combat. The gun's sights were set to a range of up to 4,000 metres. Secondary armament c final models also mounted a machine gun on the turret roof, while the first ones had a grenade and smoke laun ge in close combat conditions.

The other outstanding feature of the tank was its armour. The mantlet was 110 mm thick and there was 100 mr superstructure was 26 mm thick. Apart from the thickness of its armour, the tank was also very structurally solid, w It was virtually invulnerable to any gun in allied service in 1942, and continued to be so until the second half of 19

At first it was decided that each *Panzer Division* would have a battalion of 50 *Tigers*, but this was never accompli talions, depending on the needs of the different combat scenarios.The *Tiger 1* made its combat debut in the Lening ted in the first mission were all put out of action, one being captured by the Russians. It made a far more impress

On the Eastern Front it soon became feared by the Russians, and on many occasions a small group of *Tigers* we but also its ability to take so much punishment. As an example, in February 1943, a Tiger survived the impact of e rifles... It maintained its ascendency over over other tanks until the end of the war, and it was respected by its ene

Several variants of the *Tiger I* were developed, such as the already mentioned *Ferdinand*, the outstanding *Berget* red box which housed a 380 mm rocket launcher. This vehicle received its baptism of fire in Warsaw and took part

The successor to the *Tiger I*, the *Tiger II* or *Königstiger*, became the most formidable fighting machine of World W as 150 mm at the front of the hull and 180 mm in the turret, making it almost invulnerable to any allied gun. It had of the war. It carried 72 projectiles and had a crew of five men. There were two turret versions, the first fifty were r to March 1945 caused terror on all the battlefields on which they were present.

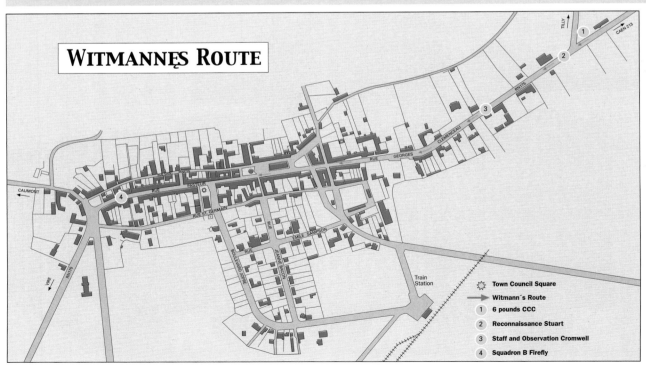

WITMANNƎS ROUTE

Town Council Square

→ Witmann´s Route

1 6 pounds CCC

2 Reconnaissance Stuart

3 Staff and Observation Cromwell

4 Squadron B Firefly

Amidst the devestation of Villers-Bocage, it is possible to see the remains of a *Sherman* artillery forward observation tank of *3rd Rgt. Royal Horse Artillery*, which was destroyed by Wittmann. (IWM).

Queens finally received the order to enter the town, and began their advance. The first units to arrive were the *carriers* and 6pdr AT guns, followed, some way behind, by four companies of infantry. They immediately took up positions in the outskirts, exchanging shots with the German infantry (from both *«Panzer Lehr»* and *2.Panzer-Division*), who had also begun to make their way into the town. When he was most needed, Brigadier Hinde, who should have been coordinating the actions of his Brigade, and taking decisions based on a first hand appraisal of the situation, was notable for his absence, and the British forces moved according to the directions of the company commanders bogged down in Villers-Bocage.

At the same time all this was going on, Wittmann and his crew reached Orbois, five kilometres away, where they found the General Headquarters of *«Panzer Lehr»*. They made their report, and a detachment of fifteen *Panzer IV's* were sent towards the fighting (the majority of the Division was engaged at Tilly).

T260030

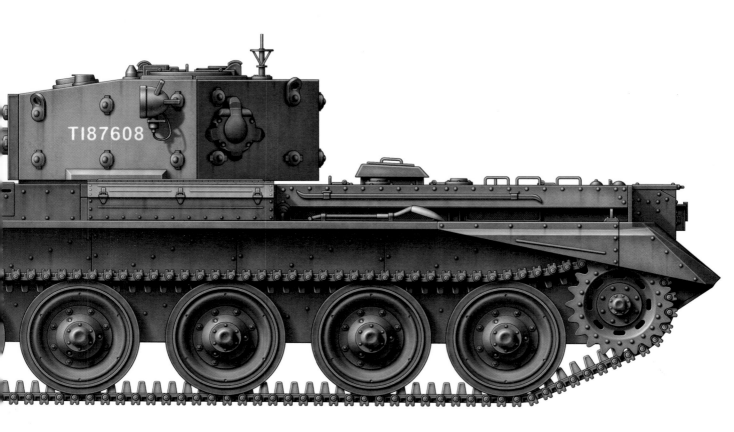

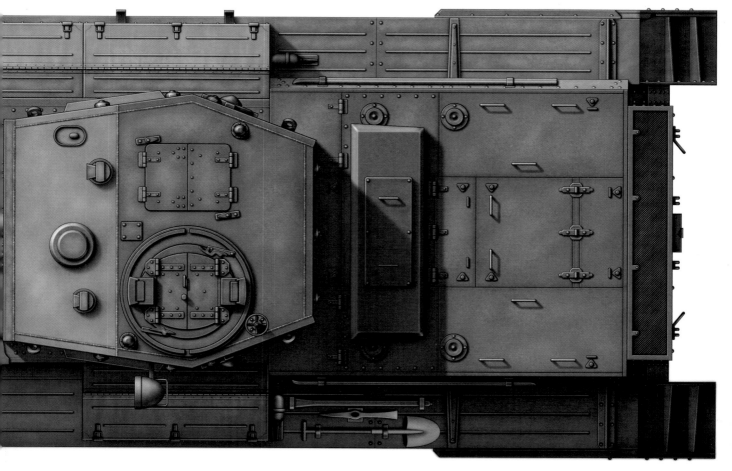

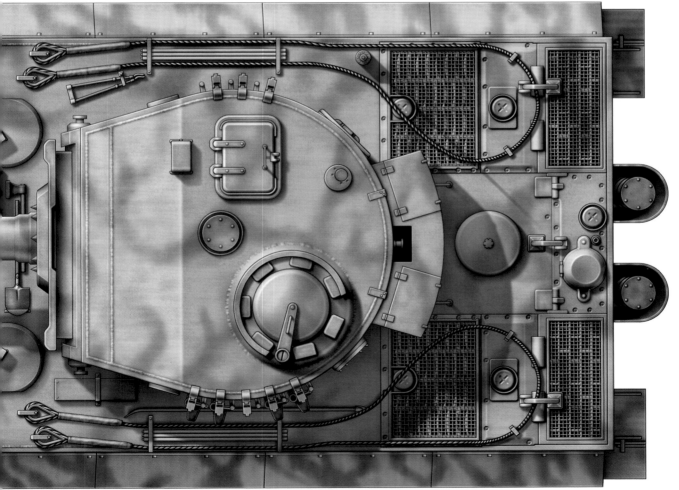

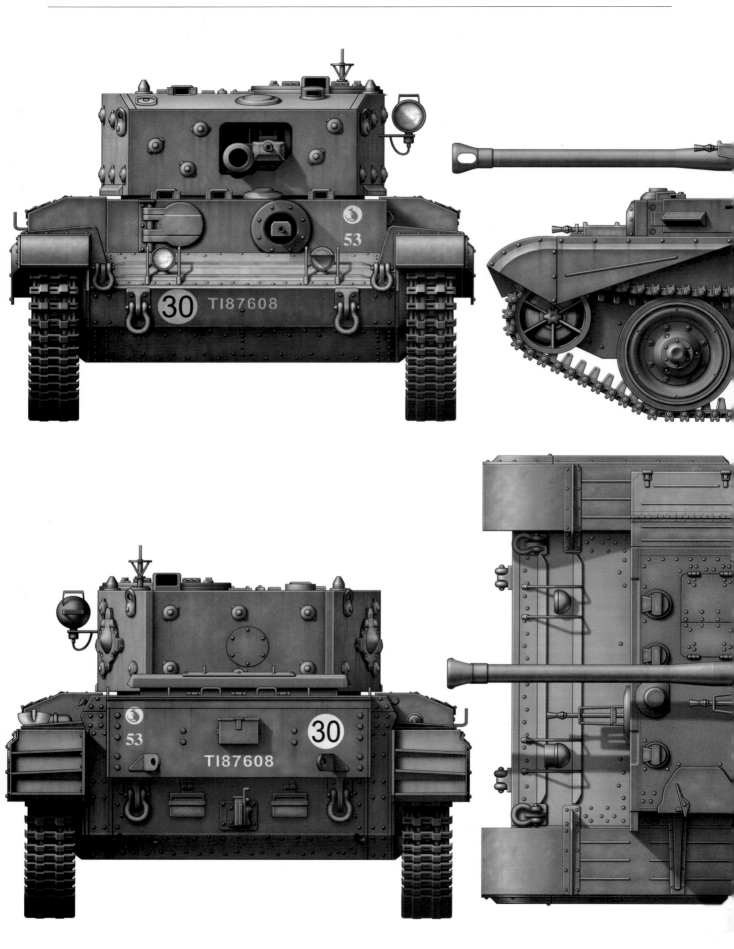

THE LAST BRITISH TANKS TO ENTER SERVICE IN EUROPE

British policy regarding tank production varied considerable during the Second World War, with the result that it was not until the very end of the war that they finally produced what they needed. Before 1939, the British had designed three types of tanks; light tanks for reconnaissance and patrolling, cruisers for exploiting a breakthrough, and infantry tanks. Light tanks such as the *Mk VI*, soon showed their limitations, and to make matters worse, were often used as cruisers. The various types of cruiser tanks were rushed into service and suffered from technical problems that took time to resolve. Furthermore, their design had many limitations that prevented the early models from adapting to new scenarios and threats. When they adopted the 6pdr gun, enemy tanks were being fitted with the 7.5 cm. The final development of the cruiser tank, the *Cromwell*, also suffered from the problem of limited space, which prevented it from fitting a more powerful gun than the 75 mm. The attempts to aument firepower resulted in the development of the *Challenger*, which up to a point was satisfactory. However, the best British tank of the war was in fact based on the *Sherman*, an American design, but mounting the highly effective 17pdr (an option the Americans, ironically, had ruled out). The Firefly was only really bettered in 1945 by the *Comet*, the best British tank to see combat in the Second World War.

British infantry tanks also evolved, from the useless *Matilda I*, armed only with a machine-gun, then on to the *Matilda II*, and later the *Churchill* and its many variants. The Churchill also showed its limitations when it became necessary to fit it with a heavier main gun. Nevertheless, the *Churchill VII* proved its worth on the European battlefields, its thick armour and manouevreability over rough ground made it adapt well to the traditional British prudence in attacks. Its numerous variants also achieved notable success. Following the failure of the *Black Prince* project, and the cancellation of the monsterous *Tortoise* (armed with a 32pdr gun, its armour was up to 225 mm thick, it weighed 86 metric tons and had a maximum speed of 20 kph), British designers finally reached the conclusion that they needed a tank that had the mobility of a cruiser, but with the capacity to evolve, and with all the virtues of the previous types. This led to the *Centurion*, which by a small margin did not see combat, and which went on to become one of the best tanks of the Sixties. The first *Centurion* (A 41) weighed 50 metric tons and had a crew of four, three of whom were positioned in the turret. Its main armament was the 17pdr, which was soon replaced by a 20pdr, it had 152 mm of armour. Maximum road speed was 35 kph, and its off-road mobility was notable for a tank of its weight. Following successive improvements, it remained in service until the nineteen-seventies, demonstrating the quality of its design on many battlefields around the world.

The *Cromwell* became the most representative of British tanks in Europe during 1944, together with the ubiquitous *Sherman*. It was fitted with a 600 hp V12 *Rolls-Royce Meteor*, adapted from the legendary *Merlin* aircraft engine, which gave it, along with its *Christie* suspension, a maximum road speed of 60 kph, and 30 kph off-road, something outstanding for a tank weighing 30 metric tons. Its armour had a maximum thickness of 76 mm (101 mm on some models), which gave it better protection than the *Sherman*, despite its square angles. Its worst defect was its armament. At the end of the day the tank was derived from the cruisers, and it had serious limitations in space. Its 75 mm gun posed no threat to German tanks, and there was no way of mounting a heavier gun without completely redesigning the tank. It had a five.man crew, with three of them in the turret.

There were several variants, including the very British CS, an infantry support version armed with a 95 mm howitzer, a command tank, recovery tank, a mine-clearing tank, and two rather unsuccessful versions, equipped with a larger main gun, the *Challenger*, with a 17pdr, and the *Charioteer*, (after the end of the war) with a 20pdr. The 17pdr also appeared mounted on the Cromwell chassis in an open turret, called the *Achilles*, which was more successful than its American counterpart.

The best British tank of the war was without doubt the A 34 *Comet*. Based on the *Cromwell*, but attempting to improve on its deficiencies, the new tank was armed with a 77 mm OQF gun, a compact version of the 17pdr, (weighing less and with a shorter breach and barrel) which did not lose any of its power, but could be mounted in the A 27. It had a crew of five men and weighed almost 40 tons. Its armour had a maximum thickness of 101 mm, and its 600 hp engine gave it a maximum road speed of 50 kph. It was the first allied tank capable of almost meeting the *Panther* on equal terms. However, it did not enter service until March 1945, to late to be completely evaluated.

of the situation and his ten *Tigers* started along the fifteen kilometres that seperated them from Villers-Bocage. Soon after, another ten recently repaired *Panzer IV's* were found (also from *"Panzer-Lehr"*), and were immediately sent on their way. Wittmann got in a *Schwimmwagen* and caught up with Möbius, bringing him up to date on the situation.

On Hill 213, the situation was becoming more and more critical. The only support the besieged British on the hill received was artillery fire from the Brigade's *Sextons*. At ten o'clock that morning, they were informed by radio that the *Queens* were entering Villers-Bocage, and would soon get them out of their predicament. But time passed, casualties began to mount and the reinforcements failed to arrive. At 1235, Colonel Cranley became aware that time was running out, and he requested a smoke screen and to attempt to break out. But the

A *«Leibstandarte» Tiger* Tank in a Norman village, with the crew appearing in a relaxed mood. Something very unusual in the daytime (Bundesarchiv)

ned round when they found themselves blocked by the railway embankment, re-entering the town by the side of the Town Hall, taking up ambush positions in the small square in front of the building. They switched off their engines and waited. Next to them was one of the 6pdr AT guns.

The first *Panzer IV's* of *«Panzer-Lehr»* to arrive on the scene began entering the eastern edge of Villers-Bocage, when two of them were knocked out by one of the 6pdrs. Möbius' *Tigers* were also arriving at this moment, and realizing what was occurring, four of them entered the town in order to neutralize the anti-tank gun. One of the *Tigers* was hit, but without being damaged, and returned fire, destroying the AT gun. After eliminating the threat, the German tanks continued on their way along the main street, rue Clemenceau, the same as Wittmann a few hours before, hoping to tempt the British into making a precipitated move. The *Tigers* had hardly any infantry with them, their only hope being that the enemy would show themselves, but in the middle of a town and fighting at almost point blank range, the advantages given to them by their thick armour and 88 mm gun, were for the most part nullified.

The lead *Tiger* nosed its way into the Town Hall Square, and the *Firefly* immediately fired, missing, but the 6pdr was able to put the German tank out of action with its first shot. The British had revealed their position at last. Another group of four *Tigers* then tried a flanking manouvre along the adjacent streets in order to attack the Square from the other side, but without infantry they were very vulnerable in the narrow streets of Villers-Bocage. Nother Tiger was knocked out by a 6pdr, hidden in an alleyway, while another two were put out of action by *PIATs*, although only one was destroyed. The *PIAT*, normally useless, proved very effetive when used from a concealed position at very close range.

infantry would not move, and a *Cromwell* that ventured out into the open was immediately destroyed. With more than thirty men wounded, surrounded and under fire from enemy machine guns and high explosive, and with no sign of help coming fom their own forces in Villers-Bocage, with the arrival of Möbius' *Tigers*, the British officers on Hill 213 found themselves with little option other than surrender, which in due course they did, without first pausing to put their own remaining vehicles out of action.

The Second Attack

Major Aird, who had remained in charge of the *"Sharpshooters"* in Villers-Bocage, decided he would look for alternative routes to the

south of the town. To this end, he detached a section of B Squadron under Lieutenant Cotton, consisting of two *Cromwells*, a command vehicle (a *Cromwell* armed with a 95 mm howitzer), and a *Firefly*. Meanwhile, the *1/7th Queen's* were taking up positions in the centre of the town, the same time German infantry, still few in number, began to infiltrate into the town from its eastern end, consolidating their own positions around the railway station. The Battalion's six 6pdr anti-tank guns were positioned to cover the way in from the east. Three companies took up position while a fourth was held in reserve.

Lieutenant Cotton's section, unable to find another route, tur-

Panzerkampfwagen IV Ausf H of the 3rd Company I. /Pz.Rgt. 130, "Panzer-Lehr Division".
Illustration: Luis Fresno Crespo

The *Firefly* in the Square spotted another *Tiger* and fired at it through the windows of a house, managing an impact, but without causing any damage. The German tank quickly accelerated, passing in front of the Square without giving the British time to fire. One of the *Cromwells* came out behind it and fired, hitting the *Tiger* in the rear and causing it to crash into a house a few dozen metres away. The *Cromwell* returned to the Square just as a *Panzer IV* appeared, which was soon knocked out by the *Firefly*.

While this game of cat and mouse was going on, the German infantry were advancing from the railway station in ever increasing numbers, forcing the British to withdraw, and closing in on the Town Hall Square. Their advance was accompanied by effective artillery support. A British mortar platoon and several *Bren Carriers* were destroyed, and the *Queen's* HQ platoon was cut off, suffering heavy casualties.

It was now afternoon and the Germans forces were gradually increasing, not only in Villers-Boca-

The *Tiger* that got the furthest into Villers-Bocage. After being hit next to the town square, it continued until it crashed into the house. (Bundesarchiv)

ge, but also in the surrounding area. It was now clear to the British that they had lost their opportunity and Brigadier Hinde, in one of the few decisions he made that day, ordered a withdrawl under cover of an artillery barrage. This was accomplished at nightfall without further complications. Villers-Bocage was left in German hands, and the breakthrough had been prevented.

The next day, 14th June, saw bloody fighting in the sector, a salient had been created in the front which the Germans were attempting to reduce, and the British maintain, using their air power and artillery. Since the afternoon of the 13th, the fighting had become generalised between Tilly and Villers-Bocage, taking place in a drizzle that hindered air operations, until engagements finally ceased that night.

At nine in the morning, an attack by German infantry on the 1/7th's positions was repulsed with the help of tanks using their machine guns. A devestating artillery bombardment, using all the British and American guns in the sector settled the issue, supressing the German attacks. The attacks were renewed in the afternoon supported by mortar fire,

and although costly for the Germans, who were concious of the danger the British salient presented, their intensity and persistance persuaded the Staff of 7th Armoured Division that the position was untenable, and that the line had to be re-established in the rearguard. One final attack took place at nightfall, this time with artillery support, just as the withdrawl was about to start. However, the allied artillery proved superior, and although the Germans managed to make a little headway, they were eventually repulsed, with *"Panzer-Lehr"* losing a score of tanks and a lot of its infantry. The *Tigers* lost one of their number. At last, in the darkness, the British were able to complete their redeployment. The battle of Villers-Bocage was over.

Conclusions

It is not easy to establish a clear winner of the battle of Villers-Bocage. Five *Tiger I's* were put out of action, although most were recovered later, and a number of *Panzer IV's* were also lost. British losses were worse with sixteen *Cromwells*, four *Fireflies*, three *Stuarts*, thirteen half-tracks and two anti-tank guns completely lost. They had also suffered 80 casualties, a third of them dead. The greater part of their losses occurred

during Wittmann's initial attack. In fact Wittmann had been responsible for hitting 25 targets himself. This had been achieved by charging with complete surprise into the middle of an enemy column, then entering the town alone, without support from other tanks or infantry, all of which had occurred in ten minutes. However, that the *Tiger* was not invulnerable had been made clear in the second attack, when four were lost. Which can only serve to emphasize Wittmann's feat.

Nevertheless, allied logistics were able to soon replace the British losses, while the German losses were irreplacable. What cannot be denied, however, is that 22nd Armoured Brigade's advance, which could have broken through at a critical moment, was brought to a halt, and the front line was stabilized for some time. This was the main consequence of Wittmann's action.

On the other hand, Wittmann did no more than exemplify German doctrine, the *"Auftragstaktik"*, according to which commanders at all levels down to the last soldier, were free to take advantage of any opportunity that came their way in order to complete their mission. Wittmann saw such an opportunity to cut the unsuspecting British column in two, and destroy a large number of vehicles in the process, so he took advantage of this. Once he started to run into serious opposition after the initial surprise had gone, his mission completed, instead of acting recklessly, he returned to his own lines. This attitude was in contrast to the passivity with which the British initially reacted to the attack, confident as they were that no enemy forces were in such close proximity. The Brigade commander was not up to

Another of the *Tiger I's* destroyed in Villers-Bocage, following the highly destructive Allied bombardment of the town after the battle.

the situation, and did not how to react adequately to the unexpected threat, something which happened all to frequently with allied units during the Second World War. Only a few individuals were able to restore some semblance of order and common sense following the initial debacle, and avoid an even greater catastrophe.

THE DEATH OF WITTMANN

The death of somebody as legendary as Michael Wittmann can never be without controversy. He was killed together with his crew during a counterattack on the outskirts of Cintheuax, during "Operation Totalize", on 8th August. The tank, carrying the number 007, was destroyed by an internal explosion, and Wittmann's remains were found after the fighting. As none of his comrades witnessed his final moments, four theories as to how he met his death have been put forward:

The most improbable is that his tank received a direct hit from a 5.5 inch artillery shell. Another hypothesos put forward for many years was that his tank was hit by a Typhoon rocket, something else which is highly unlikely. The third explanation, which is more in keeping with the Wittmann legend, is that he was surrounded by five Canadian *Shermans* that were waiting in ambush, that fired repeatedly until his tank exploded, and after he had destroyed three of there number.

The fourth, and most plausible version, is that based on the Regimental History of thel *Northampton Yeomanry*. According to this, a platoon of *Shermans*, among them a *Firefly*, were occupying a hidden position, preparing to face a German counter-attack, when three *Tiger I's* approached, exposing their flank. The British tanks opened fire at 800 metres, and at that distance, the 17 pdr shells could penetrate the side armour of a *Tiger I* without problem. The second *Tiger*, after firing and narrowly missing the *Firefly*, exploded. This was probably Tiger number 007. And so an extraordinary career was brought to an abrupt end, and a legend began.

MICHAEL WITTMANN

Michael Wittmann was born into a rural family in Vogelthal in 1914. His life was no different to that of millions of other workers until 1937, when he enlisted in the *"Leibstandarte Adolf Hitler"*, taking part in both the Polish and French campaigns with them. He had been posted to a reconnaissance unit, and was an SdKfz 222 crewman, among other things. Later, he saw action in the Greek campaign, this time in a *Stug III*, with which he destroyed several New Zealander guns. For this he was awarded the Iron Cross Second Class.

At the beginning of Operation *Barbarossa*, commanding one of the few *StuG III's* in the Division, he immediately began making a name for himself by destroying six out of eight enemy tanks he faced in one of the earliest engagements. Later, he was wounded in the fighting around Rostov. Wittmann was awarded the Iron Cross First Class in November, and was then sent to Officer School. In December 1942 he was a Lieutenant in *Panzer Regiment* 1, with his new Tiger I tank, and the crew with whom he would share most of his most successful exploits: The mythical gunner, Baltasar Woll, the loader Kurt Berges, driver Gustav Kirshner and Herbert Pollman the radio operator, all taking part in the battle of Kursk together. As platoon leader, Wittmann destroyed 30 tanks and 28 anti-tank guns. Following the cancellation of the offensive, during the fighting in the Orel salient, Wittman destroyed ten Russian tanks in one day. In January 1944, his company single-handedly stopped the advance of an entire brigade of Soviet tanks. Wittmann received the Knights Cross after destroying his sixtieth tank, soon after (January 31st) receiving the Oakleaves. His gunner, Woll, also received the Knights Cross soon after this. Wittmann married Hildegard Burmester on 1st March.

In the summer of 1944, his Division was sent to France to reorganize, where they were to face the Allied landings in Normandy. Due to the chaotic state of communications, it took his unit several days before they joined the fighting, but when they did, it would go down in history. His action at Villers Bocage is now legendary, when with his company of tanks he halted a dangerous penetration by the British 22nd Armoured Brigade, preventing an eventual breakthrough of the German front. Wittmann was then promoted to Captain, and was offered a post as an instructor, but he wished to continue serving with his men and unit and so rejected the transfer. On 22nd June 1944 he received the swords to his Knights Cross. His personal tally was now at 138 enemy tanks and 132 anti-tank guns destroyed.

On 8th August he took part in an action against the Canadians at Cintheaux, during a counter-attack in the course of "Operation *Totalize*". Wittmann had just celebrated his 30th birthday. During the counter-attack, his *Tiger I*, numbered 007, was destroyed and all the crew killed. All are buried in the military cemetery at La Cambe, In Normandy.

Michael Wittmann, together with his crew, created an aura of myth around the *Tiger* tank. He was a charismatic leader, very concerned for the welfare of his men. Cold and calculating, he knew perfectly how to take the mmaximum advantage from his material. Together with Baltasar Woll, his legendary gunner, and the rest of his crew, they made a perfect combination. Woll commanded his own tank at Cintheaux, and survived the war.

OTTO CARIUS

Born 27th May 1922 in Zweibrücken. As a child, his wish was to become a musician, becoming proficient at both the piano and violin. When he finished school, he enrolled in the Engineering Faculty at university, just before the outbreak of war. Although he requested to enlist as a tanker, he was initially sent to the infantry. Thin, short and asthmatic, he suffered during infantry training, but eventually managed to get himself posted to a tank unit, as a loader in a *Panzer 38(t)*.

Carius took part in Operation *Barbarossa*, as a member of *20.Panzer-Division (Panzer Regiment 21)*, seeing action in the battles of Minsk and Smolensk. He was promoted to *Unteroffizier* on 1st August, and was then made a driver. He was sent to Officer School, but was failed and returned to his unit. He later said himself that he had not taken the course very seriously. He saw further action in the hard fighting which took place in the winter of 1942-43, and in January 1943, he was sent back to Germany again to convert to the new *Tiger*.

In the new tank, he took part in the battles around Leningrad in the summer of 1944 with the *Schwere Panzer Abteilung* 502, commanding a platoon. His tank bore the number 213. On 6th October he was attacked by a dozen T-34's, and his own tank had broken down, but within a short time he had destroyed ten of them. On 16th October, his gunner, Heinz Kramer, managed the extraordinaryl feat of bringing down a Soviet observation plane with the tanks 8.8 cm gun, something highly unusual but well documented. During January and February he was involved in numerous actions with Soviet forces, increasing his tally of victories. In April he escaped death by inches when his tank was destroyed by several high explosive shells. On 4th May he was promoted to *Lieutenant* and awarded the Knights Cross.

On 22nd July, in Malinava, together with his comrades Kerscher and Nienstedt, he halted a strong Soviet counter-attack, destroying 17 enemy tanks in 20 minutes, some of them the new model *Stalin*. A few days later, while out on a reconnaissance mission, he was seriously wounded by a Soviet patrol. He convalesced in Germany, later returning to the front as an *Oberleutnant*, commanding the 3rd Company of *Pz Abt* 512, equipped with the new *Jadgtiger*. At the end of March 1945, he destroyed his first Sherman with his 128 mm gun.

After the war, and following several months in captivity, he worked as a pharmacist. During the course of the war, Carius destroyed a total of 150 enemy tanks. Despite this high number, Carius was not the highest scoring German tank ace of World War Two. This title must go to Kurt Knispel, of *schewere Pz Abt* 503, with 168 tanks destroyed, followed by Hans Bolter with 139 and Wittmann with 138.

COBRA 1944: THE COLLAPSE OF THE GERMAN FRONT

Introduction

Once the normandy beach-head had been consolidated, there follo-wed several weeks of hard fighting as the Allies tried to widen it, and the Germans strengthened their defences, and some of the first day's objectives, such as Caen, remained untaken.This was in part due to the determined German defence, which was stiffer than had been expected given the quality of the first line troops, and also to the indecision displayed by many Allied units, who failed to take advantage of precious opportunities which pre-sented themselves in the first hours of the invasion.

The British and Canadians had tried to break through the German defences in two operations which ended in failure, *Epsom*, and above all «*Goodwood*». «*Goodwood*» was the most ambitious, a personal pro-ject of Montgomery, which put the greatest number of tanks of the war on a single battlefield. The lack of infantry combined with the bad coor-dination between the different arms, as well as an effective German defence, resulted in the attack, which was made almost exclusively by tanks, failing in its objective, and cost the British high material losses, although few casualties. Neverthe-less, these operations did achieve at least one important objective,

which at the end of the day proved decisive, which was to keep a large number of the best German forces fighting the British and Canadians, which left the Americans more free-dom of action.

The Americans, meanwhile, spent June and the beginning of July figh-ting to make progress in the difficult terrain of the bocage, without making any significant advances. An attack by VIII Corps on the 3rd July, towards Coutances and St Lô, meant to achieve a breakthrough, made little more than a few kilome-tres progress, at a high cost in men, which fell on the already depleted 79th and 90th Infantry Divisions. After twelve days of combat, the attack was halted with little more than fifteen kilometres gained at a cost of ten thousand casualties. The only good news for the Americans was the failure of the advance by the *"Panzer Lehr"* Division on the 11th, demonstrating that the bocage made operations difficult for both sides. The defender held all the advantages. However, all these ope-rations resulted in the gradual attri-tion of the exhausted German tro-ops, something they could barely afford. But the Americans were not aware of this, and Bradley faced the problem of how to penetrate onto Brittany, and break the stalemate that was developing.

An American Sherman *passing the remains of a destroyed German Sdkfz 251 half-track.*

Bradley also had internal pro-blems, as his infantry units, who were taking most of the casualties, were showing signs of losing their combat effectiveness. In actual fact, more than 25% of the troops were showing signs of "battle fati-gue" during 1944, something very worrying and significant. One of the reasons for this was the poor qua-lity of many officers at all levels. Only a few had sufficient charisma to motivate their men, one of these being Patton.

Therefore, Bradley and Collins, commander of VII Corps, developed a plan that would finally get them out of the bocage, and allow them to penetrate not only into Brittany, but also right behind the German rear-guard, opening up the way to Paris. Bradley's aim was to send mechani-zed columns to Avranches, following a break through in the German front, which would enable him to take the vital Breton ports and then turn east towards Paris. The war of attrition in the bocage had to be replaced by a war of movement.

Collins' VII Corps was a powerful formation made up of the 1st, 4th, 9th and 30th Infantry Divisions, and the 2nd and 3rd Armoured Divi-sions. Bradley concentrated the

organic artillery of various divisions in the sector chosen for the attack, including nine heavy artillery battalions, five medium and seven light, giving a total of 258 pieces of all calibres. A total of 150,000 men and approximately 500 tanks were

An M-7 *Priest* advances through a ruined Norman village. Artillery was one of the Americans' strong points, and they employed it effectively throughout the war, at a time when what is now called "collateral damage" had less significance.

to take part in the attack. The breakthrough was to be made by the infantry divisions while the armoured units were to exploit the breach and penetrate deep into the German rearguard.

"Operation Cobra"

The objectives of Operation *Cobra* were as follows:

- capture St Lô and Coutances.
- advance towards Vire, Mortain and Avranches.
- capture Cherbourg

Although American doctrine professed otherwise, what is certain is that cooperation between tanks and infantry left a lot to be desired in Normandy, and elsewhere during the war.

If a breakthrough could be made, then the way would be open for Patton's 3rd Army to sweep into Brittany and onto the French plain, enabling the American armoured divisions to put the doctrine of a war of movement into practice.

On 20th July, as had happened previously at the beginning of the offensive, the Americans took St Lô, after two days of hard fighting. Although casualties were quite heavy, they managed to achieve their primary objective, and furthermore, during the course of the battle, the German 352nd Division, or at least what was left of it, which had caused so much suffering for the Americans at *Omaha*, along with Meindl's paratroopers, had ceased to exist.

Contrary to American doctrine, the main attack took place in a very narrow sector only some six kilometres wide, preceded by a massive air bombardment of a magnitude

THE AMERICAN ARMOURED DIVISION

The American armoured divisions of World War Two were conceived according to the traditions of the cavalry, namely as units to exploit a breakthrough in the front line and create havoc in the enemy rearguard. Direct combat with other tanks was not foreseen as part of their task. The breakthrough was to be made by the infantry divisions, supported by independent tank battalions, while combat with enemy tanks was to be the function of the tank hunter battalions and anti-tank guns. However, this doctrine contained various defects. In the first place, it denied the American armoured division the same potential as a *Panzer* Division, severely limiting its use and restricting it operationally. Another serious defect was that the tank hunter battalions (equipped with M10 tank destroyers) were not adequate to the task of confronting the German tanks, and also proved vulnerable to enemy infantry.

Due to an insufficient number of infantry, the armoured divisions adapted badly to a defensive role, and were only, therefore, apt for offensive operations, having more mobility and firepower than an infantry division. In fact, according to the 1944 manual, their primary role was "*to carry out missions requiring great mobility and firepower*".

In March 1942, following various reforms, the units received the new designation of Heavy Division, and were equipped with 232 medium tanks and 158 light tanks, organised into two regiments, each with two battalions of medium tanks and one of light tanks. The armoured infantry regiment was strengthened with a further battalion, and a Staff unit was created for the divisional artillery. The logistics units developed considerably. Each division had two *combat commands* (designated CCA and CCB), designed to control ad hoc combat groups (*task forces*). One of these formations was typically made up of an armoured regiment, several armoured infantry battalions and some units of self-propelled artillery (each division having three battalions), as well as reconnaissance and engineer units. It could, roughly speaking, be termed a brigade. Often, depending on necessity, another combat command could be created, the CCR, organised from the reconnaissance units. During the war, the original divisional structure went through six reorganizations, although only two were significant. Following bitter experience in North Africa, the armoured divisions were reorganized in September 1943, reducing the number of tanks to 245 (168 *Shermans*), and adding another combat command. This new organization was termed a Light Division. This was again slightly modified in February of 1944.

Successive reorganizations looked to increasing the number of infantry, eliminating unnecessary steps in the chain of command, increasing the number of medium tanks to light tanks, and reducing the disproportionate logistics element. The final reorganization, which resulted in a new Heavy Division, did not come into effect until 1948.

unseen up to then. The air attack was complimented by a thousand artillery pieces of differing size.

A particular feature used by the Americans in this attack (and in successive ones), and which made a notable contribution to its success, was the fitting of metal plates, which were welded to the front of the hulls of the tanks, known as "*Rhinos*", an ingenious invention thought up by Sargeant Culin and Private Roberts of the 2nd Armoured Division. The "*Rhino*" was like a giant hoe that allowed the tanks to force their way through the

Anti-tank missions in the American Army in France were mainly the responsibility of the *M10 Tank Destroyer*, until the arrival of the M18 and M36, which was not until after the Normandy battle had finished. A mid-production M10 TD of the *612th US Tank* Destroyer Battalion.

Illustration: Julio López Caeiro.

CORSAIR II

Two examples of the powerful artillery support available to the Americans: Above, an M8, on a *Stuart* chassis, with a 75 mm. howitzer. Bottom, an M7 *Priest*, armed with the 105 mm gun.

The plan to deceive and confuse the enemy worked well, with fourteen German divisions, six of them *Panzer* Divisions, remaining in the east facing the British and Canadians, while von Kluge only had eleven weak divisions to confront the Americans, only two of which were *Panzer* Divisions. For example, «*Panzer Lehr*», commanded by Fritz Bayerlein, started the attack with 2,200 men (a few more than 3,200 if units which had attached themselves to the Division are included), and less than 50 tanks. The other divisions present were in a similar condition. The 17.SS-*Panzergrenadierdivision* only had fifteen *StuG III's*, while «*Das Reich*» had 60 tanks operational. The situation was no better in the infantry divisions. The *353rd Infantry Division* had no more than 1,500 fighting men, the *243rd Infantry Division* was reduced to a weak *Kampfgruppe* of approximately 800 men, while the *6th Fallschirmjäger Regiment* (paratroops) consisted of a hundred men.

thick hedges of the bocage, instead of movement being limited to the roads and tracks, where they were very vulnerable. In this way, a tank could be through a hedge in a matter of two or three minutes, at the same time it only exposed its frontal armour, leaving the way open for the rest.

The M8 reconnaissance vehicle, although overly vulnerable and with limited mobility, it performed its tasks adequately on the Western Front. The one illustrated was assigned to *82nd Reconnaissance Battalion, 2nd Armored Division*.

Illustration: Luis Fresno Crespo

U. S. A. 6015304-S

D-11

Following several days of delay due to intense rain and low cloud which inhibited air operations, on the 24th July, almost 1,600 four-engined bombers took off to make the initial air attack. However, while they were on their way, the weather suddenly worsened, and the order was given to cancel the operation. But it was too late to turn many of the squadrons back, and 352 *Liberators* dropped 985 tons of bombs, some of which fell on the positions of the American 30th Division, causing 200 casualties. This was confirmation for the Germans that the main Allied effort would take place around the St Lô-Périers sector. The effort made by the 8th Air Force was colossal, with perhaps 900

A column of reconnaissance vehicles advances through the streets of a battle-damaged French town. Without infantry support, the M8 was extremely vulnerable in a built up area.

B-17 *Flying Fortresses* and 677 Consolidated B-24 *Liberators* taking part. Almost 500 P-38, P-47 and P-51 fighters acted as escort.

The weather was fine the next day and the devastating bombardment of the German positions located along the route of advance went ahead as planned. In the wake of an attack by fighter-bombers, 1,800 medium and heavy bombers of the 8th Air Force unloaded their bombs over a six-by-two-kilometre area. As before, many bombs fell on their own units, causing more than 600 casualties (including General Mac-Nair), but «Panzer-Lehr» suffered the effects of an aerial bombardment without precedent. The Division's losses and those of attached units were 350 killed, 1,144 wounded and 1,480 missing (most of whom were taken prisoner during the hours

American tankers inspect a *Panzer IV* that had been abandoned after suffering damage to its running gear.

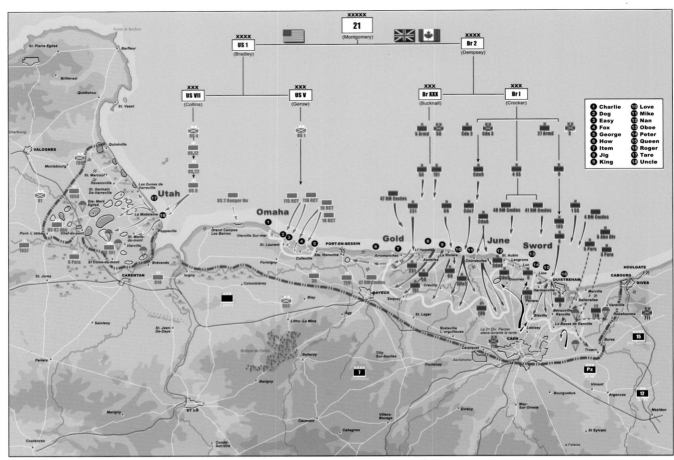

that followed, after being left isolated and completely disorganized). Curiously, none of the Division's *Panzer IV's* were destroyed. However, this was not the case the next day when the 5th tank company was almost completely annihilated by a new air attack. «*Panzer-Lehr*» had been wiped out as an effective combat unit from the air. Only five bombers were lost during the operation.

However, not everything had gone to plan. When Collins' troops, specifically the 1st Infantry Division (the *Big Red One*), reached the German lines, they were unpleasantly surprised to find that there were still defenders in the German positions ready to make a fight of it. But the carefully prepared defences had been severely damaged, and no longer offered a continuous defence in depth, only isolated positions that could be flanked with relative ease.

As the day came to an end on the 25th, troops of the 1st Division had reached Marigny, which was defended by a small group of panzergrenadiers and paratroops, and on the morning of the 26th, the first American units finally started making their way out of the bocage. During the

night, the defenders abandoned the destroyed town, and in the morning the Americans entered the ruins. One of the fastest moving units in the advance was the CCA of 2nd Armoured Division, under the command of the energetic Brigadier General Maurice Rose (who died in 1945, during the battle for the Ruhr pocket). By dawn on the 27th, one of *Cobra's* initial objectives had been achieved, a crossroads to the north of Le Mesnil. In the middle of this frenetic advance, there were many close range firefights between the advancing American units, those protecting the vital supply convoys and German units that in the middle of all the chaos were trying to fall back and form something resembling a defensive line in order to stabilize the front.

In the midst of this situation, a *Panther* was able to demonstrate once again the qualitative difference between American and German material, as well as the tactical gulf which still seperated the two armies at this late stage in the war. On the 27th, a *Panther Ausf G*, commanded by *Obersharführer* Barkmann, while trying to withdraw to Coutances in the face of the avalanch that was outflanking them, ran into an Ameri-

can armoured column. In the minutes that followed, nine *Shermans* and several half-tracks, as well as a number of *jeeps* and trucks, were destroyed. Despite coming under attack by fighter-bombers, the Panther was able to reach its own lines in Coutances safe and sound. Another similar episode occurred on the 29th during the fighting around Percy. The *Panther* commanded by *Leutnant* von Knebel, of the «*Panzer Lehr*» Division, destroyed at least thirteen *Shermans*, almost with

A *Panzerkampfwagen IV Ausf H* of 5.Kp of *"Panzer Lehr" Division*. The tanks of 5.*Kompanie* were totally destroyed in an aerial bombardment by the USAAF on 26th July.

Illustration: Julio López Caeiro.

impunity, in the course of a brief engagement.

On the 28th, 4th Armoured Division's CCB, commanded by *Brigadier* General Middleton, reached Coutances, which the Germans abandoned under strong pressure from the Americans. Over the next few days a small pocket was formed in the Roncey sector, where a number of units belonging to «*Das*

An example of the ubiquitous M7 *Priest*, advancing along a Breton street. As well as serving as field artillery, they were also very useful when used in the direct fire role against particularly tanacious defensive positions.

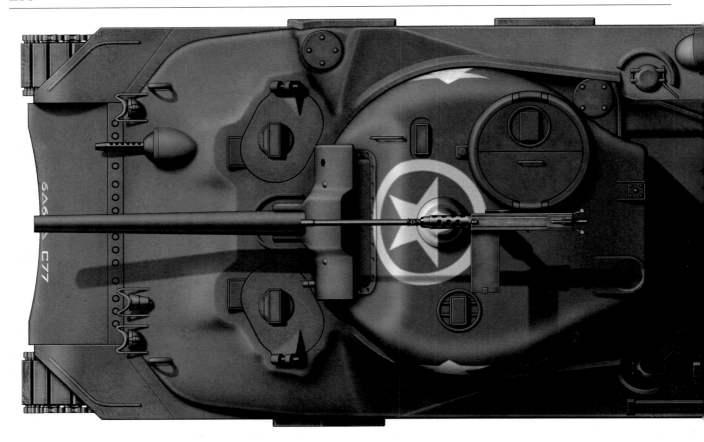

The M-4 General Sherman Medium Tank.

The United States had relegated the tank to a secondary role during the 1930s to such an extent that the tank that was to be adopted as standard in the summer of 1940 was the M2A1, which was completely inadequate for anything. The lessons of the campaign in France showed that a tank had to be armed with at least a 75 mm gun, and that its armour had to be capable of withstanding the impact from a 37 mm projectile. The first tank to be developed following these guidelines was the M3 *Lee/Grant*, of which 5,000 were built.

Using the same chassis and drive train, they developed the M4, which had been designed around a cast turret that could house a 75 mm main gun. Production began in February 1942. The first models were cast, but to speed up production, from July welded hulls were manufactured. The original engine was the voluminous *Wright Continental R-975 Whirlwind* radial, an aviation engine that was in great demand, so it was soon replaced by the *GM Twin 6-71*diesel, which was fitted in the M4A2, but this model was almost exclusively delivered to the Marine Corps. The final engine to be adopted was the gasoline driven *Chrysler A57*, which equipped the M4A4. In any case, these were also large engines which elevated the tanks silhouette considerably, but which at the same time gave more space inside for the five-man crew, three of whom were positioned in the turret.

The first unit to be equipped with the M4 was the 2nd Armoured Division, who were soon deprived of their tanks, which were sent to the British 8th Army for the El Alamein offensive. Later, after being re-equipped, the 2nd Armoured Division took part in the North African campaign following Operation *Torch*. The M4's debut with the American Army was disasterous, when on 6th December 1942, in Djebel bou Aukar, a section of the 66th Regiment was annihilated by German anti-tank guns. More fighting at the end of that month, and in the battle at the Kasserine Pass, did not see better results.

Following a complete reorganiztion, the units equipped with the M4 took part in the fighting in Sicilly and Italy, and then in the rest of Europe following the Normandy landings. Although in tank on tank combat it was inferior to the German tanks, its large numbers and the change in doctrine made the *Sherman* synonymous with the Allied advances across Europe. The Sherman also saw service with the British, French and Russians, although the last mentioned were not so enthusiastic about the tank when compared to their own models.

The M4 *Sherman* was armed with the M3 75 mm gun, with stabilized elevation. It could fire an effective high explosive shell, a smoke round, or an armour piercing projectile capable of penetrating 68 mm of armour at 500 metres. Furthermore, its spacious three-man turret also had a co-axial .30 MG. It often mounted a .50 AA machine gun as well, but in order to use this the tank commander had to expose himself to enemy fire. The tank carried eighty 75 mm shells, although many crews carried many more than that, which increased the chances of blowing up considerably if the tank received an impact.

The installation of the M1A1C 76 mm gun was an attempt to increase its rather poor anti-tank capability, with the weapon being capable of penetrating 98 mm of armour at 500 metres, but its high explosive shell was inferior to that of the 75 mm. A high velocity projectile was developed which could penetrate up to 150 mm at 500 metres, but this was issued in very limited quantities. The tank's telescopic sights were adequate for targets under 1000 metres, but they never managed to match the optical quality and power of the German sights. The British made the wise decision to fit the formidable 17pdr gun on some of their models, making the necessary modifications to the turret. The *Firefly*, as it was called, gave the Allies a tank capable of taking on the German models.

The tanks armour was one of its most controversial points. It was 51 mm thick at the front of the hull with a sloping surface of 47º, at the sides it was 38 mm thick. The turret had 89 mm of armour on the mantlet and 51 mm on the sides. Later on, the frontal armour was increased to 63 mm. This armour was inadequate when faced by the German 75 mm, or even 50 mm guns, as well as hollow charges. In order to try and improve this, many crews resorted to their own methods, such as the indiscriminate use of sandbags on the hull, something which Patton was to prohibit among his units. The only model which had adequate armour was the *Jumbo*, developed as an assault tank, which at the price of losing some mobility, had frontal armour 100 mm thick.

The *Sherman's* speed was acceptable for that time, being capable of reaching a speed of 40-45 kph over flat terrain. However, due to its narrow tracks, its speed through snow or mud was poor, as was its performance over uneven or broken ground. These limitations on its mobility were not solved until the introduction of the *HVSS* suspension in the M4A3E8 at the very end of the war. The M4A3 was the version fitted with the most powerful engine, as well as being the most appreciated by the crews, although all the engines fitted to the tank were very reliable, as was all the tanks mechanics in general, above all when compared to German or Soviet equivilents. This mechanical reliability was one of the tanks main virtues that, coupled with the simplicity of its design, made it easy to mass produce. The balance obtained between the tanks mobility, firepower and protection, made the *Sherman* an outstanding tank, which allowed the units equipped with it to make considerable advances.

As can be imagined, many variants were built using the M4 chassis, such as recovery vehicles, self-propelled artillery (the M12 and M40), mobile mortar platforms, rocket launchers, mine-clearing vehicles, amphibious tanks (the DD), those fitted with flamethrowers, and many more. Since the end of the Second World War, several versions of the Sherman have seen service with many countries, often being adapted locally, in conflicts as varied as the Korean War, the Arab-Israeli wars, a multitude of conflicts in South America and Asia, and even recently in the former Yugoslavia and Lebanon, a tribute to its design and mechanical reliability.

Reich», the *17.SS-Panzergrenadier*, and the 91st, 243rd and 353th Divisions were trapped. The Germans made several attempts to break out, resulting in confused and bloody close quarter fighting with the Americans. One of the more successful attempts at breakout occurred at St-Denis-le-Gast, in the course of which Colonel Coleman, commander of the American 41st Mechanized Infantry Regiment, was killed leading his men in an attempt to close the breach.

Both the CCB of 2nd Armoured Division and the CCA of 6th Armoured Division joined in the battle for the pocket. The Germans had lost 650 casualties, as well as 5,200 men taken prisoner by the 31st. However, in spite of this, the majority of the *Waffen* SS had managed to escape the trap, as well as the 91st and 243rd Divisions, and these were able to establish a new front line.

On the afternoon of the 30th, Rose's CCA reached Percy with *Shermans* and several infantry companies, where they met strong resistance, coming under a heavy German artillery barrage, which in itself was an unusual event on the Western Front at that stage in the war. After losing nine tanks as well as suffering heavy casualties among the infantry, the Americans withdrew. During the battle, the American tank units experienced heavy losses in material, but casualties among personnel were lighter. For example, the 66th Battalion lost 50% of its tanks, while the 743rd was reduced to 13 *Shermans*. However, the situation was no better for the Germans, as they had nothing with which to respond to the Allied artillery and air power, and counter-attacking through the difficult bocage was, as the Americans had already discovered, very difficult in deed. The heavy rate of attrition was taking its toll, and most of the German divisions were now a mere shadow of their former selves. Morale was also declining rapidly, and German commanders were beginning to notice that their panzergrenadiers were becoming more and more reticent to attack without the support of tanks or artillery. In spite of all this, however, the Germans were not yet defeated, and overconfident American

units that ventured out with optimism, frequently ran into ambushes or met with pockets of organised resistance, suffering heavy casualties and being stopped in their tracks as a result, until either the artillery or Air Force cleared the way for them to continue.

On the 31st, Granville was taken by elements of 6th Armoured Division, which then immediately began advancing towards Avranches. The *Big Red One* and the 3rd Armoured Division established a bridgehead over the River See, while the 4th Infantry Division and 3rd Armoured Division continued west. A determined counter-attack in Pontaubault by *Kampfgruppe* Bacherer, consisting of 14 *StuG III's* and two weak infantry battalions was eventually repulsed. The road to Brittany was open and the American 1st Army

had captured almost 28,000 prisoners in two days.

Cobra had resulted in a triumph for the Allies, and at last a large breach had been forced in the German lines, after long weeks of stalemate. Collins had shown his potential as an aggressive and determined commander. However, the success of Cobra would probably not have been possible without the previous weeks of heavy attrition which had weakened the Gernans considerably, and the costly pressure kept up by the British in the east. Furthermore, long painful weeks of learning lessons the hard way had been necessary for both soldiers and commanders to reach the required level of operational capability in order to defeat such a determined enemy, and of course, the Germans were unable

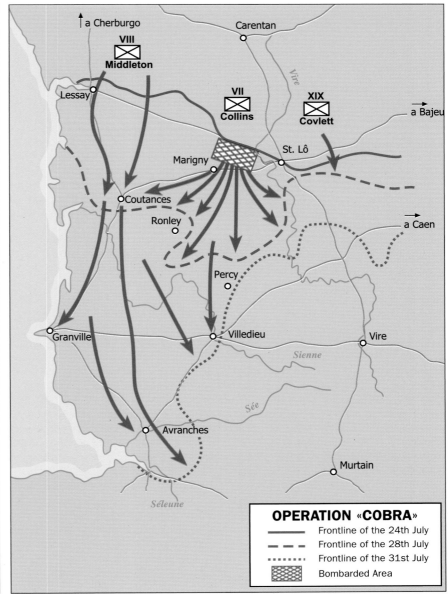

OPERATION «COBRA»
— Frontline of the 24th July
- - - Frontline of the 28th July
······ Frontline of the 31st July
▨ Bombarded Area

Once a breakthrough had been achieved, columns of German prisoners began to appear.

Mittlerer Schützenpanzerwagen Sd.Kfz 251/9 Ausf D Stummel, armed with a 7.5 cm KwK 37 (L/24) gun, «Panzer-Lehr» Division.
Illustration: Julio López Caeiro

to match the material superiority, especially the overwhelming air power, of the Allies. If the «Panzer Lehr» had not been wiped out by the heavy bombers, history may have turned out differently...

Once the breakthrough had been made, it was time for the exploitation phase. Patton's great moment had arrived. On 1st August, the Allied command had been restructured so that 1st Army passed to Hodges, and Patton's 3rd Army was activated (until then it had stayed in the shadows, its presence hidden from the Germans, rather like a virtual Army). Both 1st Army and 3rd Army were under Bradley's direct command, and together they formed 12th Army Group. The situation was becoming desperate for the Germans. Ten of their divisions had disintegrated, and morale was seriously declining. Few of them still believed a victory was possible, and added to this were the disasterous events occuring on the Eastern Front, where Operation «Bagration» had annihilated 28 German divisions and caused the collapse of Army Group Centre, allowing the Soviets to reach the frontier of Germany itself. The failed attempt on Hitler's life on 20th July also did nothing to improve the situation, only increasing the pressure on senior commanders and creating distrust between the different units.

Patton's hour arrives.

Bradley did not want to take unnecessary casualties, and so he would not consent to an advance to the south-east which could have been susceptible to a counter-attack on its flank. Instead of this, he wanted to conquer Brittany, even though the German troops there had no offensive capability, and could hardly be considered a threat to the American advance. So, in spite of Montgomery's opinion to the contrary, Bradley decided to send two of Patton's corps into Brittany. The objective assigned to 3rd Army was ambitious, as well as being prudent. Patton had to launch his four corps in four directions simultaneously: The VIII Corps towards the west to capture the ports on the north coast of Brittany, with Brest as the final objective; The XX to the south to consolidate the rest of Brittany; The XV east to Le Mans, and finally, the XII to the north-east, to widen the narrow Avranches corridor. Interpreting Bradley's orders his own way, it was clear to Patton that instead of advancing cautiously across Brittany, taking great precautions ready for an eventual German counter-attack in the bottleneck at Avranches, his objective was Quiberon bay, to cut off the retreat of the German forces in Brittany, and to take the vital port of Brest. Later, he would turn east towards Paris, his final objective in this campaign. Quiberon Bay, with the beautiful Gulf of Morbihan, was a vital strategic objective as it could become the key point for unloading supplies (the Americans expected to bring 7,000 tons ashore there daily). The same can be said for the city of Brest, which was one of the main French ports,

and which had excellent docks, which the Germans themselves had been taking advantage of up until then.

3rd Army's passage through the Avranches bottleneck was a wonder of organization, determination and lodistical efficiency. Two roads ran through Avranches, but only one emerged at the other side of the town, across a narrow bridge. Using this one single road, Patton was able to send two infantry and two armoured divisions on their way into Brittany in less then 24 hours.

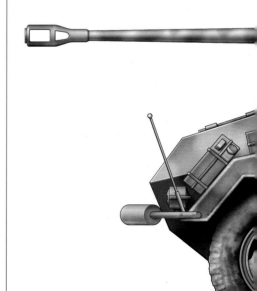

Grow's 6th Armoured Division began its advance across Britany at all speed, whereas Patton's favourite unit, The 4th Armoured Division, headed for Rennes (which at the time was only defended by 2,000 men of the *Luftwaffe*). The 4th Armoured Division was commanded by one of the most capable American Generals, Major General Wood, and on the 2nd August they reached Rennes, after advancing almost 80 kilometres in four days. The small German garrison in the city was too weak to suppose a serious threat, but at the same time suffient to complicate any attack by the Americans. Wood, concious of the situation, and wary of incurring heavy casualties, turned east, and on the afternoon of the third day his tanks were more than 50 kilometres south of Rennes, after having cut seven of the ten roads leading into the town. At this point he decided to make a direct assault on the city. The first attack made by the 4th Division's 13th Infantry Regiment was repulsed, losing them approximately twenty tanks in the process, but they eventually took Rennes on the 4th August, although they were unable to prevent the Germans from withdrawing. Their next objective was Vannes, in

Schwerer Panzerspähwagen (5 cm) Sd.Kfz 234/2 Puma. Only three pre-series examples and one hundred series models of this heavy reconnaissance vehicle were actually built; this made it exceedingly difficult to equip all the *Pz.Aufkl.Abt* of the *Panzer* Divisions with 25 vehicles of this type, as was tabled in their organization. A unit that was thus equipped was the *Pz.Aufkl.Abt 130* of the *«Panzer Lehr»* Division.

Illustration: Julio López Caeiro

order to isolate Brittany. Patton's rapid advance was proving too much for Bradley to keep up with, as the American flanks became exposed to a possible counter-attack. However, this did not seem to worry Patton in any way. An example of the disagreements within the American command is the order to halt sent to Grow by Middleton, the VIII Corps commander. Patton wanted the 6th Armoured Division to cover 320 kilometres in five days in order to take Brest, Middleton and Bradley ordered them to halt in Dinan and St Malo. When he became aware of this, Patton ordered the advance to continue at all cost. However, it was one thing to arrive at the objective, taking it was another. Although St Malo and Brest were encircled according to schedule, the German garrison in Brest did not capitulate until 19th September (after the port installations had been completely dismantled), and St Malo remained in German hands until 2nd September (the Isle of Cezembre), such was the German resistance. All this occurred despite the Americans being well aware that both ports were strategically vital if their mechanized units were to maintain their rythm of advance.

Seen in retrospect, the advance through Brittany, while appearing spectacular, was strategically speaking a failure, using up resources which would have been better used in Normandy in conjunction with the British and Canadians. The newspaper headlines about Patton's lightening advance could not make up for the stalemate which had developed around Caen. What is more, the Germans had only four second rate divisions in Brittany, with the exception of Ramcke's parachute troops, and overall control of the territory was in the hands of the Resistance, who gave a great deal of assistance to the American advance. Apart from this, Patton's method of advance involved moving at great speed and avoiding contact with the enemy. This led to the paradox of over-running large areas of territory, while causing the the enemy few casualties. The result of this was that it gave the Germans the opportunity to redeploy, and consolidate themselves in the ports which were Patton's overall objectives... the capture of Brest was prolonged more than a month, and cost the Americans 10,000 casualties, long after Patton had turned east. Following this bitter experience, Eisenhower

A Panzerkampfwagen V Ausf A Panther, of 3.Kompanie I/SS-Panzer Regiment 2, 2.SS-Panzerdivision «Das Reich». Illustration: Julio López Caeiro

Another Panzerkampfwagen V Ausf G Panther this time belonging to SS-Panzer Regiment 1, 1.SS-Panzerdivision «Leibstandarte SS-Adolf Hitler». Illustration: Julio López Caeiro

decided to leave Lorient and St Nazaire to one side, and avoid risking a frontal assault.

During the Brittany campaign, Patton's tanks had acted very independently, often under his direct command, and he often found himself in the vanguard. These units had instructions to take advantage of any advantage that would aid their progress, independent of the original plan. This had the advantage of allowing them to make local gains, but at the same time perhaps endangering neighbouring units, or even compromising the success of the entire front. This apart, they followed the American armoured doctrine of the time, pinning down the enemy with the infantry while the tanks infiltrated the rearguard to disorganize the defence.

The Advance to the East.
On the 3rd August, Bradley had already given Patton instructions to secure the north-south line along the Mayenne river. To this end XX Corps advanced towards Nantes and Angers, having the breakthrough between Paris and Orleans as their final objective.

The 5th Division reached Vitre amidst enormous traffic congestion on the 7th. From there, Patton planned for a regiment to take Angers, some 80 kilometres away, while an infantry battalion did the same with Nantes, 100 kilometres away, with the rest of the Division advancing on Segre, forty kilometres from Angers. The 11th Regiment advanced without meeting opposition to the outskirts of Angers, but then found that all the bridges along the Sarthe and the Mayenne had been blown, and they redeployed to join the rest of the Division. The Division's commmander was very reluctant to divide his forces and set off on risky ventures, as he supposed the Germans would be deployed in force at the two locations, and he feared they would counter-attack at any moment. Because of this he lost 48 hours in preparing positions for the attack on Angers (which in fact had very few defenders). Finally, on the 11th, the Americans decided to attack, and entered the city supported by fighter-bombers, with little opposition, and in a few hours had taken control of the city. Nantes was also lightly defended, and it fell without difficulty once they had decided to attack, after having had the city surrounded for almost two days.

General George S. Patton Jr. Used this specially adapted *M20 command car* while he was commanding the US Third Army during the campaign in France, 1944. Patton's M20, flew the pennant of Third Army Commander , while the glacis was painted with the command insignia for that unit.

Illustration: Luis Fresno Crespo

Third Army's next operations were to secure the area around Evreux, Chartres and Dreux, where excellent airfields could be established to support ground the operations. On the 13th, Patton ordered XV Corps to take up positions to close the gap between Argentan and Falaise, to surround the German forces and prevent them from escaping along the Seine valley. In such a fluid situation, and given the level of experience of the Allies, Patton ordered his corps commanders to be ready to move north, north-east or east, something highly unusual. However, Patton wanted his forces (four corps, with approximately two divisions each) to advance beyond their initial objectives, Bradley ordered them to halt in Dreux, Chartres and Orleans, worrying that such long lines of communication would be open to a German counter-attack, and that the operation would end in disaster. On August 16th, Orleans fell following an attack by XII Corps. The city was virtually undefended, and was taken without difficulty. Only in Chartres, where the divese German forces were regrouping, was there any resistance, and the city was not secured until the 18th. Paris was now only 80 kilometres away. This time Patton,

worried of a possible German counter-attack, constantly requested air support, as well as the destruction of the bridges over the Loire that the Germans could have used for a counter-attack. However, in spite of the closeness of the French capital, the allied objective at this point was not Paris, but the Seine.

In spite of everything, Patton wished to continue, but Bradley, worried about Third Army's exposed left flank, and the difficulty in maintaining the flow of supplies, ordered him to stop. On the 18th, Patton was given permission to continue his advance with some of his units. By the end of the day, XV Corps was only five kilometres from the river Seine, and the following morning, a patrol from the 79th Infantry Division crossed the river at Mericourt. Presented with this situation, Eisenhower decided to change the initial invasion plans, and instead of stopping on the Seine to regroup, he ordered Patton to pursue the enemy. On the morning of the 20th, two infantry battalions had crossed the Seine and established a firm bridgehead. By the afternoon a pontoon bridge had been set up and vehicles were crossing the river.

On the 21st, both XII and XX Corps were advancing east, with the objective of crossing the Seine

south of Paris. On the morning of the 22nd, *7th Armoured Division* advanced more than 50 kilometres

and reached Melun, finding an intact bridge over the Seine. An attack was immediately launched to take it, but was repulsed, as was another that afternoon. While the Americans were preparing to attack again the next day, the Germans blew the bridge that night. Another attack launched the following day over the remains of the destroyed bridge was also repulsed with the Americans suffering heavy casualties. Finally, the following day, engineers succeeded in setting up a pontoon bridge a few kilometres to the north, allowing the Division's CCA to cross the river on the 24th. Melun was taken the next day.

In spite of the overwhelming superiority of the Allied air force during the Normandy campaign, and given the fear that the *Luftwaffe* continued to invoke, the US Army mobilised several anti-aircraft artillery battalions (ATP) equipped with motorised multiple M15 and M16 mounts for the mobile protection of the armoured columns. Each of these battalions was equipped with 32 M15s and 32 M16s, organised into four companies with eight vehicles of each type in each company.

The general lack of aggression by the *Luftwaffe* usually left the M16s free for land-based support fire. Their devastating firing power earned them the macabre name of "*the meat-chopper*".

The first of these vehicles consisted in the installation of an M-54 mount (combining a 37 mm M1A2 automatic cannon with two 12.7 mm Browning M2HB machineguns) over the chassis of an M3 half-track. 680 M15 units and 1,652 M15A1s were produced. Both varieties had an almost identical appearance, though the M15 carried its machineguns on top of the main cannon while the M15A1 carried them below.

M16 was the name given to an M3 half-track, which was installed with a Maxson mount with four 12.7 mm machineguns by way of anti-aircraft mount, which had a seat for the marksman, two circular optical mounts for aiming, a front armoured shield and a small generator behind the marksman to provide assisted turning and elevation while the vehicle was stopped, without having to keep the engine running to provide a power supply. A total of 2,876 new units were manufactured; an additional 777 units were converted from other types of half-tracks.

The illustration above shows an M16 from an unknown unit.

The lower illustration shows an M15A1 from the *467th AAA Battalion*, France 1944.

Illustration: Luis Fresno Crespo

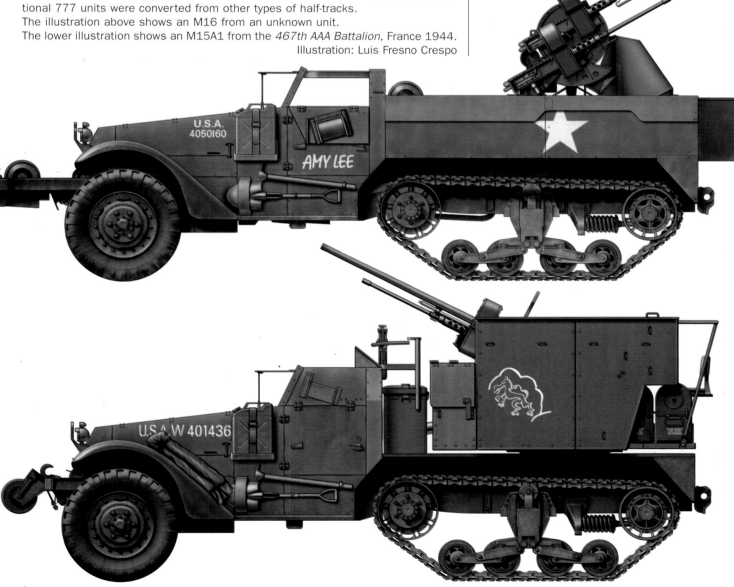

Throughout these few days, the Seine had been reached at several points, which allowed the infantry regiments to establish bridgeheads. 4th Armoured Division's CCA crossed the river to the north of Troyes, and took the city on the 26th. By the 25th, the Third Army

M4A Sherman Tank. Tenth vehicle in the C Company of the 70th Tank Battalion of the 1st Armoured Division.

Illustration: Julio López Caeiro

Among the numerous variations of the M4 Sherman medium tank, the recovery models known as M32 *Tank recovery vehicles* were built. Being equipped with a crane and winch, these vehicles had the mission of withdrawing the tanks damaged by enemy fire from battle.

Illustration: Julio López Caeiro

had been able to establish five bridgeheads over the Seine: the XV Corps had one north of Paris, in Mantes, the XX Corps, three to the south, in Melun, Vulaines-sur-Seine and Montereau, and the XII Corps one in Troyes. That same day, elements of 2nd Armoured and 4th Infantry Divisions entered Paris.

The rapid advance across France had caused the Allies enormous logistics problems, which they dealt with to a greater or lesser degree of success. Patton's famous phrase: "*my men can eat their belts, but my tanks need gasoline*", is representative of the problem. An American Armoured Division had more than 4,000 vehicles and required more than a million litres of gasoline to enter in combat (300 truckloads).

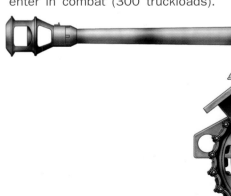

7.5cm Sturmgeschütz III Ausf G from the *316th Funklenk Kompanie*. In July 1944, this unit was aggregated to the «*Panzer Lehr*» Division.

Illustration: Luis Fresno Crespo

The rail system had been so devastated by air raids that it was necessary to transport everything by road, which caused the network to collapse. Furthermore, given the typical abundance of material the Americans had, there was enormous wastage. Each Divisional command consumed 650 tons of provisions daily, more than triple a German unit of comparable size. Bradley had had to halt and restrict objectives due to the inability of the logistics units to keep pace with the rythm of the Armoured units' advance. The main problem was not so much munnition, as fighting had not been that heavy and objectives rather limited, but rather fuel and food.

The counter-attack at Mortain.
On the night of 6th August, von Funck's *XLVII Panzerkorps* launched a sudden counter-attack, without an initial artillery bombardment, against the 30th Division's positions in the area of Mortain, which had been taken three days earlier. Three armoured columns had been tasked with advancing along narrow corri-

AMERICAN LIGHT TANKS

The United States began the war with a rather poor array of armoured vehicles, and the light tanks were no exception. The first models, the M1 and M2, were only used for training purposes, with the M2A4 being the version to see combat in the early campaigns in the Pacific theatre. A later development of this same vehicle resulted in the M3 *Stuart*, which was also used by the British, seeing service in North Africa and Europe. With a weight of 14 tons, the Stuart had a crew of four men and was armed with a 37 mm main gun and as many as five machine guns. The maximum thickness of its armour was 51 mm, and it had a road speed of 55 kph. It was often used as a medium tank and suffered high losses as a result.

In an attempt to overcome the tanks defects, the M5, and M5A1 were developed, which used two commercial Cadillac engines, had sloping frontal armour up to 67 mm thick and a newly designed turret. Despite these improvements, these tanks found themselves to be at a serious disadvantage when facing enemy reconnaissance units, due to their vulnerability and lack of a decent main gun, which made the development of a new light tank a priority.

The new M24 *Chaffee* entered service at the end of 1944, progressively substituting the *Stuart*. The M24 weighed 20 tons and had a crew of five. Its sloping armour had a maximum thickness of 25 mm, which was too thin. Maximum road speed was 70 kph, and its main armament was a 75 mm gun, which had been derived from one designed for the B25 medium bomber. Although it was not an ideal vehicle, it was at least an improvement on the Stuart, and it saw many years of service with other countries, such as France and Spain.

dors towards Avranches, approximately thirty kilometres from the starting point. Two *Waffen SS* columns advanced along the southern bank of the river See, while *2.Panzer-Division* advanced in another column along the north bank. A fourth column was awaiting the arrival of the *«Leibstandarte»*, which had been held up due to air attacks.

Armoured elements of *2.SS-Panzerdivision «Das Reich»* and *17.SS-Panzergrenadierdivision* advanced in two columns in a north-south direction. Achieving a degree of surprise, they continued advancing towards the city, overwhelming several companies from the 30th Division. During the morning they were joined

by units of *«Leibstandarte»*, which had just arrived in the theatre. The *116.Panzer-Division*, which was supposed to join in the attack, was unable to break contact and disengage from the enemy and therefore did not take part. A few hours after the commencement of the attack, the German vanguard had arrived within fifteen kilometres of Avranches. If they could reach the coast, they would be able to cut the vital flow of supplies to the American divisions.

The codename for the counter-attack was Operation *«Luttich»*, and was to prove itself to be another of Hitler's wild schemes which the German High Command had neither the ability or valour to prevent. The three

weak panzer divisions (*2.Panzer-Division*, *«Das Reich»* and *«Leibstandarte»*) that made the attack had only

Next page. The abundant self-propelled artillery deployed by the American Army in France is represented here by three of the most well-known types. From top to bottom:
- M7 *Priest* 105 mm Howitzer Motor Carriage of 14th Field Artillery Battalion, 2nd Armoured Division.
- M8 75 mm HMC assigned to the 82nd Armoured Reconnaissance battalion, 2nd Armoured Division.
- M12 155 mm Gun Motor Carriage serving with 991/987th Field Artillery Battalion.

  Illustration: Julio López Caeiro.

Note: The vehicles are not reproduced to the same scale.

U.S.A.4037722
BABOON

LAXATIVE
3-9
USA 4052227

Avant
Le Char de Mort
U.S.A. 4,081,019

June
Gil

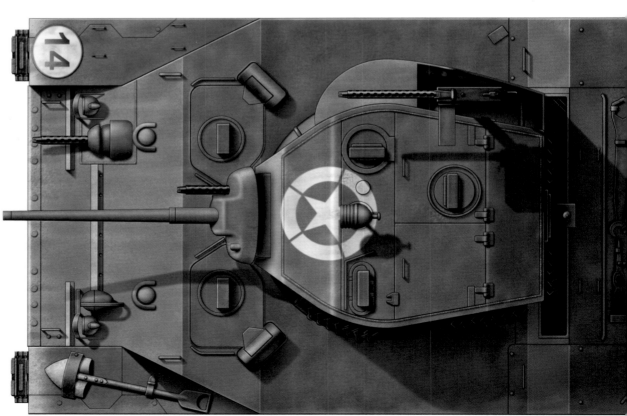

American soldiers inspecting german material abandoned after Mortain´s unsuccessful counterattack.

75 *Panzer IV's*, 70 *Panthers* and 32 assault guns and tank hunters (*StuG III's* and *Panzerjäger IV's*) between them. The «*Leibstandarte*» began its attack late due to hold ups caused by air attacks, and was stopped that afternoon by the 3rd Armoured Division. The *116th Panzer Division* by an anti-tank screen set up by the *9th Division*, with only *2.Panzer-Division* progressing according to plan.

Curiously, however, Bradley, was not overly worried, and he saw a great opportunity to achieve a decisive victory, being fully aware as he was, courtesy of *Ultra* (the German decoding machine which had been captured by the British), of the enemy's intentions. At no time did he have any intention of detaining Third Army's advance, and so he left Collins VII Army and the formidable

Allied air power to take care of the situation. 3rd Armoured Division's CCB was immediately sent to support the beleaguered 30th Division. In fact several infantry battalions had deployed on Hill 317, establishing a

desperate defensive position, until the American artillery began firing on its own positions. The next morning the weather improved, and Allied fighter-bombers appeared overhead, the *Luftwaffe* by this time being almost non-existent. The German attack disintergrated. Some American infantry units remained surrounded for up to five days, but the situation was kept under control at all times. The Allied command reacted with a maturity that was unusual up to that time, as they remained calm, waiting for the air support to resolve the crisis, which is exactly what happened. By the 8th, Operation «*Lüttich*» had turned into a failure. The Germans had lost around one hundred irreplaceable tanks during the operation, and what was worse for them, they had lost their last opportunity to turn around the situation in Normandy.

The M3 White was the Standard American half-track during the Second World War, seeing service not only as an armoured infantry transport vehicle, but also in many other roles, from tank hunting to mobile mortar platform. Robust and reliable, protection could have been improved, and its off-road performance was not as good as German equivalents, but it was effective. Proof of the design's longevity is that it remained in service with many countries, including Israel, until the nineteen-seventies.

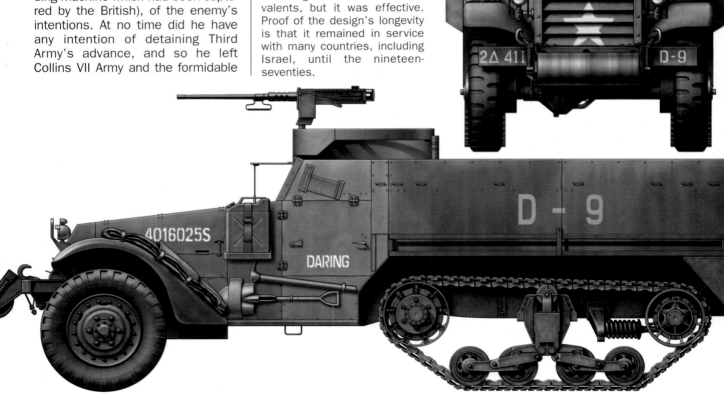

Conclusions

The Americans had finally managed to sink the German front in Normandy, and make the long awaited breakthrough, following the British failure in Operations «Epsom» and «Goodwood». Brittany had been liberated, although its most important ports remained in German hands, and the road to Paris was open. The German defensive system had been broken and the Falaise pocket brought an end to the Normandy campaign.

However, this overview warrants a more cautious analysis. The defenders who had confronted the Americans had been weakened by long weeks of attrition, and the majority of the German forces were being used to hold up the British and Canadians around Caen. The aerial bombardment that had signalled the start of the attack was without precedent and could call on unimagined resources for such an operation. The Americans had begun to accumulate combat experience in the weeks following the invasion and were becoming profficient in coordinating the different arms. The avalanche of fire that fell on the German defenders was extraordinary, but even then, the advance was slow, and the initial objectives took several days to achieve. A few resolute defenders were able to achieve disproportional results. However, in the end weight of numbers told, and the front collapsed.

Nevertheless, it needed Patton's energy to make the breakthrough, a commander who knew how to imbue his troops with a sense of speed and urgency. Brittany was crossed in a very short time, and the later advance east was also rapid. But at the same time it must be said that the American forces making the advance avoided all opposition, which resulted in them taking a lot of ground, but not defeating the enemy, and above all in the case of Brittany, when they arrived at their main objectives, the vital ports of Brest and St Malo, they came to a halt and were content to simply encircle them. The battle for the control of these ports was to last for weeks, and when they were finally taken, the destruction made them useless as points of entry for the much needed supplies. The speed with which the Americans advanced along the magnificat French roads did not by itself signify victory. But there can be no doubt that without Patton, they would have surely taken a lot longer.

GEORGE S. PATTON JR.

Born on 11th November 1885, in San Gabriel, to a wealthy California family. At the age of 18 he entered the *Virginia Military Institute*, and a year later went to West Point. He graduated in 1909 as a cavalry officer, coming 46th in a class of 103 cadets. A little later he married a wealthy Massachussets heiress. He took part in the 1912 Stockholm Olympic Games in the Modern Military Pentathalon, coming fifth. Later, he studied fencing in Saumur (France), and went on to design a sabre following this experience, the *M-1913*, which became the regulation sabre of the US Cavalry.

Patton took part in Pershing's 1916 campaign against Pancho Villa, and during the course of which there was a fire-fight with some of Villa's men, three of whom were shot, and two of these, according to tradition, by Patton himself with his pearl-handled *Colt .45*. The bodies were transported over the mudguards of Patton's vehicle.

When Pershing left for France at the head of the American Expeditionary Force, he took the energetic Patton with him. Anxious to see action, Patton was posted to the *US Tank Corps*. He himself wrote manuals and developed the doctrine on tank warfare, and he also took personal charge of training the crews. He received a serious thigh wound during the first day of the Argonne offensive, and almost bled to death. At the end of the war, without seeing further action, he decided to rejoin the cavalry, as the US Congress had approved hardly any funds for the development of the armoured branch.

Following various posts during the twenties and thirties, he took command of the *2nd Armoured Brigade* in 1939, which was stationed at *Fort Benning*, and which soon after became the 2nd Armoured Division. In 1942 he created the *Desert Training Corps*, in the Mojave Desert, where he developed the doctrine and tactics that the US

Palermo (Sicily), 23rd July: Patton contemplating a column of Italian prisoners, who, demoralised, have surrendered almost without a struggle.

Army's tanks would later use. The first unit trained there was designated the *Western Tank Force*, and took part in Operation *Torch*, the Allied landing in North Africa, in November 1942. Following the disaster at the Kasserine Pass, Patton, with his habitual energy, took command of II Corps. Patton reorganized his forces and managed to bring them to an adequate state of readiness in time for the Sicily campaign, during which he began his rivalry with Montgomery, which lasted to the end of the war. Commanding the VII Army, he won the race to Messina, something Monty would not forget.

One of the most famous incidents involving Patton occurred that August, which was to have an effect on his future career. During a visit to a field hospital, he came across two soldiers suffering from "battle fatigue", whom he slapped and insulted in front of their comrades. Although he attempt to have the incident covered up, the press got hold of it and as a result some congressmen demanded he be made an example of. Eisenhower backed Patton up as he considered him indispensable, but he did relieve him of his command for several months, until January 1944.

In the spring of 1944, Patton took command of the US Third Army in the UK, ready for the invasion of France. When the Allied offensive become bogged down and following the failure of the *Epsom* and *Goodwood* offensives to break out in Normandy, the Americans finally achieved success when Patton's Third Army was let loose. In effect, following Operation «*Cobra*», and backed up by overwhelming air superiority, Patton's Third Army advanced across France in four different directions. Political reasons impeded his entry into Paris. His next objective was the German frontier and the Rhine, but before that there was some hard fighting for Lorraine, and its most emblematic city, Metz, where the first two assaults made by his troops were repulsed. During the course of this fighting, he attacked several of the Maginot Line fortifications from the rear. At the end of the year, again with massive air and artillery support, he stopped a German counter-attack in Lorraine. In

December, Third Army took part in the counter-offensive in the Ardennes, where they broke the siege of Bastogne, with Patton's forces attacking towards the north after he had changed their direction of approach. In the spring of 1945 Patton crossed the Rhine, penetrating into Austria and Czechoslovakia, where again, for political reasons, he was denied permission to take Prague. In the course of his advance across Europe, he covered more kilometres in less time and captured more prisoners than any other Allied unit in the Second World War.

Patton was very concious of the fact that the next enemy would be the Soviet Unon (he called them "*those savage Mongols known as Russians*"), and his bellicose attitude cost him some heated arguments with his superiors, who although they had an unpolitically correct General in Patton, realised that in wartime they could not do without him. Patton died in an obscure traffic accident in Mannheim in December 1945. He was sixty years old. He was buried in the military cemetary in Ham, in Luxemburg.

Patton's personality was complex and controversial. He alternated between a refined sensitivity and toughness combined with an extreme coldness. Boastful, despotic, proud and haughty, he despised weakness and believed himself to be above either good or evil. He was even implicated in dark episodes involving the massacre of prisoners, as well as a failed mission to rescue his son-in-law, at that time a prisoner of the Germans. But he was a real leader. He knew how to encourage his men and get the best from them; without doubt he was the most charismatic American General of the Second World War, and perhaps, with some exceptions, in American military history. Patton represented like no other the fighting spirit and desire for victory, and he was a defender of the tank arm. He maintained a certain contemporary spirit of the cavalry, which he knew how to bring to a war of movement, using tanks and knowing perfectly the potential of his units. He also knew very well how to combine the abundance of weapons at his disposal. However, it must be said that he was able to act in conditions of material superiority, usually with formidible air support, and on the occasions that the logistics failed, his units suffered. What he could have done if he had been in the same conditions of inferiority as his German counterparts is a matter of conjecture.

26th August 1944: Patton going to inspect the units fighting in Brittany, in a Stinson liaison aeroplane.

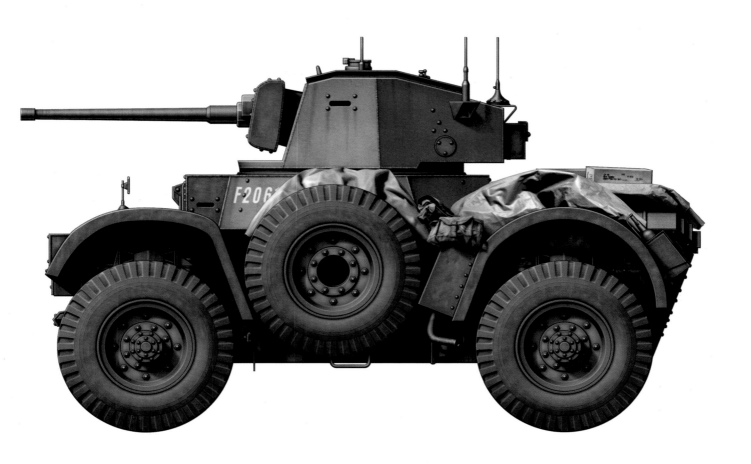

SUMMARY

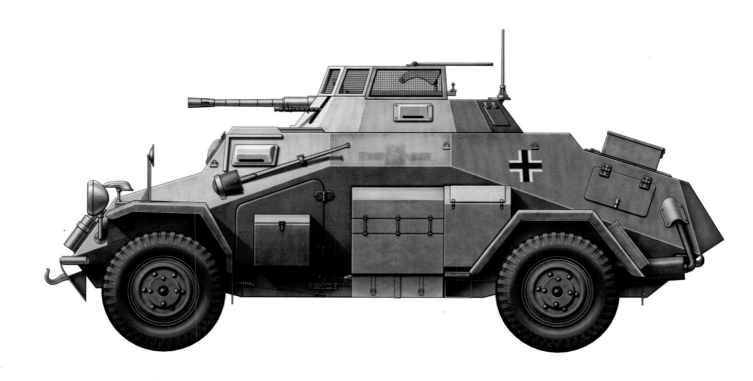